Routledge Revivals

A Critical Edition of Robert Davenport's THE CITY-NIGHT-CAP

A Critical Edition of Robert Davenport's THE CITY-NIGHT-CAP

WILLIS J. MONIE

Routledge
Taylor & Francis Group
ROUTLEDGE REVIVALS

First published in 1979 by Garland Publishing, Inc.

This edition first published in 2018 by Routledge
2 Park Square, Milton Park, Abingdon, Oxon, OX14 4RN
and by Routledge
52 Vanderbilt Avenue, New York, NY 10017, USA

Routledge is an imprint of the Taylor & Francis Group, an informa business

Publisher's Note

The publisher has gone to great lengths to ensure the quality of this reprint but points out that some imperfections in the original copies may be apparent.

Disclaimer

The publisher has made every effort to trace copyright holders and welcomes correspondence from those they have been unable to contact.

A Library of Congress record exists under ISBN:

ISBN 13: 978-0-367-14400-5 (hbk)
ISBN 13: 978-0-367-14401-2 (pbk)
ISBN 13: 978-0-429-03186-1 (ebk)

A Garland Series

RENAISSANCE DRAMA

A COLLECTION OF CRITICAL EDITIONS

edited by
STEPHEN ORGEL
The Johns Hopkins University

A Critical Edition of Robert Davenport's THE CITY-NIGHT-CAP

WILLIS J. MONIE

GARLAND PUBLISHING, INC.
NEW YORK & LONDON • 1979

All volumes in this series are printed on
acid-free, 250-year-life paper.

Library of Congress Cataloging in Publication Data

Davenport, Robert, fl. 1623–
A critical edition of Robert Davenport's The city-night-cap.

(Renaissance drama)
Bibliography: p.
I. Monie, Willis J., 1945– II. Title. III. Title: The city-night-cap. IV. Series.
PR2479.D3C5 1979 822'.3 78-66832
ISBN 0-8240-9739-4

PRINTED IN THE UNITED STATES OF AMERICA

TABLE OF CONTENTS

CHAPTER I

INTRODUCTION

1. The Man

Almost nothing is known about the life of Robert Davenport outside of his writings. There is no Robert Davenport listed at Cambridge, and none after 1515 at Oxford.[1] The *DNB* lists him as "fl. 1623," but this is based on Malone's erroneous assignment of 1623 to the publication of *A Crown for a Conqueror and Too Late to Call Back Yesterday*, actually published in 1639.[2]

To learn anything of Davenport, one must turn to his works. The earliest possible play in which Davenport could have had a hand is the lost comedy *The Woman's Mistake*, which the *Annals of English Drama* dates c. 1620-1624.[3] Humphrey Moseley entered the work in 1653 as by "Drew and Davenport."[4] Gerald Eades Bentley, however, speculates that this is Thomas Drue's lost play on the murder of Joan Tindall, licensed September, 1624.[5] *The Fatal Brothers*, a lost tragedy, is listed in the *Annals* as c. 1623-1636.[6] Moseley entered it in the Stationer's Register in 1660 as by Davenport,[7] but nothing else is known about the play. Another lost tragedy, *The Politic Queen or Murder Will Out*, is dated in the *Annals* as c. 1623-1636,[8] and was also entered by Moseley in 1660.[9] Alfred Harbage speculates that Mountfort's *Edward III, with the Fall of Mortimer* (1690; printed 1691) is an adaptation of Davenport's *Politic Queen*.[10]

The first positive date known for Davenport is 1624, when *The City-Night-Cap* was licensed by Sir Henry Herbert on October 14: "For the

Cockpit Company; a new play called The City Night-Cap: Written by Davenport."[11] It is also listed in Halliwell-Phillipps's Scrap-Books for the same date, adding that there was a one pound licensing fee, which was usually the charge for new plays.[12] Also licensed in 1624 by Herbert for the King's Company on April 10 was The History of Henry the First, by "Damport."[13] Moseley entered "Henry the first, & Hen. the 2d, by Shakespeare, & Davenport" in the Stationer's Register in 1653.[14] Warburton lists Henry I, by Shakespeare and Davenport, as one of the manuscripts supposedly burned by his cook.[15] Henry II, mentioned only by Moseley, was probably listed with Henry I to save a fee, and most likely closely followed Henry I in composition. Professor Harbage speculates that the 1692 tragedy Henry II, King of England, with the Death of Rosamond is an adaptation of this lost play.[16]

A New Trick to Cheat the Devil, Davenport's first published play in 1639, is entered in the Annals as c. 1624-1639.[17] Humphrey Blunden entered the play, by "Mr. Damport," in the Stationer's Register for March 28, 1639,[18] and it was entered in the Lord Chamberlain's list on August 10, 1639, for Beeston.[19] Another play entered at the same time for Beeston is the lost A Fool and Her Maidenhead Soon Parted,[20] listed without author between two Davenport plays, and given, on this basis, a questionable attribution by Fleay.[21] The third play listed for Beeston is King John and Matilda,[22] written around 1628-1629 (a date for which Davis argues convincingly).[23] The play was published in 1655, and again in 1662, and was reentered in the Stationer's Register for March 13, 1675 by William Cademon,[24] though he apparently brought out no edition.

The only reference to a lost play The Pirate is by Samuel Sheppard in his Epigrams, Theological, Philosophical and Romantic (1651).

Epigram 19, addressed "To Mr. Davenport on his Play called the Pirate," perhaps suggests that Davenport was alive when Sheppard wrote it:

> Make all the cloth you can, haste, haste away,
> The Pirate will o'ertake you if you stay:
> Nay, we will yield our selves, and this confesse,
> Thou Rival'st Shakespeare, though thy glory's lesse.[25]

The Pedler is listed twice by Herbert in 1630,[26] and the second entry only ascribes the play to Davenport; this may be another lost play by the playwright, but it is more probable that the play is The Conceited Pedler by Thomas Randolph.[27]

Two surviving anonymous plays have been ascribed to Davenport, although neither attribution is widely accepted. James G. McManaway argues for Davenport's authorship of Dick of Devonshire on the basis of plot and stylistic similarities.[28] McManaway also ascribes The Bloody Banquet (published in 1639 as by "T.D.") to Davenport, on "considerable internal evidence,"[29] which he has yet to publish. Neither attribution can be accepted on the facts and arguments now available.

Besides his dramatic output, Davenport was the author of several poems and dialogues. A Crown for a Conquerour; and Too Late to Call Back Yesterday, published together in 1639 and dedicated to the actors Richard Robinson and Michael Bowyer, indicates a connection with the theater as late as 1638-1639. The dedication supplies an additional biographical fact: "These poems...being some expence of my time at Sea..."[30] Davenport thus spent some time on board ship, perhaps between England and Ireland as other evidence suggests.

The address to the reader in A New Trick to Cheat the Devil (1639) states: "But the Poem it selfe, being now an Orphant, and wanting the Father which first begot it...." This seems to suggest that

Davenport was dead, and there exists no conclusive proof to contradict this idea.[31] Two commendatory verses by Davenport, one for Thomas Rawlins' *The Rebellion* and one for Nathaniel Richards' *Messallina*, were published in 1640, but both plays were produced earlier and these poems could also have been written before 1640. An epistle by the author to the reader (and signed "R.D.") in the 1655 edition of *King John and Matilda* (but omitted in the 1662 edition) seems to indicate that the playwright was alive in that year, but it has been suggested that this conventional statement could have been written by anyone.[32] Even Davenport's year of death, then, has not been determined.

The rest of Davenport's rather conventional poetic output exists in seventeenth century manuscripts. *A Dialogue between Policy and Piety* is partly concerned with Irish problems, and one copy of the manuscript is dedicated to the Bishop of Londonderry, John Bramhall, and signed "a servant and poore neighboure,"[33] perhaps suggesting Davenport's residence in Ireland. A second manuscript contains the prose character "A Martyr" and several religious poems.[34] Another poem, reprinted by Bullen in *The Works of Robert Davenport* from the manuscript in the Cambridge University Library, is "A Survey of the Sciences."

2. The Works

The extant works definitely attributable to Robert Davenport, then, include three plays, *The City-Night-Cap*, *King John and Matilda*, and *A New Trick to Cheat the Devil*, several poems largely in the form of dialogues, and one short prose character.

The poems can safely be called undistinguished. Two poems,

"A Crown for a Conquerour" and "Too Late to Call Back Yesterday," were published together in 1639. The first is a religious dialogue based on Revelations 22,12: "Behold I come quickly, and my reward is with me." Christ explains to a suffering Christian how to win the crown of salvation, through faith and works. The second poem is also a dialogue, between a lover and the day. The lover has found the vows of his mistress to be false, and he wants to call back yesterday or call forth tomorrow, all to no avail. Finally, Christ appears and offers comfort and salvation. A third poem, also in the form of a dialogue, is "A Dialogue between Policy and Piety." Policy ("wisdome, experience, Learning, knowledg, witt") and Piety ("Celestiall," "all grace") are married at the instigation of Hibernia (Ireland); the poem is also incidentally concerned with Irish affairs. The last poem of significance is "A Survey of the Sciences," in which a Body (the speaker throughout the poem) goes in search of its Soul among the various sciences. Finally, the soul is found sheltered by Christ, where the Body leaves it in contemplation, since "obedience is no bondage where wee love."[35]

The prose character and the short poems, reprinted by Thorn-Drury from a manuscript dedicated to the popular patron of the arts William Earl of Newcastle, are interesting to the reader of *The City-Night-Cap,* since each work casts light on Davenport's attitude toward several characters of the play. "A Martyr," the short prose work, illustrates the character of a person much like Abstemia, willing to suffer to the point of giving his life for his belief. "A Spiritual Coward" illustrates Lorenzo's character, struck by the devil's dart, "Distrust." Given a second chance in prison, Lorenzo begs for life and dishonor rather than a martyr's death. So with a spiritual coward:

So in o[u]r Gods great battailes, oft we see,

the bouldest boasters, frequent failers bee [,]
Promise is due debt; yet, in his brave fight,
ffaith is our promise, but our payment--fflight. (p. 14)

The other two poems, "A Weeping Convert" and "A Sacrifice," also are concerned with the theme of winning the crown of salvation through suffering, a central concern of The City-Night-Cap.

As J.O. Davis points out, the interest of these poems to a student of Davenport's drama "lies in their very conventional and pious moral sentiments, as well as their undistinguished poetic quality."[36] In The City-Night-Cap Davenport's moral viewpoint is in every respect conventional, and the play is distinguished far more for its plot and dialogue than for any poetic quality.

In the comedy A New Trick to Cheat The Devil, Slightall, rejected by Anne in favor of Lord Scales, gives himself to squandering his fortune, and finally signs his soul to the devil for money to pay his debts. When Anne meets the Lord, however, she realizes that "I have seen a thousand private gentlemen Both better fac'd and featur'd," and prefers Slightall. But all seems lost when the devil comes to claim Slightall's soul; however, a cunning friar argues that the devil has not kept his part of the bargain, since Slightall has not been able to discharge all his debts, and in fact is indebted now as much as ever, to the devil. Slightall and Anne are married, finally with the blessings of Anne's silly mother and even Lord Scales.

In the historic tragedy King John and Matilda, John faces two problems: some of his nobles are plotting a rebellion since he has not kept the Magna Charta, and he desperately desires Matilda, daughter of one of the rebelling nobles. The rebellion finally fails, but Matilda is killed on the orders of John in a moment of jealous anger, who finally repents his evil ways and forgives all.

Endnotes: Chapter I

1 Gerald Eades Bentley, The Jacobean and Caroline Stage (Oxford: Clarendon Press, 1956), III, 225.

2 Ibid.

3 Alfred Harbage, Annals of English Drama, rev. S. Schoenbaum (London: Methuen and Co., 1964), p. 110. Referred to in the text as Annals. See also: Bentley, III, 237.

4 A Transcript of the Registers of the Worshipful Company of Stationers; from 1640-1708 (1914; rpt. New York: Peter Smith, 1950), I, 428.

5 Bentley, III, 238, 286.

6 Harbage, Annals, p. 116.

7 A Transcript of the Registers of the Worshipful Company of Stationers; from 1640-1708, II, 271.

8 Harbage, Annals, p. 116.

9 A Transcript of the Registers of the Worshipful Company of Stationers; from 1640-1708, II, 271.

10 Alfred Harbage, "Elizabethan-Restoration Palimpset," Modern Language Review, 35 (1940), 310-318.

11 Joseph Quincy Adams, ed., The Dramatic Records of Sir Henry Herbert ([1917]; rpt. New York: Benjamin Blom, n.d.), p. 29.

12 Bentley, III, 227-228.

13 Adams, pp. 27-28.

14 A Transcript of the Registers of the Worshipful Company of Stationers; from 1640-1708, I, 429.

15 Bentley, III, 230.

16 Harbage, "Elizabethan-Restoration Palimpset," pp. 310-318.

17 Harbage, Annals, p. 120.

18 Edward Arber, ed., A Transcript of the Registers of the Company of Stationers of London 1554-1640 (1877; rpt. New York: Peter Smith, 1950), IV, 436.

19 Bentley, I, 331.

20 Ibid.

21 Frederick Gard Fleay, A Biographical Chronicle of the English Drama 1559-1642 (London: Reeves and Turner, 1891), I, 105.

22 Bentley, I, 331.

23 Joyce Outten Davis, "Robert Davenport's King John and Matilda: A Critical Edition," Diss. Tulane 1969, p. xv.

24 A Transcript of the Registers of the Worshipful Company of Stationers; from 1640-1708, II, 502.

25 Bentley, III, 236. Sheppard must have been born after April, 1623, his parent's marriage date, suggesting a composition date after 1640.

26 Arber, IV, 197, 198.

27 Bentley, III, 236.

28 James G. and Mary R. McManaway, eds., Dick of Devonshire (Oxford: Malone Society, 1955), pp. viii-ix.

29 James G. McManaway, "Latin Title-Page Mottoes as a Clue to Dramatic Authorship," Library, 4th series, 26 (1945), 35.

30 A. H. Bullen, ed., The Works of Robert Davenport, Old English Plays, NS, III (London and Redhill: Hansard Publishing Union, 1890), p. 311.

31 It has been suggested that this passage merely means Davenport was away, perhaps at sea or in Ireland. See: Bentley, III, 226; DNB.

32 Bentley, III, 226.

33 Folger Library MS. 1919.3. The Folger Library kindly furnished a photocopy of this document.

34 Rpt. in: G. Thorn-Drury, ed., A Little Ark (London: P.J. and A.E. Dobell, 1921), pp. 11-15. He dates it between 1629 and 1643 on the basis of the dedication.

35 This same line ends both this poem and "A Dialogue between Policy and Piety."

36 Davis, p. xi.

CHAPTER II

SOURCES

The source for the Lodovico-Francisco-Dorothea plot of The City-Night-Cap is the seventh tale of the seventh day in Giovanni Boccaccio's Decameron, probably from the English translation of 1620.[1] This source was first noted by Gorard Langbaino,[2] and has not been questioned. In this tale, Lodovico, the only son of a wealthy merchant, hears a knight proclaim that the most beautiful of women is Madam Beatrix, wife of Egano de Galluzzi of Bologna. Lodovico assumes the name Anichino, and enters Egano's service. Finally, alone with Beatrix, he reveals his identity and his love, which she promises to reward if he comes to her that night.

When he enters her chamber, however, she wakes her husband and announces that Anichino has attempted to seduce her. But instead of exposing him in the chamber, she sends Egano, disguised in her night-gown, to the garden, where she says she has promised to meet the servant, so her husband can personally chastise Anichino.

After enjoying his love, Anichino goes to the garden, armed with a cudgel. He declares his faithfulness to his master, and beats the lustful "Beatrix." Egano flees back to his bedroom, where his wife praises his servant's loyalty. The lovers are now able to enjoy their love, while Egano remains a dupe and cuckold.

Davenport changes the ending for his purposes, to draw a parallel with his other plot, in order to contrast the rewarded chaste wife with the punished unfaithful wife. He also adds the character of Pambo, the clown, whose comments add to the comedy, and put Dorothea's hypocrisy and Lodovico's blind trust into proper perspective. Otherwise, the playwright follows Boccaccio's story quite closely, while developing potentially dramatic situations more fully. For example, Davenport changes the relatively short incident where Beatrix sends Egano to the garden into a longer, comic scene, with Francisco attempting to hide without pulling Dorothea, who has a tight hold on his hand, out of bed, while a drunk Lodovico is finally sent to the garden. And the garden incident is transformed from a few lines in Boccaccio to a scene with humorous dialogue between Pambo, who is disguised as Dorothea, and Francisco, with Lodovico making asides while observing them.

Davenport does not borrow any of the language of the English translation. This is understandable, however, since the novel is eight pages in length, with the actual gulling of the husband only four pages, and the form is narrative rather than dramatic, with almost no dialogue.

The source of the Lorenzo-Philippo-Abstemia plot has presented more problems to critics. Gerard Langbaine in 1691 noted that this plot was "borrow'd from the novel of the _Curious Impertinent_ in the Romance of _Don Quixote_."[3] This conclusion was included in the 1744 and 1780 editions of Dodsley, as well as the 1810 edition of _The Ancient British Drama_. But the 1827 edition of Dodsley emended this note to say, "The plot . . . is taken partly from _Philomela, the Lady Fitzwater's Nightingale_, by Robert Greene . . . which resembles the novel of the _Curious Impertinent_ in _Don Quixote_ . . . ."[4] The 1875 edition of Dodsley retained this change, while Bullen accepted this new source and added, "It will be noticed that the euphuistic passages in the play are borrowed almost word for word from Greene."[5]

A.S.W. Rosenbach, in tracing the early influence of the "Curious Impertinent" episode in English drama, concludes that Davenport "was not obliged to go to _Don Quixote_ for material for this incident." He refers to lines 6-7 (I, i) to suggest that the playwright most likely derived the plot from either another play, or from a work like Greene's Philomela, "as Mr. Bullen has shown."[6] The possibility of another play as source will be discussed shortly. However, the standard English drama surveys still continue to list Cervantes as Davenport's source.[7]

John Clark Jordan, in the first extensive treatment of Greene's Philomela as a source, discusses the name borrowings by the playwright, the plot similarities and differences, and several parallel passages. He does not extensively analyze Davenport's verbal borrowings from Greene, and concludes merely that there are "in The City Nightcap many passages which resemble in style work written thirty-five or forty years before . . . ."[8] James S. Dean, Jr., develops Davenport's verbal borrowings more fully, listing the six Jordan noted, and adding twenty-four more. His list "shows the great extent to which Davenport drew upon Greene's romance."[9] A more complete list of verbal borrowings is included later in this chapter.

The reason why there has been disagreement is the similarity of the plots of the "Curious Impertinent" episode and Philomela. In Cervantes' story, set in Florence, Anselmo asks his close friend Lothario to test his wife Camila to see if she is as virtuous as she appears.[10] Lothario, though hesitant, finally tests Camila, whose beauty has captured his heart, and is successful almost immediately. They enjoy each other's love without interference, until Lothario, seeing a man leaving Camila's house, suspects her faithfulness to him and reveals all to Anselmo; afterwards, deciding this revenge is unreasonable, he reveals his actions to Camila. He discovers that she has not had another lover (the man is her maid Leonela's lover), and she tells him to come to her chamber the next day, after making sure Anselmo is hidden in the room. Anselmo overhears Camila's sorrow; finally, she makes a mock attempt to stab Lothario, and then stabs herself, in the shoulder. Anselmo is now convinced of her virtue, while Camila and her lover are free to continue their affair. Eventually, threatened by the possibility that Leonela will reveal all, Camila flees to a convent, while Lothario flees the kingdom. Anselmo dies after forgiving Camila and admitting that his curiosity caused the tragedy, Lothario shortly afterwards is killed in battle, and Camila soon dies of sorrow.

In Greene's romance, the jealous Count Philippo Medico, kinsman of Lorenzo, Duke of Venice, asks his close friend Giovanni Lutesio to test his wife Philomela Celii, daughter of the Duke of Milan.[11] Lutesio tries to seduce Philomela, but the latter proves completely virtuous. However, Philippo now suspects his friend and wife, and seeing them standing hand in hand is enough to convince him of his dishonor. He bribes two slaves, and the three of them testify against Lutesio and Philomela. The Duke of Venice sentences the couple to death, but at Philippo's insistance, lighter sentences are handed out, and Philomela is divorced while Philippo alone can remarry, and Lutesio is banished. Philomela, under the assumed name Abstemia, travels to Palermo, where she bears Philippo's child, Infortunatus. Lutesio goes to Milan to seek help from Philomela's father.

The Duke of Milan and Lutesio lead an army to Venice and force Lorenzo to agree to a retrial. When the Duke of Milan produces one of the slaves who readily admits his perjury, the second slave also confesses, and Philippo is sentenced by the Duke of Milan to banishment, during which time Philippo swears to search for Philomela.

In Palermo, the Duke's son, Arnoldo Frozzo, has exchanged identities with his slave in order to slip away to visit a lover. Petro Salmo, also of Palermo, who had a grudge against Arnoldo, kills the slave dressed as Arnoldo thinking it is his enemy, maiming the face beyond recognition. The body is discovered, and Philippo, failing in his search for Philomela and on the point of despair, is found nearby. He readily admits guilt, seeing this as an opportunity to die. At his trial, Philomela steps forward and also claims guilt, but before the Duke can act, Arnoldo reappears to clear them both. Philippo dies of ecstasy, and Philomela, though offered marriage by Arnoldo, ends her days as a grieved widow in Venice, the "Paragon of vertue" whose fame is "canonized" to this very day.

The parallels between Cervantes' and Greene's stories are evident. Both husbands ask their best friends to test a supposedly virtuous wife. Anselmo's motive, however, is curiosity, and the motive for Philippo is jealousy. One wife, Camila, and one friend, Lothario, prove faithless, while the others, Philomela and Lutesio, prove virtuous. From the standpoint of plot alone, the Lorenzo-Philippo-Abstemia plot in _The City-Night-Cap_ is closer to _Philomela_ than the "Curious Impertinent."

Several other dramas before 1624 deal with a similar story. The anonymous _Second Maiden's Tragedy_[12] follows the Cervantes' plot very closely, with only minor changes and a mass slaughter at the conclusion where everyone dies. The wife fails her chastity test, and the results are tragic. Davenport, however, does not follow this play, which is based on the Cervantes' tradition of the story.[13] The Antonio-Mercury-Maria plot in _The Coxcomb_ bears so slight a resemblance to the episode of the "Curious Impertinent" "that one is quite safe in asserting that [Beaumont and Fletcher] made use of other material than Cervantes' novel."[14] _The Coxcomb_ has even less resemblance to _The City-Night-Cap_. The reason Antonio allows Mercury to make love to his wife is not to test her, but rather to prove his friendship for Mercury.

Nathan Field's Amends for Ladies (ca. 1611), on the other hand, is much closer to Davenport's play. In the husband-wife subplot, the husband asks Subtle to test his wife's virtue; the wife, however, resists the temptation, and proves her honor to her husband's satisfaction, and he concludes: "Thus false friends are made true, by a true wife."[15] William Peery questions Rosenbach's conclusion that the subplot is from Cervantes,[16] and instead suggests that Field more likely borrowed from the Second Maiden's Tragedy, or simply heard the story. Amends for Ladies is a comic version of the Cervantes plot, and is therefore more similar to The City-Night-Cap than any of the other plays, but still the similarity is superficial. There are no verbal parallels, and numerous plot and character differences, particularly in the characters of Subtle and the wife, and in the actions of Subtle. There is no evidence that Davenport directly used Amends for Ladies.

Davenport, then, very likely borrows the plot directly from Philomela. In fact, beside numerous plot parallels, the playwright uses some of the same character and place names. He adopts the names Philippo (for the friend instead of the husband), Lorenzo Medico (for the husband instead of the Duke), and Abstemia (except during the exile, when she assumes the name Millicent), and uses a Duke of Venice (for Abstemia's brother rather than Lorenzo's kinsman), a Duke of Milan (for the father whose son is supposedly killed instead of Abstemia's father), and a Duke of Verona (Lorenzo's kinsman, substituted for Greene's Palermo). The setting is primarily Verona, with the conclusion in Milan, while Philomela is set in Venice, Milan (briefly), and Palermo.

Davenport makes several changes in plot, and sometimes shifts the emphases. He omits Abstemia's actual trip into exile, pregnancy, and child. He has her stay in exile in a brothel, and greatly expands the love of the Duke's son for her, barely suggested in Greene. And, while Philippo in Philomela dies, Lorenzo remains alive, having finally learned of his wife's true virtue. Below is a comparison of the space used to develop each of the major actions of the plot of both Philomela and The City-Night-Cap:

Philomela (page numbers)	The City Night-Cap (line numbers)
1. introduction, two seduction attempts (115-155).	1. I, i--introduction, one seduction attempt (1-162).
2. suspicion and arrest of friend and wife (155-164).	2. I, iii -- same (366-453).
3. trial (164-170).	3. II,iii--same (670-906).
4. exile trip of wife (171-180).	4. omitted.
5. friend at Abstemia's kinsman's court to gain redress (180-184).	5. omitted.
6. retrial (184-191).	6. III,ii--same (1076-1317).
7. Abstemia in exile, with child, before being reunited with her husband (191-193).	7. IV,i--Abstemia in exile, in brothel; tempted by Antonio (1465-1627).
8. events leading up to conclusion (193-204).	8. V--same (1930-2522).

Davenport greatly shortens the introduction, condensing the test to one attempt, with an immediate planting of the seeds of Lorenzo's jealousy toward Philippo. The suspicion of Lorenzo, the mistaken interpretation of Abstemia's and Philippo's words, and the arrest of the couple, are also significantly condensed. The trial and retrial, each one scene in the play, are short episodes in Philomela. Abstemia's problems with Antonio, her stay in the brothel, and the prison scene, occupy part of Act IV and most of Act V, and are not paralleled in Greene's work.

Davenport, we shall see, used a different source for this part of the plot. Greene condenses the conclusion, a part which Davenport emphasizes because of the addition of Antonio's love for Abstemia. So while Greene devotes only eight pages to the actual exile of Abstemia and events leading up to the conclusion, Davenport devotes over eight hundred and fifty lines, more than he devotes in the rest of the play to the entire Lorenzo-Abstemia plot.

In addition to name, place, and plot borrowings, Davenport borrows numerous passages directly from Philomela. Dean's list is inaccurate and incomplete, and the references are to the signatures of the 1592 edition of Philomela, and to the signatures of the 1661 edition of The City-Night-Cap, which makes the list difficult to use without these two editions. Below is a complete list of verbal parallels between the two works, with references to Grosart's edition of Greene, the standard and readily available edition of the prose, and to the lines in The City-Night-Cap, as the present edition is numbered. In addition, I have indicated in parentheses the page references for both the Hazlitt edition of Dodsley and the Bullen edition (both reprinted in 1964). References starred are additions to Dean's list.

Philomela Page	The City-Night-Cap Lines	(Bullen page-Hazlitt page)
1. 116	32-33	(94-106)
2. 116	36-38	(94-106)
3. 116	38-42	(94-106-107)
4. 118	49-50	(94-95-107)
5. 116	52-53	(95-107)
6. 118	54-55	(95-107)
7. 119	57-59	(95-107)

8.	119	59-60	(95-107)
9.	129; 145-146	91-92	(96-108)
10.	147	93-97	(96-108-109)
11.	153	98-100	(96-109)
12.	137	107-108	(97-109)
13.	143	118	(97-109)
14.	146	120-122	(97-109)
15.	146	122-123	(97-109-110)
*16.	147	131-132	(98-110)
17.	146-147	135-136	(98-110)
18.	130	140-142	(98-110)
*19.	128	147-150	(98-110)
20.	132; 189	152-156	(98-111)
21.	143 (same as #13)	371-372	(107-119)
22.	158	442-443	(110-121)
*23.	158	452	(110-122)
24.	164	695-697	(120-131)
25.	137	704-706	(120-131)
26.	169	831-832	(124-135)
27.	167	866-867	(125-136)
28.	168	872-873	(125-136)
29.	169-170	883-886	(126-137)
30.	170	896	(126-137)
31.	199	915-916	(127-138)
32.	185	1060-1064	(133-144)
33.	186-187	1080-1086	(133-134--144-145)
34.	187	1089-1090	(134-145)
*35.	128	1201	(137-148)

*36.	132; 198	2288	(178-189)
*37.	132; 198 (same as #36	2307	(178-190)
*38.	141	2335-2336	(179-190)
*39.	153	2338-2339	(179-190)

All of the verbal parallels are quoted in full in the notes to this edition, so only a few examples will be cited. Compare Davenport's "Beauty, like the herb _larix_, is cool i'th' water, But hot i 'th' stomack" with Greene's "Beauty is like the herbe _Larix_, coole in the water but hot in the stomach. . . "(number four on the list). Or, Davenport's "ye may let that slip by, Like water that ne'er meets the miller's eye" with Greene's "they may let much water slippe by the Mill that the Miller knoweth not of . . ."(number thirty-eight on the list). Those examples, only two of thirty-nine, indicate the extent to which Davenport borrows directly from the language of _Philomela._ There are, in addition, numerous parallels, some of which were discussed earlier in this chapter, that are merely plot, name or idea parallels not close enough to call direct verbal borrowings. It is safe to conclude that Davenport had a copy of _Philomela_ before him during much of the composition of _The City-Night-Cap._

For the conclusion to the Lorenzo-Abstemia plot, Davenport went to a second source. _Philomela_ suggested the exile, the murder of a slave thought to be a prince, the false confession of a husband in despair and false confession of a wife to save her husband, and a hint of the prince's love for the wife. Davenport, though, greatly expands these suggestions by adding the seduction attempt of Abstemia while the couple is in prison. She is offered the life of her husband if she will only submit to Antonio's desires. The source which most likely supplied Davenport with this idea was Measure for Measure. The playwright may have used one of Shakespeare's sources, such as Whetstone's Promos and Cassandra or Cinthio's Hecatommithi, since there are no definite verbal parallels between Measure for Measure and The City-Night-Cap, but several details argue the contrary. Davenport was steeped in Shakespeare, as W. J. Olive has shown.[17] Olive, in fact, attempts to show the direct influence of Measure for Measure: "The last scene of The City-Night-Cap. . . is rather closely modeled on Measure for Measure."[18] But his argument is based only on similarity of plot and rather dubious parallels of speeches during the prison scene between Isabella and Claudio, and Abstemia and Lorenzo. Yet Davenport does handle these speeches, and indeed the whole scene, with a technical mastery more similar to Shakespeare than to Whetstone.

Certainly the addition of the seduction attempt by Antonio has given The City-Night-Cap a greater unity and a greater depth. In Philomela the end is unified only by the two major characters, Philomela and Philippo. But in Davenport's play, Antonio has more than an incidental part; he is the central figure around whom most of the action revolves in the final two acts. He provides for Abstemia one final test, to put her concept of morality to one more proof, with the final twist of saving her husband. Lorenzo, of course, begs her to accept Antonio's offer, but she is firm. Lorenzo's final, "Thou wealth worth more than kingdoms, I am now confirm'd . . . we will die the martyrs of marriage," is necessary for the comic ending, but the reader is unconvinced by his sudden turn of mind. Much as Claudio's pleading to Isabella leaves the reader with a sense of man's shortcomings, it is his jealousy and final cowardice for which we remember Lorenzo.

Endnotes: Chapter II

[1] For a complete discussion of the English translation of *The Decameron*, see Mary Augusta Scott, *Elizabethan Translations from the Italian* (Boston and New York: Houghton Mifflin Co., 1916), and Herbert G. Wright, *The First English Translation of the 'Decameron' (1620)* (Upsala: A. B. Lundequistska Bokhandeln, 1953). All references to *The Decameron* are to the following edition: Giovanni Boccaccio, *The Decameron*, The Tudor Translations, First Series (1909: rpt. New York: AMS Press, Inc., 1967), III, 204-212.

[2] Gerard Langbaine, *An Account of the English Dramatic Poets* (1691; rpt. in facsimile, Hildesheim: Georg Olms Berlagsbuchhandlung, 1968), p. 117. It is possible that the source is one of the several tales based on the seventh tale of the seventh day, but most of them are briefer than Boccaccio's, and would have suggested even less of the plot outside of the actual cuckolding of the husband. None that I have seen use the name Lodovico. I have examined the following tales based on the seventh tale of the seventh day, none of which seem to be Davenport's source:

a. "The Smith's Tale" in *The Cobler of Canterburie* (1590; 1608). See Frederic Ouvry, ed., *The Cobler of Canterburie* (London: Frederic Ouvry, 1862), pp. 23-33.

b. The second tale in *A Hundred Mery Talys* (1526). See W. Carew Hazlitt, ed., *Shakespeare Jest-Books* (London: Willis & Sotheran, 1864), I, 12-14.

c. The third tale in *The Sackful of Newes* (1673, but known as early as 1575, and perhaps 1557). See W. Carew Hazlitt, ed., *Shakespeare Jest-Books* (London: Willis & Sotheran, 1864), II, 169-171.

3 Langbaine, p. 117.

4 John Payne Collier, ed., A Select Collection of Old Plays (London: Septimus Prowett, 1827), XI, 267. John Colin Dunlop, History of Prose Fiction, 2nd ed. (Edinburgh: John Ballantyne, 1816), III, 446, is apparently the first critic to note this source.

5 A. H. Bullen, ed., Old English Plays, New Series, III (London and Redhill: The Hansard Publishing Union, 1890), p. xii.

6 Abraham S. Wolf Rosenbach, "The Curious-Impertinent in English Dramatic Literature Before Shelton's Translation of Don Quixote," Modern Language Notes, 17 (1902), 363.

7 A. W. Ward and A. R. Waller, The Cambridge History of English Literature (N. Y.: G. P. Putnam's Sons, 1910), VI, 265. And, Felix E. Schelling, Elizabethan Drama 1558-1642 (1935; rpt. N. Y.: Russell and Russell, Inc., 1959), I, 260.

8 John Clark Jorden, "Davenport's The City-Nightcap and Greene's Philomela," Modern Language Notes, 36 (1921), 282.

9 James S. Dean, Jr., "Borrowings from Robert Greene's 'Philomela' in Robert Davenport's 'The City-Night-Cap'," Notes and Queries, 13, No. 8 (1966), 302.

10 All references to Don Quixote are to the following edition: Miguel de Cervantes, The History of Don Quixote of the Mancha, trans. Thomas Shelton, The Tudor Translations, First Series (London: David Nutt, 1896), II, 61-113.

11 All references to Philomela are to the following edition: Alexander B. Grosart, ed., Life and Complete Works in Prose and Verse of Robert Greene (n.d.; rpt. New York: Russell & Russell, 1964), XI.

12 W. W. Greg, ed., The Second Maiden's Tragedy, The Malone Society Reprints (1909; rpt. Oxford: University Press, 1964), p. v follows the

Stationer's Register in dating the play 1611.

13 Rosenbach, pp. 358-359, also reaches this conclusion.

14 Rosenbach, p. 362.

15 William Peery, ed., The Plays of Nathan Field (Austin: University of Texas Press, 1950), p. 226.

16 Ibid., p. 149.

17 W. J. Olive, "Davenport's Debt to Shakespeare in The City-Night-cap," Journal of English and Germanic Philology, 49 (1950), 333-344; and W. J. Olive, "Shakespeare Parody in Davenport's A New Tricke to Cheat the Divell," Modern Language Notes, 66 (1951), 478-480.

18 Olive, "Davenport's Debt to Shakespeare in The City-Night-Cap," p. 336.

CHAPTER III

THEATRICAL HISTORY (1624-1700)

The City-Night-Cap was licensed October 14, 1624, for the Cockpit Company, that is, Queen Henrietta's Men.[1] The title-page states, "As it was Acted with great Applause, by Her Majesties Servants, at the Phoenix [i.e., Cockpit] in Drury Lane." When the company became Beeston's Boys in 1636 or 1637, the play apparently remained in the repertory, for when the Lord Chamberlain issued his edict protecting those plays which evidently represented the repertory of the King and Queen's Young Company on August 10, 1639, The City-Night-Cap was on the list.[2]

The play was first printed in 1661, at which time many pre-Restoration plays were issued as the reopening of the theaters led to an increased demand among the reading public. The London Stage attributes a production of the play to sometime in the 1660-1661 acting season, but this date seems to be based only on the date of publication.[3] Whether or not, then, the play was performed at this time in its pre-1642 form is in doubt, but there exist two adaptations of The City-Night-Cap, and several other plays using the same story, attesting to the continual popularity of the plot.

One adaptation, although it is not known whether actually produced or not, consists of a combination of The City-Night-Cap with Sir William Lower's The Enchanted Lovers, surviving in a manuscript presently in the Folger Library.[4] The Folger date for it, c. 1665, is only approximate, and no attempt at a careful examination of paper or watermark has yet been made.[5] The original binding of this manuscript, included with six other plays, dates from c. 1725,[6] and nothing is known of the history of this text before that time. The Enchanted Lovers was first printed in 1658, though its composition date is not known.

The manuscript play is a strange combination, totally disunified. The Enchanted Lovers is a pastoral romantic comedy, The City-Night-Cap a domestic tragi-comedy. In the plot taken from Lower's play, set on an island kingdom of shepherds and shepherdesses, Toulmoso (whose actual name is Celia), who seven years previously had been washed ashore from a shipwreck after her mother had taken her from Seville to prevent her abduction by a courtier, is still grieving over the loss of her lover, Cleon. Cleon, thinking Celia dead, had killed the courtier and fled Seville, a hunted man. Lorina, Toulmoso's friend, soon discovers that Cleon is none other than Leander, a recent arrival on the island. Lorina brings them together; afterwards, the lovers pose as long lost brother and sister to hide their love from the ruler Melissa who is also in love with Leander, hoping to escape the island, but a merchant recognizes them. Melissa, who is also an enchantress, puts a spell on them which makes each die in turn while the other is forced to mourn. Melissa soon repents her anger, but only the goddess Diana, who decends from the heavens, is able to break the spell, and all live happily ever after.

These scenes are interspersed with the Lodovico-Dorothea-Francisco plot from The City-Night-Cap, and virtually no connection is made with the plot from The Enchanted Lovers.[7] In fact, the cuckolded-husband plot takes place in Verona, not on the island located near Portugal, and none of the characters figure in both actions, except for a few lines at the end. The play must act as if two separate plays are being performed. The plot from Davenport is an almost verbatim rendering of the six scenes of the Lodovico plot, with some cuts and some elimination of minor characters and action. In this play, the name Roderigo is used for

Lodovico, Livia for Dorothea, and Jerome for Francisco. Following is a comparison of this plot in the two plays:

MS (pages; number of handwritten lines)	*The City-Night-Cap* (number of lines)
1. Roderigo leaves, while Jerome and Livia reach agreement (6-9; 102 lines).	1. I, ii--Lodovico leaves, while Francisco and Dorothea reach agreement (202 lines).
2. bedroom scene (13-17; 114 lines).	2. II, i--same (93 lines).
3. garden scene (17-21; 135 lines).	3. II,ii--same (121 lines).
4. Roderigo reveals the faithfulness of his wife, and friar disguise set up (34-39; 171 lines).	4. III, i -- friar disguise set up (149 lines).
5. confession scene (47-51; 154 lines).	5. III,iii--same (146 lines).
6. penance scene, with non-speaking masque (63-68; 233 lines).	6. IV,ii--penance scene, with masque entitled "The City-Night-Cap" (301 lines).

In the first scene reference to meeting the Duke, and the characters of the four Lords, are eliminated, that is, lines 163 to 272, but the rest of the scene is given almost verbatim, including even Roderigo's motto, *Crede quod habes et habes.* The next scene, in the bedroom, is a very close rendering of the same scene from Davenport, with slight cuts. The same is true for the garden scene, except in the part preceding Jerome's entrance, which has been cut by more than half, eliminating of course all reference to the Lorenzo plot of *The City-Night-Cap.* Lodovico's recounting of the incidents is again slavishly followed, even to the introducing of two new characters, gentlemen of Verona. The slighting reference to Puritans (ll. 934-935) is retained. In the confession scene, the source again is closely followed. The manuscript play and the 1661 edition both read "far more" at l. 1389, suggesting perhaps that the 1661 edition and not a manuscript was followed. The final scene, where Livia must perform her penance, eliminates the spoken masque (substituting a dance of masquers) and the part of Pandulpho, and changes the conclusion, but otherwise closely follows the original. The two Dukes, Verona and Venice, are present, though they never appear earlier. The conclusion, after l. 1918, has been changed by the addition of a dance performed by the shepherds, the welcoming back of Count Cleon to court, and a reversal more in keeping with a comic treatment of the plot. The play ends on a note of reconciliation and promise:

> Vero. Count Roderigo if you have so much Charity as to Receive your Lady againe we'll gratifie that desire of our Welcome ffreinds, and revoke our Sentence
>
> [Rod.] Uppon Condition my wife Dreams no more I fforgive her
>
> Vero. Come then our noble ffreinds the rest of this night we'el Dedicate to our ffull Mirth, Madam Lett your ffuture honesty Deserve your Lords Pardon, Bad women are Natures Clouds eclipsing her ffaire shine the good all gratious Saint-like & Divine (p. 68).

The conclusion is more in keeping with the comic treatment of the plot, yet Roderigo's sudden forgiveness, like Lodovico's, seems too easy. Leander's return to his home (now apparently not Seville but Verona) is the only connection with the plot from Lower's play, and considering that Leander had fled under threat of death, his entrance and immediate request to revoke the sentence seems somewhat presumptuous if not preposterous. It is interesting to note that Verona's last two lines are taken from the conclusion to The City-Night- Cap, the only lines from the Lorenzo-Abstemia plot.

Since the manuscript has not been dated, the question of whether the text was copied from the 1661 edition of Davenport's play, or an earlier manuscript remains open. The Folger manuscript differs considerably in spelling from the printed edition; more extensive capitalisation but less punctuation is used. There are a few corrections and changes, as at lines 941, 1361, 1783, and 1883, but the textual problems at lines 466 and 1389 are repeated in the manuscript. It seems more likely that the reviser imposed his own spelling, capitalization, and punctuation on the text in an otherwise careful rendering of the 1661 edition.

A second adaptation, based entirely upon The City-Night-Cap, though in a greatly condensed form as a droll, was printed in 1680 as The Politick Whore: or, The Conceited Cuckold. The title page indicates that it was acted at Newmarket, before the Court and possibly by Robert Parker's Strollers.[8] In its printed text, the play is only twenty-one pages, plus a prologue, epilogue, and list of characters, and is included with two other drolls in The Muse of Newmarket (London, 1680).

The Lorenzo-Abstemia-Philippo plot, here Sir Isaac Jealousie-Innocentia-Fido, is reduced to 186 lines. The first scene begins with Sir Issac giving the background of the test, which has already taken place, and his suspicions of Fido, at which point he misinterprets Innocentia and Fido's conversation and in a fury accuses them. The next scene of this plot centers entirely on Innocentia, who has fled her husband and taken refuge in a whorehouse, where a pimp and bawd try to corrupt her. Much of this scene, the longest involving this plot (66 lines), is devoted to the dialogue of Drudgeo the pimp and the Bawd, and is taken almost verbatim from The City-Night-Cap, as is most of the dialogue in the entire play. The third scene involving the chaste wife is again set in the whorehouse, where the disguised Sir Isaac tries Innocentia, only to be lectured on virtue and the sin of lust--in a total of seven lines. Finally, at the end of the last scene, they are reunited, both forgiving and accepting each other, and presumably live happily ever after. This takes thirteen lines.

The faithless wife plot, here Sir Cornelius Credulous-Policia (the politick whore)-Mutchcraft, on the other hand, runs for 611 lines, over three times longer than the Isaac-Innocentia plot. The Credulous plot follows Davenport even more closely in both action and language. It omits the masque, eliminates the minor characters except for the clown Mocko, and cuts some of the dialogue. A comparison of The Politick Whore and The City-Night-Cap, to give an indication of the length and action parallels, follows:

The Politick Whore (number of lines)	The City-Night-Cap (number of lines)
1. I, i -recounting of test; accusation of Fido and Innocentia (45 lines).	1. I, i and iii-test; arrest of Philippo and Abstemia (249 lines).
2. I,ii -omission of Duke, with Fido replacing Lords; agreement between Policia and Mutchcraft (115 lines).	2. I, ii -Lodovico, four Lords, and Clown leave to meet Duke; Dorothea and Francisco reach agreement (202 lines).
3. II, i -bedroom scene (78 lines).	3. II, i -same (93 lines).

4.	II,ii-garden scene (97 lines).	4.	II,ii - same (121 lines).
5.	omitted (none suggested).	5.	II, iii - trial (236 lines).
6.	II, iii - Cornelius discusses faithful wife with Fido, who suggests friar disguise (87 lines).	6.	III, i - Lodovico discusses faithful wife with Lords, who suggest friar disguise (149 lines).
7.	omitted (none suggested).	7.	III, ii - retrial (260 lines).
8.	III, i - confession scene (78 lines).	8.	III, iii - confession scene (146 lines).
9.	I, iii - Innocentia, Bawd and Pimp in whorehouse (66 lines).	9.	Iv, i - Abstemia, Bawd, and Pimp in whorehouse, with Antonio (162 lines).
10.	III,iii - penance scene, and conclusion, with Cornelius handing out punishment, and Isaac reconciled with Innocentia (169 lines).	10.	IV,ii - penance scene, with masque (301 lines).
11.	III,ii - Isaac in disguise tests Innocentia in the whorehouse (62 lines).	11.	V, i - iv--Antonio plot, with Lorenzo and Abstemia in prison, and conclusion (593 lines).

It is obvious, then, that the Lorenzo-Abstemia plot, except for the scenes set in the brothel, suffered huge cuts, while the sensuous Lodovico-Dorothea plot is presented much more fully. Eliminated altogether are the Dukes, the Lords, the trials and divorce, and the masque (for which a silent banquet of "all sorts of Horns in Dishes" is substituted). Every slighting reference to Puritanism is eliminated in The Politick Whore. For example, Pambo, commenting on Dorothea's fast for her dead confessor, says, "She'll munch the more in a corner, that's the Puritan's fast" (ll. 934-935). But Mocko says, "She'le Munch the more in a Corner, that's her Fasts"(Sig. H4). In addition, the setting is made completely English, with the names changed to emphasize various character traits.

With the reward of Innocentia and punishment of Policia, the moral order of Davenport's world seems intact, but in this adaptation, the epilogue, spoken by Policia, completely changes the moral position of the conclusion.

> Must I, because I have to some been kind,
> For ever be secluded from Mankind,
> . . . .
> . . . Not I by Jove.
> Thanks to my Stars, our Sex as yet is free,
> Kind England grants us Christian Liberty;
> And some of you, no doubt, would be so good,
> To pity and relieve poor Flesh and Blood
> . . . .
> Then 'faith reverse my Sentence; if you don't
> When e're you'd do the Feat, be sure we wont.
>
> (lines 9-10; 12-16; 26-27)

The entire moral structure of The City-Night-Cap, then, had been undermined. The emphasis on the Credulous-Policia plot suggests the revisor's interest, and the epilogue makes his position explicit. Sexual fidelity implies restraint of our "Christian Liberty," a wasting of "Beauty," and an unfair demand on our frail natures. And, by extension, the faithfulness of Innocentia is not worth the reward which comes with it.

Several other Restoration plays related to The City-Night-Cap may be discussed more briefly. Edward Ravencroft's The London Cuckolds (1682), Act V, scenes iii and v, use the same bed trick as Davenport's play, but the plot follows Boccaccio closely, and probably derives directly from the seventh novel of the seventh day.[9] Sir Francis Fane's Love in the Dark, or The Man of Business (1675) complicates the bed trick, but once again Boccaccio, not Davenport, seems to be the source. The same is true for Thomas Durfey's Squire Oldsapp: or, the Night Adventurers (1679), though once again a new twist (a second lover) is added. Montague Summers identifies the Lorenzo-Abstemia plot as a source for Aphra Behn's The Amorous Prince (1671): "Mrs. Behn has taken her episode of Antonio's persuading Alberto to woo Clarina from Robert Davenport's fine play, The City-Night-Cap. . . ."[10] However, the source of this subplot is neither Davenport nor Greene, but probably Cervantes' episode of the "Curious Impertinent," which the playwright follows quite closely.

The City-Night-Cap was apparently popular before the closing of the theaters, but whether the play was acted after the Restoration is unknown. The story itself was widely used in the Restoration period, although Davenport's moral viewpoint is changed, with the Dorothea-character not longer severely punished, nor the Abstemia-character amply rewarded.

Endnotes: Chapter III

1 Joseph Quincy Adams, ed., The Dramatic Records of Sir Henry Herbert ([1917]; rpt. New York: Benjamin Blom, n.d.), p. 29.

2 Gerald Eades Bentley, The Jacobean and Caroline Stage (Oxford: Clarendon Press, 1941), I, 331.

3 William Van Lennep, ed., The London Stage 1600-1700 (Carbondale: Southern Illinois University Press, 1965), I, 16.

4 MS. 1478.2 (J.b.2). The Folger Library kindly furnished a photocopy of this document.

5 I am indebted to Folger librarian Laetitia Yeandle for this information.

6 From Giles Dawson's description of the Lambarde manuscript at the time the plays of the original volume were individually bound.

7 It should be pointed out that in addition to the plots from Lower and Davenport, there are elements of other sources in the play, such as the first scene of Act V between Ciss and Madge, and Frank and Anthony, which has nothing to do with either of the other plots, aside from the subject love.

8 Alfred Harbage, Annals of English Drama, rev. S. Schoenbaum (London: Methuen and Co., 1964), p. 180; and Sybil Rosenfeld, Strolling Players & Drama in the Provinces 1660-1765 (1939; rpt. New York: Octagon Books, 1970), pp. 39-40.

9 Interestingly, II,ii, where Loveday conjures a supper for Dashwell, is apparently taken from A New Trick to Cheat the Devil, so Ravenscroft was familiar with at least one play by Robert Davenport.

10 Montague Summers, ed., <u>The Works of Aphra Behn</u> (London: William Heinemann, and Stratford - On-Avon: A.H. Bullen, 1915), IV, 119.

CHAPTER IV

THE PLAY

1. Characterization

Davenport's sources provide the basic traits of most of the characters, with the possible exception of Pambo, yet the playwright does not slavishly follow his sources. The changes that Davenport makes from his sources in some of his characters reveal his interpretation of them.

For Abstemia, Davenport closely follows Greene's Philomela, with one important exception. Abstemia is totally virtuous; it is part of her essential nature. She cannot consider adultery under any circumstances, even to save her husband's life, and she never questions her husband or her duty to him. This is not true of Philomela. While she too is virtuous and faithful, to the point of never remarrying after her husband dies, she shows anger toward Philippo and questions her duty to him. After her husband's capture in Palermo, Philomela thinks, "now maiest thou triumphe in the fall of thy Jeliouse husband, and write thy chastitie in the characters of his bloode, so shall he die disgraced . . . ."[1] After this initial bitter reaction, she has an internal debate, trying to decide whether to simply curse Philippo, who is getting what he deserves, or to sacrifice her life for his, finally concluding that" . . . even so ought a good wife to be kind to her husband midst his greatest discourtesies, and rather venture her life, then suffer him incur any prejudice, and so will I doe by Philippo . . . I wil justifie him with mine owne death, so shall my ende bee honorable, as my life hath beene wonderfull."[2] The motivation of Philomela, then, is twofold: to save Philippo, and to preserve her own honor. Abstemia, on the other hand, never questions her duty to Lorenzo, to the point of immediately offering her life for his, and only incidentally regards the honor which she has earned,

> As I am expos'd
> To th' greatest battery beauty ever fought,
> Oh blame me not, if I be covetous
> To come off with greatest honour. . . (ll. 2397-2400)

She is a purely noble person, the ideal wife.

At the same time, Lorenzo's character undergoes an important change from Greene's Philippo. Philippo is convinced of his wife's guilt and, though he bribes two slaves, he too swears he saw the couple commit adultery. Yet, after the trial, he is "greatly tormented in his conscience."[3] And before the retrial, he "now began to feele remorse of conscience, and to doubt of the issue of his treacherie."[4] In *The City-Night-Cap* Lorenzo shows no hint of remorse or guilt until after the slaves confess their perjury. Lorenzo, therefore, appears crueler, more heartless, and as a result, should be less easily forgiven. Further, Lorenzo in the prison has a second chance which Philippo lacks, and he fails that second test, with only Abstemia emerging guiltless, and more admirable because she can yet forgive Lorenzo.

Lorenzo, then, appears a total villain, worse than Greene's Philippo, until his unconvincing conversion (l. 2406). However, he also emerges as the most human of the characters of that plot, perhaps because Abstemia is at times unbelieveable in her total virtue. But the playwright never sees her as unrealistic, although he does portray her as an ideal. In his prose character "A Martyr," Davenport describes a disciple of Christ rejoicing in his suffering, gaining salvation by his restraint and obedience.[5] Just as a guiltless Christ, though unjustly persecuted and killed, is forgiving, so the martyr must be guiltless and forgiving in order to win the crown of salvation. Significantly, Philippo says to Abstemia:

> Look up
> And see a crown held for thee; win it, and die
> Love's martyr . . . (ll. 877-879).

Lorenzo, full of doubt and all too human when facing death, reminds us of ourselves, while Abstemia wins salvation, as the ideal martyr of love.

Abstemia calls to mind Measure for Measure's Isabella, a character she may in part be modelled on. In Measure for Measure, a play also concerned with the testing of honor and virtue (of Isabella, Claudio, Angelo), Isabella's concept of chastity is challenged in a situation similar to Abstemia's in the prison scene in Act V. Claudio begs his sister Isabella to sacrifice her chastity to save his life, as Lorenzo begs Abstemia. Davenport's play has an added complication; Lorenzo, as husband and as previous doubter of his wife's virtue, ironically urges Abstemia to commit the act he most dreaded. In Act V of Measure for Measure Isabella must publicly confess to the sin she loaths and never commits; and finally, plead for Angelo's life, even though she thinks him the murderer of her brother; this is the final test of her charity.[6] But Isabella is never called upon to give her life for Claudio's, as Abstemia willingly would.

The central difference in the chastity tests in Shakespeare and Davenport lies in the arguments. Angelo argues on essentially ethical grounds; Isabella on the other hand asks for mercy for her brother, which can be granted if she commits the same offense. Antonio, with the same power of life or death that Angelo has, argues that he is merely borrowing her, and Lorenzo will not know the difference. In other words, not being a virgin, she has nothing to lose. Further, he argues, once Lorenzo is dead, his wife will probably yield with much less persuasion. To Abstemia, and finally to both Lorenzo and Antonio, his argument is mere sophistry.

Isabella has no test previous to Angelo's, and the result appears to be a shallow clinging to the mere concept of chastity. J.W. Lever therefore reasons, "Accordingly 'shame' not sin, 'honour' not charity, are seen now as the all-important considerations, and Claudio's duty to Isabella as superseding her duty to him."[7] Abstemia, on the other hand, cannot be so criticized, since her moral position is not ambiguous. She has already proved, before Antonio's test, that her virtue is deeper than a mere concept. Isabella is so unsure of both herself and Claudio that she feels compelled to convince her brother to support her, while Abstemia, assured of her position, argues that if she sinned she would be killing Lorenzo's name and her own soul; yet, she has no compunction to justify herself to either Lorenzo or Antonio.

Lorenzo too, then, is in the same position as Claudio; both have sinned and both fear death and beg dishonorably for their life. Their fates are put into the hands of others, and as a result, their weakness is, if not honorable, at least understandable as being human. Angelo too is like Antonio, although far more complex and perhaps more vicious a character; yet both become subjected to their lust and each is reformed by learning his own short-comings and seeingthe virtuous example of another. Angelo is educated about his own nature, and he marries Mariana. Antonio, hot-tempered frequenter of "*Venus'* Colledge," must prove his nobility, which he does by being won over by Abstemia's virtue.[8]

Paralleling, and contrasting with, the characters of this plot are Dorothea, Lodovico, and Francisco. Dorothea, like Abstemia, seems virtuous, but she fails her test. For her, Francisco is correct in proclaiming,

> Extreams in vertue, are but clouds to vice;
> She'll do i'th dark, who is i'th' day too nice.
> (ll. 315-316)

Both Dorothea and Abstemia are extremes in virtue, but Dorothea's virtue is easily seen through because of her comically exaggerated manner. In this respect, she is like Isabella entering the convent, upset because the strict rules of the order are too lenient, although Isabella's excess is caused by innocence, Dorothea's by cunning. For the husbands, Davenport contrasts and condemns their extremes; Lodovico, the trusting and naive husband learns that he is a fool and a cuckold, while Lorenzo, suspecting and mistrusting his wife, learns the possible tragic results of excessive jealousy. A mean between these extremes must be found. Finally, Francisco and Philippo are contrasted; the one is in the demeaning disguise of a servant to betray his trusting lord and satisfy his lust, the other proves a true friend to both husband and wife.

Pambo the clown has no predecessor in Shakespeare, since generally the jester-clown figure in Elizabethan drama was replaced by "the jesting, intriguing servant, not unlike the Italian type."[9] Pambo is a clown in name only; he is not the court jester, but rather a cynical, sophisticated, clown-knave whose comments, witty in their irony to the audience, are seldom funny to those around him. His function in the play is to put Lodovico's actions, Dorothea's feigned virtue, and Francisco's lust, into proper perspective. And he furthers the contrast of the two plots in his comments on Dorothea and Abstemia (ll. 230; 566; 569-571;

945-946). His punishment at the end is earned because of his betrayal of his generous lord, which his cynicism makes possible.

Davenport generally draws upon his sources for his characters, but he changes them where necessary to fulfill his didactic purpose, to convey the themes of The City-Night-Cap.

2. Structure and themes

Davenport employs a double plot, each one closely paralleled with, and contrasted to, the other. The one plot, Lorenzo-Abstemia, is 1499 lines long, while the other, Lodovico-Dorothea, is 1023 lines; the difference is chiefly accounted for by the elaborate conclusion to the Abstemia plot. Act I, scene i introduces the characters of the first plot, and shows how virtuous Abstemia in reality is, with the test by Philippo, and how excessively jealous Lorenzo is. I, ii introduces the characters of the second plot, and shows in contrast how hypocritical Dorothea's virtue is, with her test by Francisco, and how excessively naive and trusting Lodovico is. The explicit contrast is brought out in lines 227-245; Lodovico at one point proclaims, "ye shall have no Count Lorenzo of me," while the Clown ironically adds, "nor no Count Lorenzo's Lady of your wife." Dorothea then compares herself to Abstemia, of course to the latter's discredit. In I,iii the innocent Abstemia and Philippo are arrested for adultery at the instigation of Lorenzo, while in II, i, Francisco and Dorothea commit adultery, and make a dupe of Lodovico. II, ii is a supposed trial of Francisco in the garden, with II, iii the trial of Philippo and Abstemia, wrongly accused and unjustly convicted. The action has reached the point where the moral order is reversed, the innocent apparently punished, and the guilty free and in apparent control of the situation. Act III begins to reverse the morally unacceptable world created in the play; in scene i Jaspro proposes the disguise of friar to Lodovico so the latter can discover his wife's "pidling" sins, while in scene ii Abstemia and Philippo are cleared and Lorenzo is banished. But this only prepares the way for the resolution of this plot, since Lorenzo must find Abstemia, discover her true worth, and undergo a test of his own. In III, iii, the disguised Lodovico confesses Dorothea, and discovers her adultery and her true feelings toward himself. In IV, i, Abstemia is tempted by Antonio, whom she converts to goodness, at least temporarily. She has reached an apparent low, "miserable dispis'd Abstemia," divorced from Lorenzo, living in a brothel. In IV, ii, Dorothea is in her own home, hostess to two Dukes, apparently at the pinnacle of success. However, with the disrobing of the "frantick" friar, her world collapses and she, Francisio, and Pambo are punished for their sins. Act V is the complicated working out of the other plot, where Lorenzo learns that Abstemia will even die for him, and finally agrees to die a martyr with her. Their reward is reunion and restoration to their former positions. The Duke of Millain delivers the moral at the end:

> bad women
> Are nature's clouds eclipsing her fair shine;
> The good, all gracious, saint-like and divine.
> (ll. 2520-2522)

The two plots, then, are closely related, the scenes alternating to contrast each situation. The overall story of each, the two women, their actions and final punishment or reward, provides the basis for the parallel, and Davenport consciously extends this parallel to scene arrangement, and to the other characters.

Levin traces paralleling of this particular subject in several contrast-plot plays, perhaps suggesting a tradition in which The City-Night-Cap was composed. In discussing The Second Maiden's Tragedy (1611), Levin says: "Each plot begins with an episode that is clearly meant to function as a test of the heroine's virtue, since it requires her to choose between remaining faithful to the man to whom she rightfully belongs, legally and morally, or yielding to another whose desire for her is explicitly characterized as 'lust.' This test decides her fate, for the remainder of each plot develops the consequences of the crucial choice."[10] Levin discerns the same pattern in The Changeling (1622): "In each plot the heroine (Beatrice, Isabella) is tested by being faced with a choice between remaining faithful to her betrothed or husband (Alonzo, Alibius) or betraying him with a rival (Alsemero, Antonio/Franciscus) . . . and again, one woman fails the test and therefore, must descend along a path of deception, crime, and degradation to a shameful death, while the other passes and so emerges victorious."[11] So, while the consequences of Dorothea's wrong choice have been changed from the tragic to conform to the tragicomic atmosphere of the play, the basic pattern remains the same.

Levin, however, finds certain inherent difficulties in The City-Night-Cap, since the plot involving the failing wife is no longer a tragedy as in the earlier plays. Primarily concerned with the resolution, he says: "Since the women represent moral absolutes, Dorothea's punishment must be as serious as Abstemia's reward . . . which violates the comic mood of the subplot. And it throws the paired denouements off balance, for after the husbands are cured of their equivalent aberrations, Lorenzo is reunited with his paragon of purity . . . while Lodovico is left with nothing."[12] This judgment, however, can not be totally accepted. The resolution is merely the working out of the contrasted plots; Dorothea's punishment, as well as Abstemia's reward, is inherent in the action. The Dorothea plot begins as comedy, to be sure, but the mood changes by III, i. The consequences of her actions are tragic; she is exiled to a nunnery, and Francisco and Pambo are severely punished. Lodovico is left with nothing, but he is content. No one dies since Dorothea does nothing to deserve death; she compromises her husband's honor, but does not plot to kill him. And death, in this case, would mar the tragic-comic mood of the play. Perhaps the underlying fault is with Davenport's comic handling of scenes of a plot that is not comic, rather than condemn the plot itself. But the play is a "Tragi-comedy," as the title-page states, and the Abstemia plot which moves from the potentially tragic to the final comedy is neatly balanced by the Dorothea plot which moves from the comic to the potentially, though never fully, tragic. Levin's conclusion that "these are no doubt minor faults in a play replete with all the major ones"[13] needs qualification, a look at the play within its tradition.

Davenport, while not always faring well with some critics on this point, has carefully drawn his characters and carefully constructed his play. The plot, a balanced contrast, reinforces the themes of the play.

The main theme is that there is sometimes a difference between appearance and reality, a central theme also of _Measure for Measure._ In Shakespeare's play the Duke says, "Hence shall we see . . . what our seemers be" (I, iii, 53-54), and the word "seem" rings throughout _The City-Night-Cap_ as well. For Abstemia, "seem" is equated to "is"; she says no one will cuckold a husband "Whose wife seems honest, and no hypocrite." (l. 157) But for Dorothea, "seem" must be contrasted with reality. In the words of Francisco, who knows Dorothea:

. . . as he who fain would know
The real strain of goodness, may in her read it,
Who can seem chaste, and can be what she seems;
So, who would see hell's craft, in her may read it,
Who can seem too, but not be what she seems.

(ll. 541-545)

For Abstemia, there is no separation between appearance and reality; for Dorothea, her whole life seems to be one thing but in reality is the opposite.

This difference between appearance and reality extends beyond Abstemia and Dorothea to other characters and situations. So Abstemia and Philippo, walking hand in hand (ll.379-383), seem to be returning from committing adultery ("Philippo, you have fully satisfied me"). In the brothel, Abstemia appears to be a whore, but in reality she is an angel who converts Antonio from his hellish intents. On the other hand, Dorothea seems chaste, railing against intemperance and immodesty, going to confession twice a week. Related to this theme is the frequent use of disguises and false names in the play. Abstemia, Philippo, Lodovico, Francisco, the slave, and Antonio all assume false identities, in an attempt to be someone other than each really is.

A second central theme is that the best marriage involves a certain amount of trust, yet the husband must place some restraint on his wife. And the wife has her duties. The only ideal marriage depicted is Abstemia-Lorenzo at the end of the last act; Lorenzo now trusts his wife and is willing even to sacrifice his life for her virtue. She respects his honor and knows her duty to him, which includes offering her life to save his.

Another theme is the ultimate triumph of justice. The events naturally lead to the moralistic ending; Abstemia's virtue must be rewarded, Dorothea's adultery must be punished. This is obvious enough, except that Davenport's source for the Dorothea-plot does not have the same ending. Boccaccio ends his tale with the gulled husband an unsuspecting cuckold, and the clever wife in complete control. Davenport probably could not have left the Dorothea-plot as his source had even if he was not consciously contrasting the two plots, since his moral view-point is in all respects traditional and conventional,[14] and therefore out of moral necessity he departs from his source.

3. Setting

The setting of The City-Night-Cap is Venice and Milan, but no dramatic use is made of these locations. Davenport's sources, Greene and Boccaccio as well as Measure for Measure, are all set in Italy, which may account for the playwright's choice. Many contemporary tragi-comedies were also set in Italy or similar locations, and Davenport could be following this convention. By 1624, the Italian setting was conventional not only as a place of sexual intrigue, murder, and revenge, but as a setting of true love and actions and tests concerning honor, as depicted in Boccaccio, Candello, and Cinthio, frequent sources of English drama. Philippo, in fact, refers to the frequency of the trying of a wife in "most of our Italian Comedies" (1. 7).

Robert C. Jones, in discussing Italian settings in Elizabethan tragedy, notes that many times the scene is seldom described at all.[15] In fact, it is "simply not part of [the Jacobean playwright's] poetics to work up the landscape or atmosphere of an actual region in detail, even when commonly known details might suit their themes. . . ."[16]

Davenport too makes no use of his setting other than the mention of some place names, most of which are repeated from Greene. Where he has the opportunity to use a specific setting, as in Act V, scenes i, ii, and iii, the actual setting is merely "a wood."

The same is true for other background of the play. There are very few references within The City-Night-Cap to any specific customs or people, and none to any historical events. Other than the references to Lodovico's pamphlet of his wife's virtues, apparently alluding to the very popular Overbury poem "A Wife," to the use of yellow starch and the wearing of cork heel shoes, and to Puritan hypocrisy, there are no references to contemporary people, events, or customs.

There is only one reference in the play which contrasts England and Italy. Lodovico discusses an English gentleman, whom he brings home to see a horse and who tries to kiss Dorothea. She does not like that, and says, "Though confidence made cuckolds in England, she could no coxcombs in Italy." To which the Englishman retorts, "Confidence makes not so many cuckolds in England, but craft picks open more padlocks in Italy." (ll. 197-198, 201-204). Italy then, in contrast to England, is a place of craft and deception, a commonplace convention of Jacobean plays.

Jones is correct, for Davenport at least, in saying that the playwrights were not symbolizing the viciousness and moral sickness of their plays through the Italian setting itself.[18] Davenport, while setting The City-Night-Cap in Italy, does not dramatically use that setting. He does not give specific descriptions, nor does he seem to be making an indirect attack on any contemporary object or person.

4. Style

Davenport's style, as has been pointed out often enough, is "undistinguished."[19] The City-Night-Cap is written in both prose and verse, and the style is unpoetic, yet functional.

The prose style needs little discussion. There are no distinguishing features, except perhaps a tendency to omit pronouns and to elide unstressed letters. Such devices, which sometimes make the dialogue hard to understand, must have been closer to the way in which the lines were spoken, and in fact make the dialogue seem more domestic and informal, in harmony with the story.

It is likely that at least some of the lines that are set in verse in the 1661 edition should be prose, since they are so unpoetic, lacking meter and rhythm. Line 177, for example, is set as verse, with the first word of the next line capitalized in the 1661 edition, but the rest of the speech is set as prose, as is much of the rest of the scene. It is more likely that this entire scene should be set as prose, not both verse and prose.

The euphuistic passages, usually set in verse, have been the concern of several critics. Swinburne, perhaps too enthusiastic on the whole, disliked the passages from Greene: "Was it modesty, sheer laziness, or inveterate admiration for an early favorite, which so woefully misguided a poet who could write when it pleased him with such masculine purity and simplicity? The barren and cumbersome profusion of these faded artificial flowers [the euphuistic passages], colourless now and scentless always . . . ."[20] Perhaps Swinburne overstates his case for the poetic beauty of The City-Night-Cap, but he does raise the problem of whether the euphuistic passages are intergral within the play. We, perhaps, agree with Swinburne and can see a disparity of style between the rather simple informal dialogue, particularly evident in the Dorothea plot, and the elaborate formal euphuistic dialogue, but Davenport did not. He did like this style, and in A New Trick to Cheat the Devil there are examples of euphuism which the playwright seems not to have borrowed from any source. In The City-Night-Cap the euphuistic passages are used almost entirely in the Abstemia plot, and usually either describe her or are spoken by her. Davenport, then, perhaps in an attempt to set the ideal Abstemia apart from the other characters, associates with her this distinctive style, which certainly the playwright would not want to be regarded as "artificial."

The play is, on the whole, devoid of image motifs. The conventional crown image, symbol of Abstemia's salvation, is one, but it is not very extensively used. The most effective image is the sun-cloud contrast, which runs throughout the play. Francisco describes Dorothea's virtue as "but clouds to vice" (l. 315), while Philippo describes Abstemia (in the brothel) as "like the sun behind a cloud" whose "beams do give intelligence it is there." (ll. 1547-1548) At the same time, truth is compared to "heaven's sun" (l. 1928), revealing virtue. Lorenzo, however, describes Abstemia as "Like a silver cloud" (l. 2019), and the Duke of Millain describes Antonio's face as "sunlike" (l. 2040). Both these characters are wrong; Antonio is the "displeasant black cloud" (l. 2265), as he describes himself, while Abstemia remains a sun, surviving the various eclipses of "nature's clouds" (such as Antonio and "bad women," like Dorothea) only to shine forth once again as bright and constant as always. This sun-cloud contrast is used consistently; some characters have trouble in the darkness of an eclipse to see the true sun, but in the end, truth and Abstemia, "the good, all gracious, saint-like and divine" shine again in all their glory.

One device used by the playwright in his verse is an occasional couplet, not only to end a scene (e.g., ll. 162-163, 1316-1317), but within scenes, especially in a long speech at the second and third lines from the end (e.g., ll. 86-87, 117-118) or the second and third lines from the end of a stopping point in the action (e.g., ll. 451-452, 904-905), though Davenport also uses an occasional couplet in the middle of a speech too (e.g., ll. 152-153, 154-155, 156-157). Not only does the use of couplets indicate Davenport's conscious attempt to render his verse more poetic, but it keeps any longer speech from becoming monotonous.

The one lyric which is apparently sung by Francisco is functional. This song (ll. 216-217, 221-222, 224-225) serves a thematic function: truth is seldom found today (in the case of Dorothea at least). In addition, Bowden points out that "Dorothea's overvirtuous response is immediately evident as a pose, and her husband Lodovico's approval of her conduct stamps him as a born cuckold. This song, then, combines plot function with characterization."[21]

Several other lyrical couplets, perhaps also sung, serve plot, character, or thematic functions as well. At ll. 315-316, Francisco "unravels" Dorothea's pose:

> Extreams in vertue, are but clouds to vice;
>
> She'll do i'th' dark, who is i'th' day too nice.

This accurate summary of Dorothea's character shows that she is afraid not of sin but of shame. As long as she can safely sin without discovery, she will keep her "virtue."

An extensive section of couplets, though not lyrical, is the masque in Act IV, in which the humor is in the wit of the lines and the stumbling delivery of Pambo, probably sensing something amiss and feeling most uncomfortable. The masque is entitled "a City-Night-Cap" and thematically connects the play title and theme. The masquers, disguised as horned animals, symbolic of both the horned cuckold and animal lust, dance around Lodovico's banquet hall, where the chief masquer, Lodovico, sprouts his cap, a large head of horns. It is in the city, "where have women most their will" (l. 1750), that a husband has a great likelihood of gaining a city night-cap, and the jest of the poets is that the husband may not ever know it (an irony which provides the humor of this plot through the first three acts of the play).

Closely related to this irony is the extensive use of double entendres in the Dorothea plot, where the second meaning is humorous and usually sexual in nature. The clown's lines oftentimes have this double meaning, as in ll. 576-578 with a play on "prick." At only one point is there a double meaning in the Abstemia plot, where Lorenzo in a potentially tragic mistake misunderstands his wife's "satisfied," psychologically perhaps as he wanted to understand it.

While Davenport's verse is, then, on the whole devoid of what might be called poetic quality, it is functional; it prevents monotony in most of the longer speeches, provides humor, keeps the dialogue moving forward, and usually works thematically or descriptively to forward the playwright's ideas.

Endnotes: Chapter IV

[1] Alexander B. Grosart, ed., Life and Complete Works in Prose and Verse of Robert Greene (n.d.; rpt. New York: Russell & Russell, 1964), XI, 197.

[2] Ibid., p. 199.

[3] Ibid., p. 170.

[4] Ibid., p. 186.

[5] G. Thorn-Drury, ed., A Little Ark (London: P.J. and A.E. Dobell, 1921), p. 12.

[6] J. W. Lever, ed., Measure for Measure, The Arden Edition of the Works of William Shakespeare (London: Methuen & Co., and Cambridge: Harvard University Press, 1965), p. lxxix, argues that Isabella lacks this virtue.

[7] Ibid.

[8] Perhaps an inconsistency exists in The City-Night-Cap. Philippo says to Antonio:

> you are noble, just and true;
> My hate was at your cloathes, my heart at you.
>
> (ll. 2510-2511)

Either Philippo is lying (which might be the courtly thing to do), since it was Antonio who kicked him, or the plot is inconsistent, at this point confusing the disguised slave and Antonio's actions. If we assume the former, Antonio's temper, as well as his other actions, have been forgiven.

[9] Olive Mary Busby, Studies in the Development of the Fool in Elizabethan Drama (London: Oxford University Press, 1923), p. 86.

10 Richard Levin, *The Multiple Plot in English Renaissance Drama* (Chicago: University of Chicago Press, 1971), p. 27.

11 *Ibid.*, p. 36. The details of the plots of these plays and *The City-Night-Cap* are of course different, each coming from a different source.

12 *Ibid.*, p. 49.

13 *Ibid.*

14 Davis concurs for Davenport's other work and points out: "The main interest of these poems to a student of Davenport's drama lies in their very conventional and pious moral sentiments . . . [for] the moral order which underlies *King John and Matilda* is at all points a traditional and conventional one." Joyce Outten Davis, "Robert Davenport's *King John and Matilda*: A Critical Edition," Diss. Tulane 1969, p. xi.

15 Robert C. Jones, "Italian Settings and the 'World' of Elizabethan Tragedy," *Studies in English Literature*, 10 (1970), 255.

16 *Ibid.*, p. 261.

17 Frederick Gard Fleay, *A Biographical Chronicle of the English Drama* 1559-1642 (London: Reeves and Turner, 1891), I, 104.

18 Jones, p. 257.

19 To use Davis's description. See, p. xi.

20 Edmund Gosse and Thomas James Wise, eds., "Robert Davenport," *The Complete Works of Algernon Charles Swinburne* (1925; rpt. New York: Russell & Russell, 1968), XII, 310.

[21] William R. Bowden, The English Dramatic Lyric, 1603-42 (New Haven: Yale University Press, 1951), p. 160.

CHAPTER V

TEXTUAL INTRODUCTION

1. Textual History

The first edition of The City-Night-Cap was printed in 1661 by James Cottrel for Samuel Speed. Cottrel was a London printer from 1649 to 1670, and at the time of the survey of the press (July, 1668), he employed two presses, two compositors, and no apprentices, so that Plomer concludes Cottrel's business was not a large one.[1] Speed, a London bookseller from 1658 to 1667, was, as Plomer states, located in St. Paul's Churchyard and the two Temple Gates, although only the first location is noted on the title page of The City-Night-Cap.[2]

Copies of this edition are relatively common. Wing locates English copies at the British Museum (the BM Catalog indicates three copies--vol. 49, p. 29), the Bodleian, in the Dyce Collection (Victoria and Albert), at Dulwich College, and at Worcester College (Oxford). In addition, there is a copy in the Bute Collection in the National Library of Scotland (Studies in Bibliography, 15 (1962), p. 102). American copies, locations updated by the National Union Catalog, Pre-1956 Imprints, (London and Chicago: Mansell, 1968--), are at the Library of Congress, Yale University, Chapin Library at Williams College, Harvard University (two copies), the University of Texas at Austin, Newberry Library, Huntington Library, Princeton University and the Boston Public Library (vol. 134, p. 118). I have examined the originals or photocopies of all of these American located copies except for the last two, which were unavailable at the time.

A second edition of The City-Night-Cap appeared in volume IX of the collection of plays entitled A Select Collection of Old Plays, edited and published in 1744 by Robert Dodsley, who followed the 1661 edition rather closely, although making numerous changes in punctuation and spelling.

The next edition appeared in volume XI of the second edition of Dodsley's collection published in 1780 by James Dodsley, and was edited by Isaac Reed. Reed added "notes critical and explanatory." The third edition of Dodsley again included The City-Night-Cap in volume XI. It was published by Septimus Prowett in 1827, and was edited by John Payne Collier, who added further notes and offered further emendations. The last edition of Dodsley published in the years 1874, 1875 and 1876 by Reeves and Turner was edited by W. Carew Hazlitt. Volume XIII (published in 1875) included The City-Night-Cap, again with additional notes and emendations. This edition has been photographically reprinted and is readily available.[3] Hazlitt examined both a 1661 edition and Collier's edition, adopting many of Collier's suggested emendations and adding many more of his own.

The National Union Catalog, Pre-1956 Imprints, volume 134, p. 118 (item ND 0062420), lists what appears to be a unique copy of The City-Night-Cap at Harvard University. I have examined this copy, and it is actually a copy of Hazlitt's edition, removed from the 1875 printing, and differs in no way from two other copies of Hazlitt's edition which I have examined.

In 1810, The Ancient British Drama set was published by William Miller, and edited by Walter Scott; volume III includes The City-Night-Cap. This is a reprint of the 1780 edition of Dodsley, using the same text and the same notes. Finally, in 1890, A. H. Bullen, in his Old English Plays, new series, volume III, edited the "complete" works of Davenport. It was privately printed by the Hansard Publishing Union, Ltd., of London and Redhill, and limited to one hundred and fifty copies. This edition has been photographically reprinted.[4] Bullen has examined at least Hazlitt's edition, but independently edits. His edition is the most fully annotated, with a conservative following of the 1661 edition, except for extensive rearrangement of the lines. There is a general lack of textual notes, and some inaccuracies and many inconsistencies in the text itself.

2. Treatment of the Text

The only edition with possible authorial textual authority is the 1661, of which there is only one issue. In the seven copies of this edition which I have examined, there is only one correction during printing.[5] I have therefore based this critical edition on the 1661 edition, examining the later editions to see what variants they contain and what emendations their editors made. Because of the large number of variants in these later editions, only changes in words, changes in spelling or punctuation which affect meaning, and additions and omissions are given in the textual notes.

This edition contains the edited text, under which are the annotations, consisting of meanings of obscure or obsolete words, alternate spellings when in question, parallels with sources, and other general explanatory matter. Textual notes are at the end, and indicate changes of substantive readings of the text[6] in this edition as well as changes in later editions which affect the meaning or reading of the text.

The text of the present edition is based on conservative principles. Those accidentals of the copy-text (the 1661 edition) which have been silently standardized to Davenport's most frequent usage, where this can be determined, are spelling, capitalization, punctuation, and typography. For example, the word modesty is spelled "modestie" and "modesty" in the 1661 edition. The most common spelling, both in this edition and in Davenport's other work is "modesty", and this spelling is therefore used throughout the play. In mid-sentence, both "Sir" and "sir" occur, but "sir" is by far the most common, hence the text is standardized to the lower case form throughout. In questionable cases, the NED was consulted for accepted spellings, serving as the final arbiter. If any standardization possibly affects the meaning, it is included in the textual notes. This edition also silently modernizes the old ʃ form throughout, and the capital W, whenever printed VV, is silently altered to W throughout. With these exceptions, all departures from the copy text are recorded in the textual notes.

Italics are indicated by underlining. All proper names and song lyrics are italicised, following the copy-text. Speech prefixes and stage directions too are italicised, with additions to the copy-text enclosed within brackets. All speech prefixes have been silently standardized. The spacing of the text has also been silently standardized.

The 1661 text is divided into five acts, but not into scenes. This edition numbers each scene, considering a new scene as beginning each time the stage is cleared. The lines are consecutively numbered from beginning to end, omitting only act numbers and stage directions; stage directions are indicated by the preceding line number followed by a lower-case letter, beginning with a. Thus 286a would refer to the first line of a direction after line 286 of the dialogue. Bullen, following the partial efforts in the earlier editions, attempts to regularize the lines, and frequently divides lines, but *The City-Night-Cap* is not primarily in blank verse, nor are the lines as they stand in the 1661 edition particularly corrupt. This edition maintains the original lineation, without "regularization," unless otherwise noted.

Endnotes

[1] Henry R. Plomer, A Dictionary of the Booksellers and Printers Who Were At Work in England, Scotland and Ireland from 1641 to 1667 (1907; rpt. The Bibliographical Society, 1968), p. 54.

[2] Ibid., pp. 169-170.

[3] rpt. New York: Benjamin Blom, Inc., 1964.

[4] rpt. New York: Benjamin Blom, Inc., 1964.

[5] at line 2262; see the textual notes.

[6] Here I use W.W. Greg's distinction of "substantive" and "accidental." See "The Rationale of Copy-Text," Studies in Bibliography, 3 (1950), p. 21, and The Editorial Problem in Shakespeare (Oxford: the Clarendon Press, 1942), pp. 1-lv.

Abbreviations

Editions of _The City-Night-Cap_:

1661: London: James Cottrel for Samuel Speed, 1661 (Wing D-369).

MS: "William Lower's _The Enchanted Lovers_ and Robert Davenport's _The City-Night-Cap_," Folger MS. J.b.2.

D1: Robert Dodsley, ed., _A Select Collection of Old Plays_, IX (London: R. Dodsley, 1744),

D2: Isaac Reed, ed., Dodsley's Select Collection of Old Plays, XI (London: J. Dodsley, 1780).

D3: John Payne Collier, ed., Dodsley's Select Collection of Old Plays, XI (London: Septimus Prowett, 1827).

D4: W. Carew Hazlitt, ed., _Dodsley's Select Collection of Old Plays_, XIII (London: Reeves and Turner, 1875).

D: All four editions of Dodsley's plays.

B: A. H. Bullen, ed., _The Works of Robert Davenport, in Old English Plays_, III (London and Redhill: Hansard Publishing Union, 1890).

Other references:

Farmer and Henley: J. S. Farmer and W. E. Henley, eds., _Slang and Its Analogues_. 7 vols. (London: n.p., 1890-1904).

Fleay: F. G. Fleay, _A Chronicle History of the London Stage_, 1559-1642, 2 vols. (London: Reeves and Turner, 1890).

NED: _A New English Dictionary_, ed. James A. H. Murray, et al., 10 vols. (Oxford: the Clarendon Press, and New York: Macmillan and Co., 1888-1933).

Olive: W. J. Olive, "Davenport's Debt to Shakespeare in _The City-Night-Cap_," _Journal of English and Germanic Philology_, 49 (1950), 333-344.

Shakespeare: Harold F. Brooks and Harold Jenkins, general eds., *The Arden Edition of the Works of William Shakespeare* (London: Methuen & Co., and Cambridge: Harvard University Press, v.d.).

Tilley: Morris Palmer Tilley, *A Dictionary of the Proverbs in England in the Sixteenth and Seventeenth Centuries*. (Ann Arbor: University of Michigan Press, 1950).

THE

City-Night-Cap:

Or,

Crede quod habes, & habes.

A

Tragi-Comedy.

By *Robert Davenport*.

As it was Acted with great Applause,
by Her Majesties Servants, at
the Phoenix in *Drury Lane*.

LONDON:

Printed by *Ja:* *Cottrel*, for *Samuel Speed*, at the Signe of the
Printing-Press in St. *Paul*'s Church-yard. 1661.

Drammatis Personae.

Duke of Verona.
Duke of Venice, Brother to Abstemia.
Duke of Millain.
Antonio, the Duke's [of Millain] Son.
Lorenzo, Husband to Abstemia.
Philippo, his Friend.
Lodovico, Husband to Dorothea.
Lords of Venice.
Senators of Verona.
Sanchio, Sebastiano, Pandulpho, — Lords of Millain.
Spinoso, Jaspro, Jovani, — [Lords of Verona].
Francisco, servant to Lodovico.
Pambo, a Clown.
Morbo, a Pander.
A Turk, Slave to Antonio.
2 Slaves to Lorenzo.
Officers and Servants.

Women Actors.

Abstemia, Lorenzo's Wife, and Sister to the Duke of Venice.
Dorothea, Lodovico's wanton Lady [wife].
Timpanina, a Bawd.
Ladies [of Verona].

ACTUS PRIMUS.

[SCENE I]

Enter Lorenzo and Philippo.

Lor. Thou sha't try her yet once more.

Phil. Fie, fie.

Lor. Thou shalt do't.
If thou be'st my friend, thou'lt do't.

Phil. Try your fair wife?
You know 'tis an old point, and wonderous frequent
In most of our Italian comedies.

Lor. What do I care for that? Let him seek new ones
Cannot make old ones better; and this new point,
Young sir, may produce new smooth passages,
Transcending those precedent. Pray, will ye do't?

Phil. Pray, fool your self no farther; twice you have swaid me,
Twice I have try'd her; and 'tis not yet, ye know,
Ten days since our reconciliation.
How will it shew in you so near a kinsman
To the Duke, nay, having woven your self into
The close-wrought mystery of opinion,
Where you remain a souldier, a man

---

9. Cannot] [who] cannot. Davenport frequently omits the pronoun. See the discussion on style in the introduction.

Of brain and quality, to put your friend
Again on such a business, and to expose
Your fair wife to the tempest of temptation?
And by the white unspotted cheek of truth,
She is———————

Lor. A woman.

Phil. A good woman.

Lor. Pish.

Phil. As far from your distrust, as bad ones are from truth.
She is in love with vertue; would not boast it,
But that her whole life is a well-writ storie,
Where each word stands so well plac'd, that it passes
Inquisitive detraction to correct.
She's modest, but not sullen, and loves silence;
Not that she wants apt words,(for when she speaks,
She enflames love with wonder) but because
She calls wise silence the soul's harmony.
She's truly chaste, yet such a foe to coyness,
The poorest call her courteous; and which is excellent,
(Though fair and young) she shuns to expose her self

---

30. passes] exceeds.

32-33. She's modest . . . apt words] Cf. Greene's *Philomela* (p. 116): "she was modest without sullennesse, and silent not as a foole, but bicause she would not be counted a blab . . ."

36-39. She's truly . . . eyes] Cf. Greene's *Philomela* (p. 116): "[she's] chast, and yet not coy, for the poorest of all held hir courteous: though she was young, yet she desired neyther to gad nor to gase, nor to have hir beautie made common to every bad companions eie . . ."

To the opinion of strange eyes; she either seldom
Or never walks abroad but in your company,
And then with such sweet bashfulness, as if
She were venturing on crack'd ice; and takes delight
To step into the print your foot hath made,
And will follow you whole fields; so she will drive
Tediousness out of time, with her sweet character.
And therefore, good my friend, forbear to try
The gold has past the fire.

Lor. Thou foolish friend,
Beauty, like the herb *Larix*, is cool i 'th' water,
But hot i 'th' stomack; women are smooth flatterers, but cunning injurers.

Phil. Thou wonderous yellow friend,
Temper an antidote with antimony,

39-42. she either. . . ice] Cf. Greene's *Philomela* (p. 116): ". . . for she never would goe abroad but in the company of hir husband, and then with such bashfulnesse, that she seemed to hold hir owne mansion. . ."

46. my good] All other editions read: good my

46-47. forbear to try. . . the fire] alluding to the proverb, "Gold is tried in the fire" (Tilley, G284).

49-50. Beauty . . . stomack] Cf. Greene's *Philomela* (p. 118): "Beauty is like the herbe *Larix*, coole in the water but hot in the stomach. . ."

larix] the herb *Camphorosma monspeliacum*; this line cited in *NED* as one example.

51. yellow] jealous.

52-53. Temper . . .infectious] Cf. Greene's *Philomela* (p. 116): "But as there is no Antidot so pretious but being tempered with Antimonie is infectious. . ."

antimony] a brittle metallic element of bright bluish-white color and flaky crystalline texture. Perhaps Greene and Davenport are referring to the popular etymology of the word, "monks-bane" (*NED*), or perhaps they are confusing it with arsenic, a similar compound related in appearance and physical property.

And 'tis infectious; mix jealousie with marriage,
It poysons vertue; let the child feel the sting,
He'll fly the honey-comb. Has she one action
That can expose you to distrust?

Lor. Oh! When the Elesander leaf looks most green,
The sap is then most bitter; an approv'd appearance
Is no authentick instance; she that is lip-holy,
Is many times heart-hollow.---------Here she comes.

Enter Abstemia.

A prayer-book in her hand! Oh hypocrisie!
How fell'st thou first in love with woman? Wilt try again
But this one time?

Phil. Condition'd you will stand
Ear-witness to our conference, that you may take
In at your ear a vertue that will teach

---

53. infectious] unhealthy.

54-55. let the child . . . honey-comb] Cf. Greene's *Philomela* (p.118): ". . . a child stunge with a bee wil fly from the hunnicombe . . ." Not in Tilley, but similar to the proverb, "the burnt child dreads the fire" (C297).

57-59. Oh! When . . . instance] Cf. Greene's *Philomela* (p. 119): ". . . the greener the Alisander leaves bee, the more bitter is the sappe, every outward appearaunce is not an authenticall instance . . ."

57. elesander] Alexander, a plant, also called horse-parsley, once cultivated and eaten like celery. *NED* does not record this variant spelling.

59-60. she that . . . heart-hollow] Cf. Greene's *Philomela* (p. 119): ". . . then are women most hart hollowe when they are most lip-holie . . ."

lip-holy] merely from the lips, and not heart felt; *NED* cites this line as one example.

64. Condition'd] on the condition, provided.

Your erring soul to wonder.

Lor. [*Aside*] He would wittal me,
With a consent to my own horns. [*To Phil.*] I will;
I'll give thee a new occasion. There lurks in woman's blood
A vindicating spirit.

Abst. I came, sir, to give you notice,
Count *Lodovico*, *Stroimo*, *Spinoso*, and *Pandulpho*, with the rest
Of the consiliadory, certifie
They are setting forth to meet the Duke your kinsman
Returning from *Venice*.

Lor. Oh, there he has seen the Duke your brother.

Abst. Yes, sir, and they stay but for your company.

Lor. And you're cloy'd with't.-----*Kicks her and exit*. *She weeps*.

Phil. And will you still be used thus? Oh Madam,
I do confess, twice I have batter'd at
The fort I fain would vanquish, and I know
Ye hold out more 'cause ye would seem a souldier,
Than in hate to the assailant; I am again
Inflam'd with those sweet fountains from whence flow
Such a pair of streams. Oh strong force of desire!
The quality should quench, hath set on fire:
I love you in your sorrows.

---

68. wittal] wittol, to make a fool or cuckold of; *NED* cites this line as the unique instance of wittol used as a verb. Farmer and Henley (VII, 360) also cite this line as an example.

74. consiliadory] governing or advisory counsel; *NED* cites this line as a unique example (but Cf. l. 1108, and Greene's *Philomela* (p. 167), "Consigladiori").

79. cloy'd] burdened.

Abst. And I sorrow in nothing but your love; twice, *Philippo,*
Have I not beat back the impetuous storm
Of thy incessant rudeness? Wilt thou again
Darken fair honour with dishonesty?
Thou know'st my Lord hath long and truly lov'd thee
In the wisdom of a friend in a fair cause;
He wears his good sword for thee, lays his heart
A lodger in thy bosome, proclaims thee partner
In all he hath, but me. Oh be not counterfeit.
We all conclude, a diamond with clouds
The goldsmith casts into his dust; and a gentleman
So blemish'd in his honour, blots his name
Out of the herald's book, stands a lost man
In goodness and opinion. Oh *Philippo,*
Make me once more so happy to believe
'Tis but a painted passion.

91-92. Wilt thou . . . dishonesty] Cf. Greene's *Philomela* (p. 129): ". . . darken not these honours with dishonestie . . ." And (pp. 145-146): ". . . I desire that thou mightest have mor honour and less dishonestie . . ."

93-97. Thou know'st . . . but me] Cf. Greene's *Philomela* (p. 147): "Phillippos wealth is at thy will, his sword at thy commande, his hart plast in thy bosome, he reserveth of all that he hath for thee, save only me to himselfe . . ."

97. counterfeit] false.

98-100. a diamond . . .his honour] Cf. Greene's *Philomela* (p. 153): "For as a Diamant with a clowd is cast into the Goldsmithes dust: so a Gentleman without credite, is carelesse holden for refuse."

98. clouds] impurities.

Lor. [*Aside*] Most acute witch!

Phil. Come, learn of your city-wagtail; with one eye
Violently love your husband, and with t'other
Wink at your friend.

Lor. [*Aside*] I will not trust you, brother.

Phil. He seeks; will ye not have him finde? Cries ye out,
In his mad fits, a strumpet; rails at all women,
Upon no cause, but because you are one.
He gives wound upon wound, and then pours vinegar
Into your bleeding reputation,
Poyson'd with bitter calumny. Pox on him.
Pile a reciprocal reward upon him;
Let ballet-mongers crown him with their scorns:
Who buys the buck's head, well deserves the horns.
Demur not on't, but clap them on.

Abst. You are, sir, just like the Indian Hysop, prais'd of strangers
For the sweet scent, but hated of the inhabitants

---

105. acute] shrewd. *NED* records no use of acute in this sense between 1599 and 1755.

106-109. with one eye . . . brother] related to the proverb, "He that winks with the one eye and looks with the other, I will not trust him though he were my brother" (Tilley, E 241).

wagtail] inconstant woman, hence courtesan.

107-108. Violently . . . your friend.] Cf. Greene's *Philomela* (p. 137): ". . . and fawne upon her husbands neck when she giver her lover a wincke . . ."

110. He seeks . . . finde] from the proverb, "He that seeks finds" (Tilley, S213 and F222).

118. Who buys. . . horns] Cf. Greene's *Philomela* (p. 143): "Sith Philippo [i.e., the husband] will buy the Buckes head, is he not worthy to have the hornes . . ."

For the injurious quality. Can he love the wife,
That would betray the husband? Hast thou not seen me
Bear all his injuries, as the ocean suffers
The angry bark to plough through her bosome,
And yet is presently so smooth, the eye
Cannot perceive where the wide wound was made.
And cannot this inform, I love him better
In his sow'r follies, than you in your sweet flatteries?
If *Verona* hath observed any errors in me,
I well may call for grace to amend them,
But will never fall from grace to befriend you.

Phil. [*Aside*] With what a majesty good women thunder!

Lor. [*Aside*] 'Has given her some close nod that I am here.

Abst. Rip up the end of thy intent, and see
How shame and fear do lurk where you would walk,

120-122. You are . . . quality] Cf. Greene's *Philomela* (p. 146): "Thou are like, *Lutesio*, unto the Hysope growing in *America*, that is liked of straungers for the smell, and hated of the inhabitantes for the operation . . ." Sugden, *A Topographical Dictionary* . . . (p. 265) cites "Indian Hysop," although incorrectly attributing the passage to Davenant.

122. injurious quality] hyssop is hot and dry, but no other reference was found to an "injurious" nature.

122-123. Can he love . . . the husband] Cf. Greene's *Philomela* (p. 146): ". . . how canst thou love the wife, that betraiest the husband . . ."

128-129. And cannot this inform . . .] i.e., Cannot you understand that . .

131-132. I well may. . . befriend you] Cf. Greene's *Philomela* (p. 147): ". . . and I will call for grace and amend them, but never a whit the more befriend them . . ."

134. close] secret.

135-136. Rip up. . . would walk] Cf. Greene's *Philomela* (pp. 146-147): ". . . rippe up the ende of thy attempte, and then if that shame hath not utterlye abandoned thee, thou wilt for feare of shame leave off thy lust, and grow into more grace."

Like a pair of serpents in a flow'ry mead.
Lust sees with pleasure, but with fear doth tread.

Phil. [*Aside*] Very brave, woman!

Abst. What is the pleasure thou pursu'st? A sin
Finish'd with infinite sorrows. Read and finde
How barb'rous nations punish it with death;
How a minute's sin so stolen, though in the face
Sit summer calms, all smooth, yet thou wilt hear,
From the eternal 'larum of thy conscience,
How it sets within thy soul continual tempests,
Thunder and dismal blackness. Mark but the course
Of the holy-seeming hollow-man, and see
How he that glories heaven with no honour,
Covets to glorifie himself with honesty.
And to put you past your hopes, let me leave this with you:
Thou mayst hold an elephant with a thread, eat fire
And not be burnt, or catch birds with desire;
Quench flame with oyl, cut diamonds with glass,
Pierce steel with feathers; this thou mayst bring to pass,

---

138. Lust sees . . . tread.] Cf. *King John and Matilda*, IV, i. (B, p. 60):
. . . how sweet a face hath sin!
Which but past by, a cheater she appears,
Joyes are her promise, but she paies us fears.

140-141. A sin . . . sorrows] Cf. Greene's *Philomela* (p. 130): ". . . and a sinne finished with sorrowe."

142. How barb'rous . . . death] Cf. Greene's *Philomela* (p. 130): "Barbarous nations punishe it with death . . ."

147-150. Mark but . . . honesty] Cf. Greene's *Philomela* (p. 128): ". . . that the holiest men in shew are oft the hollowest men in substance, and where there is the greatest florish of vertue, there in time appeareth the greatest blemish of vanitie."

Sooner than hope to steal that husband's right,
Whose wife seems honest, and no hypocrite. *Exit.*

[*Lorenzo comes forward.*]

Phil. What think you now, sir?

Lor. Why now I do think it possible for the world
To have an honest woman in't.----Good-buy, sir,
I must go meet the Duke. Adieu.

Phil. Farewel.
Oh jealousie! How near thou dwell'st to hell! *Exeunt.*

[SCENE II]

Enter Lodovico, Pandulpho, Spinoso, Jaspro, and Jovani, and Clown.

Lod. The Duke not seven leagues off! My horse, rogues.

Pand. Our negligence deserves just blame; and how
'Twill please his Grace to conster it, we know not.

Jasp. But where's your fair chaste wife, my Lord?

Lod. Marry, with my man *Francisco*. Oh that fellow!
She were undone without him; for indeed
She takes great pleasure in him; he learns her musick.

152-156. Thou mayst . . . right] Cf. Greene's *Philomela* (p. 132): "I tell thee it is more easie to cut a Diamond with a glasse, to pearce steele with a fether, to tye an Elephant with a thread of silke, than to alienate an honest womans love from her husband . . ." And (p. 189): ". . . that as oyle thogh it be moist, quencheth not fire . . ."

154. Quench flame with oyl] a proverbial impossibility (Tilley, F287).

166. conster] construe, interpret.

To hear what counsel she will give him! If he but screw
His look sometimes, with the pin, she will tell him straight,
'Twas an unchristian look. I love him dearly.

Spin. But can your honour never woo your Lady
To a more sociable affability?
She will not kiss, nor drink, nor talk, but against new fashions.

Lod. Oh, sir, she is my crown; nor is it requisite women should be so sociable. I have had such a coyle with her, to bring her but to look out at window; when we were first married, she would not drink a cup of wine, unless nine parts of it were water.

Omn. Admired temperance!

Lod. Nay, and ye knew all, my Lords, ye would say so. T'other day I brought an English gentleman home with me, to try a horse I should sell him; he (as ye know their custome, though it be none of ours) makes at her lips the first dash.

Clown. He dash'd her out of countenance, I'm sure of that.

---

171. screw] twist, in this case his looks, into an unnatural position; also, perhaps, he screws, or turns, the pin in l. 172, hence, with his stringed instrument.

172. with the pin] perhaps, with the turning peg of his stringed instrument (i.e., with a too happy or bawdy song); cf. Greene's Philomela (p. 126): "Giovanni hearing hir harpe on that string [love] strained it a pin higher thus." And A New Tricke to Cheat the Divell, I, ii. (B,p. 200):

Faith I was never on a merrier pinn
Nor my breast lighter hearted.

"To be on merry pin" is proverbial (Tilley, P335). Or perhaps, with a squint ("web and pin" was a cataract, which would cause squinting; cf. Lear, III, iv, 120: ". . . he gives the web and pin, squinies the eye . . .").

178. coyle] row, noisy disturbance.

185-186. he (as . . . dash.] This allusion has not been specifically identified, although the English were notorious "kissers."

Lod. She did so powt and spit, that my hot-brain'd gallant could not forbear, but ask the cause; quoth she-----

Clown. No, sir, she spit again, before *quoth she* left her lips.

Lod. I think she did indeed; but then quoth she, "A kiss, sir, is sin's earnest-penny." Is't not true, *Pambo*?

Clown. Very true, sir; by the same token, quoth he to her again, "If you dislike the penny, Lady, pray let me change it into English half-pence," and so gave her two for't.

Lod. But how she vex't then! Then she rattled him, and told him roundly, "Though confidence made cuckolds in *England*, she could no coxcombs in *Italy*."

Clown. But did ye mark how bitterly he clos'd it with a midling jest?

Lod. What was that, I prethee?

Clown. Why quoth he to her again, "Confidence makes not so many cuckolds in *England*, but craft picks open more padlocks in *Italy*."

Jov. That was something sharp.-----But here she comes.

Enter Dorothea and Francisco.

Lod. Ye shall see how I'll put ye all upon her presently.

---

188. spit] utter in a proud, spiteful, or unreserved manner.

191-192. A kiss . . . earnest-penny] This proverbial phrase, not in Tilley, is apparently related to the proverb, "Wanton kisses are keys of sin" (K104).

192. earnest-penny] a small sum of money paid as an earnest or pledge to secure a bargain (also in religious use).

196.. rattled] scolded.

200. midling] meddling, contending (with a pun intended); or perhaps, middling, meaning mediocre.

Clown. Then I shall take my turn.

Dor. *Francis.*

Fran. Madam.

Dor. Have you chang'd the ditty you last set?

Fran. I have, Madam.

Dor. The conceit may stand, but I hope you have cloath'd the method in a more Christian-like apparel.

Fran. I have, Lady.

Dor. Pray, let me hear it now.

Fran. *She that in these days looks for truth,* [*Sings.*]
Seldom or never findes, in sooth.

Dor. That's wondrous well.

Clown. Yes, in sadness.

Lod. Peace, sirrah; nay, she's built of modestie.

Fran. *Even as a wicked kiss defiles the lips,* [*Sings.*]
So do new fashions her that through them trips.

Dor. Very modest language.

Fran. *She that doth pleasure use for what 'twill bring her,* [*Sings.*]
Will pluck a rose, although she prick her finger.

Dor. Put in *hurt her finger,* good *Francis*; the phrase will be more decent.

---

212. conceit] idea, thought.

222. *trips*] moves lightly, dances.

224-225. *She that . . . her finger*] Olive suggests that "perhaps Davenport borrows even Shakespeare's bawdy word play," and cites these lines which he parallels with *Pericles*, IV, vi, 32-40.

225. *Will pluck . . . finger*] from the proverb, "no rose without a thorn" (Tilley, R182).

prick] with a pun intended, hence the change to make the song "more decent."

Pand. Y'are a wondrous happy man in one so vertuous.

Lod. Nay, ye shall have no Count *Lorenzo* of me, I warrant ye.

Clown. Nor no Count *Lorenzo's* Lady of your wife, I warrant ye.

Lod. Sweet Chick, I come to take leave of thee. Finger in nye already!
We are all to meet the Duke this afternoon, Bird,
Who is now come from *Venice*. Thou mayst walk and see
The Count *Lorenzo's* Lady.

Dor. 'Las, she's too merry for my company.

Jasp. Too merry! I have seen her sad,
But very seldom merry.

Dor. I mean, my Lord,
That she can walk, tell tales, run in the garden.

Clown. Why, then your Ladyship may hold your tongue, say nothing, and walk in the orchard.

Dor. She can drink a cup of wine not delay'd with water.

Clown. Why, then you may drink a cup of water without wine.

Dor. Nay, if a noble man come to see her lord,
She will let him kiss her too, against our custome.

Pand. Why, a modest woman may be kist by accident,
Yet not give the least touch to her reputation.

Lod. [*To Pand.*] Well said; touch her home.

Dor. Nay, but they may not; she that will kiss, they say,

---

231. Finger in nye already] crying already; nye: eye (*NED* cites this line as one example). Proverbial (Tilley, F229).

242. delay'd] weakened; diluted. *NED* cites this line as one example.

247. touch] blemish; stain. *NED* cites no example after 1616.

Will do worse, I warrant her.

Jov. Why, I have seen you, Madam, kist against your will.

Dor. Against my will it may be I have been kist indeed.

Clown. Pshew, there's nothing against a woman's will; and I dare be sworn, if my Lady kiss but any one man, 't is because she cannot do with all.

Lod. Nay, I know that to be true, my Lords, and at this time,
Because ye cannot do with all, pray kiss them in order.
Kiss her all over, gentlemen, and we are gone.

Dor. Nay, good my Lord, 'tis against our nation's custome.

Lod. I care not; let naturals love nations.
My humour's my humour.

Spin. I must have my turn too, then.

Jov. It must go round.

Dor. Fie, fie,

Lod. Look how she spits now.

Jasp. The deeper the sweeter, Lady.

249-250. she that will kiss . . . worse] D4 notes: In allusion to the proverb, "After kissing comes greater kindness." Tilley cites these lines as one example (K107).

253. Pshew] probably pshaw, although NED does not record this spelling, and no use before 1673 is cited. Used again in l. 1921.

there's . . . woman's will] from the proverb, "women will have their wills" (Tilley, W723).

255. cannot do with all] pun on "do withal," meaning cannot help it, and "do with all." B first notes this pun.

260. naturals] natives of a country; also, fools.

266. The deeper the sweeter] a proverb; this line cited as one example by Tilley (D188). Jaspro is referring to his kiss.

Clown. The neerer the bone, the sweeter the flesh, Lady.

Dor. How now, sauce-box!

Clown. Did not my Lord bid the gentlemen kiss you all over?

Lod. I have sweet cause to be jealous, have I not, gentlemen? No, *Crede quod habes, & habes* still; he that believes he has horns, has them. Will you go bring my horse, sir?

Clown. I will bring your horse, sir; and your horse shall bring his tail with him. *Exit*.

Lod. *Francis*, I prethee, stay thou at home with thy lady. Get thy instrument ready; this melancholy will spoil her. Before these Lords here, make her but laugh, when we are gone-----

Fran. Laugh before these Lords when they are gone, sir!

Lod. Pish, I mean, make her laugh heartily before we come home; and before these Lords, I promise thee a lease of forty crowns *per annum*.

Fran. Can ye tell whether she be ticklish, sir?

Lod. Oh, infinitely ticklish!

Fran. I'll deserve your lease, then, ere you come home, I warrant.

---

267. The neerer . . . the flesh] a proverb (Tilley, B520) more often applied to meat than women.

268. sauce-box] a saucy or impertinent person.

271. *Crede . . . habes*] Believe you have it, and you have it. Burton Stevenson in *The Home Book of Proverbs, Maxims and Familiar Phrases* (New York: Macmillan, 1948) cites two examples of this proverb, one in the original Latin (Erasmus, *Letter to Thomas More*) and one in English (John Heywood, *Proverbs*, pt.ii, ch. 9: Beleue will, and have well, men say.) Tilley (B265) lists four examples before 1624, including Heywood, of this same proverb.

280. lease] contract, guarantee.

Lod. And thou shalt ha't yfaith, boy.

[*Re-*] *enter Clown.*

Clown. Your horse is ready, sir.

Lod. My Lords, I think we have staid with the longest; farwel, Doll. *Crede quod habes, & habes,* gallants.

Pand. Our horses shall fetch it up again. Farewel, sweet Lady.

Jasp. Adieu, sweet mistris. And whensoere I marry, fortune turn up to me no worse card than you are.

Clown. And whensoere I marry, *Venus* send me a card may save fortune the labour, and turn up her self. *Exeunt.*

Dor. How now? Why loyter you behind? Why ride not you along with your Lord?

Fran. To lye with your Ladyship.

Dor. How?

Fran. In the bed, upon the bed, or under the bed.

Dor. Why, how now, *Francis*?

Fran. This is the plain truth on't, I would lye with ye.

Dor. Why, *Francis* !

Fran. I know too that you will lye with me.

Dor. Nay, but *Francis*!

Fran. Plague of *Francis.* I am neither *Frank* nor *Francis,*
But a gentleman of *Millain,* that even there
Heard of your beauty, which report there guarded

---

290. fetch it up again] make up lost time. *NED* records no examples used with this meaning before 1665.

293. may] i.e., which may. The clown's ironic humor here is suggesting that Dorothea is less than perfect.

295. loyter] loiter.

With such a chastity, the glittering'st sin
Held no artillery of power to shake it.
Upon which, I resolv'd to try conclusions;
Assum'd this name and fortune, sought this service.
And I will tell ye truly what I guess you.

Dor. You will not ravish me, *Francis.*

Fran. No; but unravel ye, in two lines experience writ lately:
Extreams in vertue, are but clouds to vice;
She'll do i'th dark, who is i'th'day too nice.

Dor. Indeed, ye do not well to bely me thus.

Fran. Come, I'll lye with thee, wench, and make all well again; though your confident Lord makes use of *Crede quod habes, & habes,* and holds it impossible for any to be a cuckold can believe himself none, I would have his Lady have more wit, and clap them on.

Dor. And truly, *Francis,* some women now would do't.

Fran. Who can you chuse more convenient to practise with, than me, whom he doats on? Where shall a man finde a friend but at home? So you break one proverb's pate, and give the other

---

314. unravel] make plain, reveal.

316. She'll do i'th' dark] Cf. *King John and Matilda,* III, i. (B. p. 39): Come, come, we'l do't i'th dark then.

322. clap] put or place with promptness.

325-326. Where shall . . . at home?] perhaps referring to the proverb: It is better to make one's friendships at home (Burton Stevenson, *The Home Book of Proverbs, Maxims, and Familiar Phrases,* New York: Macmillan Co., 1948, p. 900; not in Tilley). Or perhaps ironically referring to the proverb: Where shall a man have a worse friend than he brings from home? (*Ibid.*, p. 892; Tilley, M 413).

a plaister. Is't a match, wench?

Dor. Well, for once it is. But and ye do any more, indeed I'll tell my husband.

Fran. But when shall this once be? Now?

Dor. Now? No indeed, Francis.
It shall be soon at night, when your Lord's come home.

Fran. Then! How is't possible?

Dor. Possible? Women can make any of these things possible, Francis. Now many casualties may cross us; but soon at night, my Lord, I'm sure, will be so sleepy, what with his journey, and deep healths for the Duke's return, that before he goes to bed (as he uses still, when he has been hard a drinking), he will sleep upon the bed in's cloaths so sound, bells would not wake him, rung in the chamber.

Fran. The cuckold slumbers; though his wife hit him o'th' forehead with her heel, he dreams of no such matter.

Dor. Now Pambo, that makes him merry in his chamber, shall, when the candle's out, and he asleep, bring you into the chamber.

Fran. But will he be secret?

Dor. Will he, good soul! I am not to try him now.

Fran. 'Sfoot, this is brave;

326-327. So you . . . plaister] refering to the proverb, "to break one's head and give him a plaster" (Tilley, H269).

plaister] plaster, mending, with a pun on the second meaning of copulation (Farmer and Henley, V, 224).

335. casualties] uncertainties, chance events.

348. 'Sfoot] by God's foot; an oath.

My kind Lord's fool is my cunning Lady's knave.
But pray, how then?

Dor. When you are in at door on right before you, you shall feel the bed; give me but softly a touch, I'll rise, and follow you into the next chamber. But truly, and you do not use me kindly, I shall cry out and spoil all.

Fran. Use you kindly! Was lady ere us'd cruelly i'th' dark? Do you but prepare *Pambo* and your maid, let me alone with her mistris. About 11 I desire to be expected.

Dor. And till the clock strick 12, I'll lye awake.

Fran. Now ye dare kiss.

Dor. Once with my friend, or so; yet you may take two, *Francis.*

Fran. My cast is ams-ace then.

Dor. Deuce-ace had got the game.

Fran. Why then you're welcome. Adieu, my dainty mistris.

Dor. Farewel, kind *Francis.* *Exeunt.*

[SCENE III]

Enter Lorenzo, as from horse.

Lor. I have given them all the slip, the Duke and all,
And am at home before them. I cannot rest,

---

353. and] Here, as in 1.328, "and" means "an" (i.e., if).

358. strick] strike.

362-363. My cast . . . the game.] B notes: A pair of aces,--the lowest throw [of the dice]. So Francis takes two kisses, and three [deuce-ace] wins the game.

364. Why then your're welcome.] B notes: He gives her a third kiss.

Philippo and my wife run in my mind so.
I know no cause why I should trust him more
Than all the world beside. I remember
He told her that I bought the buck's head, therefore
Deserv'd the horns. Although I bid him try her,
Yet I did not bid him bid her with one eye
Love me, and with the other wink at a friend.
How we long to grow familiar with affliction!
And as many words do aptly hold concordance
To make one sentence, just so many causes
Seem to agree, when conceit makes us cuckolds.

Enter Philippo, and Abstemia.

And here comes proof apparent, hand in hand too.
Now their palms meet; that graspe begets a bastard.

Phil. By your white hand I swear 'twas only so.

Lor. [Aside] Poyson of toads betwixt ye.

Abst. *Philippo,* you have fully satisfied me.

369-370. I know . . . world beside] from the proverb, "He that trusts to the world is sure to be deceived" (Tilley, W871).

371-372. I bought . . . the horns] borrowed from the same passage in *Philomela* as l. 118.

382. Poyson of toads] toads, the devil's own animal, were popularly considered poisonous (as in the proverb: Full as a toad of poison. Tilley, T360). Cf. *King John and Matilda*, IV, i. (B, p. 58): "[Bread] coming from a Toad 'twill poyson him."

384. satisfie] Olive (p. 340) parallels Lorenzo's mistake with Leontes' in a similar situation in *The Winter's Tale*, I, ii, 232-234:

Cam. To satisfy your highness, and the entreaties
Of our most gracious mistress.
Leon. Satisfy?
Th' entreaties of your mistress? satisfy?

Lor. [Aside] Insatiate whore! Could not I satisfie ye?
I shall commit a murder, if I stay;
I'll go forge thunder for ye. Oh let me
Never more marry! What plague can transcend
A whorish wife, and a perfidious friend! Exit.

Phil. By the unblemish'd faith, then, of a gentleman,
And by your potent goodness, a great oath;
(For you are greatly good) by truth it self,
(For still I swear by you) what again hath past,
Was at the first, but tryal of her chastity
Far above time or storie. As I speak truth,
So may I prosper.

Abst. And came these tryals from your brest only?

Phil. Only from my brest; and by the sweet
Excellent blush of vertue, there is in you
Plenty of truth and goodness.

Abst. You have nobly
Appeas'd the storm o'ertook you, and you are
Again a good man.

Enter Lorenzo, Pandulpho, Spinoso,
Jaspro, Jovani, [and some officers].

Lor. Traytor to truth and friendship!
Did not mine honour hold me, I should rip out
That blushing hypocrite, thy heart, that hath break
So strong a tie of faith; but behold,
How much of man is in me! There, I cast them

From this believing heart, to the iron hand
Of law, the wrong'd man's saint.

Phil. What means this?

Pand. My Lord, here's warrant for what's done immediate from
The Duke, by force of which you're early i'th morning,
Before his Grace, to answer to such injuries
The Count *Lorenzo* shall alledge against you.

Phil. Injuries! Why friend, what injuries?

Lor. Can ye spell stag, sir? 'Tis four letters with two horns.
Good gentlemen, convey him from my furie,
For fear of greater mischief.

Phil. Thou yellow fool. *Exeunt.*

Abst. I would you would instruct me, noble sir,
But how to understand all this.

Lor. Do ye see her? Look on her, all, and wonder. Did ye ever see so foul guilt stand underneath a look so innocent?

Jov. I should have pawn'd my blood upon her honour.

Pand. Colours not in grain
Make as fair shew, but are more apt to stain.

Abst. My Lord.

Lor. Ye whore. *Kicks her; she sowns.*

Jasp. Look to the Lady.

Lor. Look to her! Hang her! Let me send her now

---

425. in grain] dyed in a fast color.

428. *sowns*] swoons.

to th' devil, with all her sins upon her head.

Spin. Bear her in gently, and see her guarded. [Exeunt.]

Pand. You are too violent, my Lord.

Lor. That men should ever marry! That we should lay our heads, and take our horns up out of woman's laps.

Jov. Be patient, good sir.

Lor. Yes, and go make potguns.

Jasp. 'Tis late, and sleep would do you good, my Lord.

Lor. Sleep! Why, do you think I am mad, sir?

Jasp. Not I, my Lord.

Lor. Then you do lye, my Lord,
For I am mad, horn-mad. I shall be acted
In our theaters of Verona. Oh what poyson's
Like a false friend? And what plague more ruinous
Than a lascivious wife? They steal our joyes,
And fill us with afflictions; they leave our names
Hedg'd in with calumny. In their false hearts

430-431. let me . . . her head.] Olive (p. 341) notes a possible allusion to Hamlet, III, iii, 89-95:

> When he is drunk asleep, or in his rage,
> Or in th'incestuous pleasure of his bed;
> At game, a-swearing, or about some act
> That has not relish of salvation in't;
> Then trip him, that his heels may kick at heaven
> And that his soul may be damned and black
> As hell, whereto it goes.

437. potguns] popguns, toy guns.

442. For I am mad, horn-mad] to be horn-mad, or a cuckold, was proverbial (Tilley, H628).

442-443. I shall . . . of Verona] Cf. Greene's Philomela (p. 158): " . . . thy whordomes to be acted in the Theaters of Venice . . ."

Crocodiles breed, who make grief their disguise,
And, in betraying, tears still through their eyes.
Oh! He that can believe he sleeps secure
In a false friend's oaths, or in a bad wife's arms,
Trusts *Circe's* witchcraft, and *Calipso's* charms.

Omn. 'Tis late, let's to the court. *Exeunt Omnes.*

Finis Actus Primi.

ACTUS SECUNDUS.

[SCENE I]

A bed thrust out. Lodovico sleeping in his cloaths; Dorothea in bed. Enter Clown leading in Francisco.

Fran. Softly, sweet *Pambo*. Are we in the chamber yet?

Clown. Within a yard of my Lady, and ye can be quiet.

Fran. Art sure my Lord's asleep?

Clown. I know not, I'll go and ask him.

Fran. No, no, no, do not wake him; we are undone then, man.

Clown. Ha, ha, ha, now do I see, cuckold-making is as ticklish a profession as cunny-catching. My Lord was so paid with

---

448. Crocodiles] Crocodile tears (false grief) are proverbial (Tilley, C831).

449. still] distil (i.e., trickle down or fall).

452. *Circe's* witchcraft, and *Calipso's* charms] Cf Greene's *Philomela* (p. 158): " . . . thou has learned with Circes to inchat, with Calipso to charm ..."

460. cunny-catching] literally, catching rabbits (conies), extended to mean catching dupes, hence swindling, gulling. Perhaps, with this spelling, a pun is intended.

healths at court, he's fast enough.

Fran. But still I pursue wonder, why my Lady should prescribe this strange, nay wonderous desperate way to her desires.

Clown. Is that a question to ask now? Would you would groap out the bed; for I sleep in my talk, I am sure of that.

Lodovico coughs.

Fran. We are lost for ever. Did he not cough?

Clown. 'Tis nothing but the last cup comes up in stew'd broath. If ever you make true whore-master, I'll be bound to resign my place up to my Lord's page. Sea-sick before you come to th' salt-water? Let me go in your stead.

Fran. No, I'll venter, stood a gulph between, belching up
A tempest. Oh valiant lust!
How resolute thou go'st to acts unjust!
Pambo, good night.
Desire drowns fear in presuppos'd delight.

Clown. Turn of your left hand, 'twill lead you to the devil, to my Lady, I should say, presently. Exit.

Fran. Let me four steps on the left hand. I have the bed, and

---

468-469. stew'd broath] stenched vomit. NED cites no examples of this meaning of stewed between 1571 and 1781.

472. venter] venture, perhaps with a pun either on the Latin meaning of womb or stomach, or on vent (to go with belching).

stood a gulph between] [even though] a gulf stood between [us].

477. of] to.

479. Let me] Let me [take]; or perhaps as in D and B: Let me [see].

on this side she lyes. 'Sfoot, there's a beard? But all's well yet,
she lyes on this side sure.
I have her, 'tis her hand, I know the touch;
It melts me into passion. I have much ado
To contain my wild desires; as the wind strains
In caverns lock'd, so through my big-swolne veynes,
My blood cuts capers.

Dor. Who's there?

Fran. 'Tis I.

Dor. *Francis*!

Fran. Fortunate *Francis*, that was wrap'd in's mother's smock.

Dor. Give me your hand, *Francis*.

Fran. There 'tis; I melt already.

Dor. My Lord, Count *Lodovico*, awake.

Fran. I am lost for ever, Madam.

Dor. My Lord, my Lord!

Fran. [Aside] If I pull too hard, I shall pull her out o'th' bed too.

Dor. My Lord, will ye not wake?

Lod. What's the matter? What's the matter?

Fran. [Aside] How I do dwindle!

Dor. Pray hear me, sir, I cannot sleep till you
Have resolv'd me one thing.

484-485. as the wind . . . lock'd] It was believed winds were originally confined in caverns, as depicted in Virgil's *Aeneid*, Book I, 52 ff.

490. that was . . . smock.] B notes: A proverbial saying applied to men who are fortunate in love. (Tilley, M1203).

492. melt] dissolve into ecstasy; pun (continued in l. 499 with "dwindle") on second meaning, to ejaculate.

Lod. What is't, sweet-heart?

Dor. Of all your men, which do you love best?

Lod. That's a strange question to ask at mid-night. Francisco.

Dor. And that same false Francisco in your absence
Most leudly tempted me to wrong your bed.

Fran. [Aside] Was ever woodcock catch'd thus?

Lod. Oh rogue, I'll go cut's throat sleeping.

Dor. Nay, I have fitted him most daintily.

Fran. [Aside] Now, now, now, now, I am spitted.

Dor. I seem'd, sweet-heart, to consent to him.

Fran. [Aside] A plague of seemings. I were best confess, and beg pardon.

Dor. And to make him sure for your revenge, I appointed
About this hour, the door left ope on purpose-----

Fran. [Aside] Ah!

Dor. To meet me in the garden.

Fran. [Aside] All's well again.

Dor. Now, sweet-heart,
If thou would'st but steal down thither, thou mightst catch him,

---

503. Of all . . . best?] Cf. The Decameron (III, 209): "Among all the men retained into your service; which of them do you thinke to be the best, most loyall, and worthiest to enjoy your love?"

507. woodcock] a bird, often trapped as food, that was popularly considered stupid. Hence the ironical proverb: As wise as a Woodcock (Tilley, W746); or the proverb: To play the Woodcock (i.e., fool) (Tilley, W748).

510. spitted]impaled on a spit, caught.

517. garden] Cf. The Decameron (III, 209): " . . . I made him promise, to meete him in our Garden . . ."

and snap the fool very finely.

Lod. Oh my sweet birds-nye! What a wench have I of thee? *Crede quod habes, & habes* still; and I had thought it possible to have been cuckolded, I had been cuckolded. I'll take my rapier as I go, sirrah; and the night being dark, I'll speak like thee, as if thou hadst kept thy word. Oh villain! Nothing vexes me, but that he should think I can be a cuckold, and have such a Lady. Do thou lye still, and I'll bring thee his heart for thy munkie's break-fast.

Dor. And would you part unkindly, and not kiss me?

Lod. I have no more manners than a goose; farewel,
My chaste delitious *Doll.* What may his life
Be compar'd to, that meets with such a wife? *Exit.*

Enter Clown.

Fran. Pish, *Pambo.*

Clown. Here, boy.

Fran. Go meet him in the garden, and hark.

Clown. Excellent! I'll play my Lady, I warrant ye.

Fran. Do't daintily.

Clown. Well, I may hope for a squire's place, my father was

---

521. snap] catch suddenly by surprise.

522. birds-nye] vulgar term of endearment, used in the same manner as pig's-nye. *NED* gives only the two examples from *The City-Night-Cap* (see 1.975).

532. delitious] delicious.

539-540. Well I . . . costermonger] D2, D3, D4, and B note: A costermonger is a seller of apples; and an apple-squire was formerly a cant term for a pimp. (Tilley, A303, also lists apple-squire as proverbial for a cuckold maker.)

a costermonger. *Exit.*

Fran. Well, now I see, as he who fain would know
The real strain of goodness, may in her read it,
Who can seem chaste, and can be what she seems;
So, who would see hell's craft, in her may read it,
Who can seem too, but not be what she seems.
In brief, put him to school (would cheat the de'il of's right)
To a dainty smooth-fac'd female hypocrite. *Exeunt.*

[SCENE II]

Enter Lodocivo and Clown.

Lod. Here's a wife, *Pambo!*

Clown. Now, *Crede quod habes, & habes,* sir.

Lod. Why right, man; let him believe he has horns, and he has 'em.

Clown. To discover upon the pinch to ye!

Lod. Oh! You kind loving husbands, like my self,
What fortunes meet ye full but with such wives!

Clown. Fortune's i'th' fashion of hay-forks.

Lod. Sirrah *Pambo,* thou shalt seldom see a harsh fellow have such a wife, such a fortunate wedding.

Clown. He will go to hanging as soon.

543-545. Who can . . . what she seems] Related to two proverbs: "Be what thou would seem to be" (Tilley, S214), and "Things are not as they seem" (Tilley, T199). Abstemia is, of course, what she seems, while Dorothea is not.

552. To discover . . . to ye!] i.e., [I should] discover [your horns] to you at the critical juncture.

555. fashion of hay-forks] i.e., which look like cuckold's horns.

Lod. No, no, we loving souls have all the fortunes.
There's Count *Lorenzo* for example now,
There's a sweet coyle to morrow 'bout his wife.
He has two servants that will take their oaths
They saw her dishonest with his friend Count *Philippo*,
Nay, in the very act. Now what was't brought her to't, but his dogged usage of her?

Clown. Nay, she never liv'd a good day with him.

Lod. How she goes flaunting too! She must have a feather in her head, and a corke in her heel.

Clown. I, that shews her light from head to heel, sir; and who have heavier heads, than they whose wives have light heels? That feather confounds her.

Lod. I shall so laugh to hear the comical history of the great Count *Lorenzo's* horns. But as I have such a wife now, what a villain did I entertain to teach her musick? 'Has done her no good since he came, that I saw.

Clown. Hang him, 'has made her a little perfect in prick-song, that's all; and it may be she had skill in that, before you married her too.

---

561. coyle] coil, disturbance, fuss.

567-568. feather in her head] perhaps referring to the proverb, "to put a feather in one's cap" (i.e., to be full of pride or aloof; Tilley, F157).

568. a corke in her heel] cork heels (i.e., light heels) were associated with loose behavior (cf. *A Chaste Maid in Cheapside*, III, ii, 190). B adds: High cork heels,--chopines; *very fashionable in Italy*, whence they were imported to England.

569. I] Aye,

576. prick-song] a written descant or accompanying melody to a plain-song. A pun is intended.

Lod. She could sing at the first sight, by this hand, *Pambo.* But hark, I hear some-body.

Enter Francisco.

Clown. 'Tis he sure, 'has a dreaming whore-master's pace; pray let me practice my Lady's part, and counterfeit for her.

Lod. Canst thou imitate to th' life?

Clown. Can I? [*To Francisco, imitating Dorothea*] Oh wicked *Francis!*

Lod. Admirable! Thou shalt do't. [*Lorenzo hides.*]

Clown. Pray be you ready with your rapier to spit him then, and I'll watch him a good turn, I warrant ye.

Fran. [*Aside*] Here they are. If *Pambo* now comes off with his part neatly, the comedy passes bravely. [*To Clown*] Who's there-----Madam?

Clown. *Francis?*

Fran. The same.

Clown. I think this place lyes too open to the air, *Francis?*

Lod. [*Aside*] Delicate *Pambo.*

Clown. And truly there's a great dew fallen to night;
The grass is wondrous wet.

Lod. [*Aside*] Sweet rogue!

Clown. Come, *Francis,*
And let us sport our selves in yonder rushes;
And being set, I'll smother thee with busses.

Lod. [*Aside*] Oh villain!

598-599. And let us . . . with busses.] Fleay (I, 104) and Olive (p.343) note an apparent parody of *Venus and Adonis,* ll. 17-18:
Here come and sit, where never serpent hisses,
And being set, I'll smother thee with kisses.

Fran. Hear me, Lady,
It is enough my Lord hath now a friend,
In these dishonest daies, that dares be honest.

Lod. [*Aside*] How is this?

Clown. Nay for thy Lord, he's a meer coxcomb, *Francis.*

Lod. [*Aside*] Out, rogue!

Fran. 'Tis but your bad desires that tell you so.
Can I contain a heart, or can that heart
Harbour a thought of injury 'gainst him,
Under whose wing I safely stretch my penions?
Has he not nobly entertain'd me? Stand I not
Next neighbour, save your self, unto his heart?

Lod. [*Aside*] I, by this hand dost thou.

Fran. And should I quit him thus? No, Lady, no.

Lod. [*Aside*] Brave *Frank*!

Fran. I am too wise to fall in love with wo,
Much less with woman. I but took advantage
Of my Lord's absence, for your tryal, Lady,
For fear some fellow (far hotter rein'd than I)
Might have sought, and sped; and I would be loath
A Lord so loving-----

Lod. [*Aside*] Shalt have five leases, by these fingers.

Fran. Should have a Lady false.

---

610. penions] pinions, wings.

616. wo] woe, with an obvious pun in the next line on *wo*men.

619. hotter rein'd] less restrained, more governed by lust.

622. five leases, by these fingers] five for the five fingers. B notes one of the frequent allusions to "the odd custom of swearing by the fingers."

Back, Lady, to your yet unblemish'd bed;
Preserve your honour, and your Lord's calf's head.

Clown. Well, *Francis,* you had been better. If I do not tell my Lord of this!

Lod. [*Aside*] He has put him to't now.

Fran. Then I am lost for ever,
You'll turn it all on me, I know; but ere
I'll live to wrong so good a Lord, or stand
The mark unto your malice, I will first
Fall on my sword and perish.

Lod. Hold, hold, hold, man. [*Lodovico comes forward.*]

Fran. Ha, who are you?

Lod. One that has more humanity in him, than to see a proper fellow cast himself away, I warrant thee. 'Tis I, 'tis I, man, I have heard all.

Clown. And 'twas I play'd my Lady, to have snap'd ye.

Fran. Has she been then so good to tell your honour?
Now am I worse afflicted than before,
That she should thus outrun me in this race of honesty.

Lod. Nay, sh'as bob'd thee bravely; sh'as a thousand of these tricks, yfaith, man; but howsoever, what I have found thee,
I have found thee. Hark in thine ear, shalt have five leases,

---

625. calf's head] i.e., without horns.

636. proper] honest.

639. snap'd] caught by surprise.

643. bob'd] made a fool of, deceived.

and mine own nag, when th'ast a mind to ride.

Fran. Let me deserve, sir, first.

Lod. Shalt have them. I know what I do, I warrant thee.

Fran. I joy in such a Lady.

Lod. Nay, there's a couple of you, for a wife and a friend. Shalt be no more my servant. I had thought to have made thee my steward, but thou'rt too honest for the place, that's the truth on't.

Clown. His superfluity is my necessity; pray let me ha't, sir.

Lod. I will talk with thee to morrow, *Pambo*; thou shalt have something too; but I'll to bed. Honest *Francis*, the dearest must part, I see; I will so hug the sweet rascal that thinks every hour ten, till I come yonder! Good night, *Frank*; to bed, *Pambo*.

What delight in life
Can equal such a friend and such a wife?
So, my dainty *Doll*, I come to thee. *Exit.*

Clown. So a city-night-cap go with thee.------But shall I not be thought on, for my night's service?

Fran. Oh look ye, pray forget not ye had something.

Clown. Well, and pray do you remember I had nothing.

Fran. Nothing! What's that?

Clown. Nothing before I had something, I mean; so you are well return'd from *Utopia*.

Fran. You're very nimble, sir; good morrow. *Exeunt.*

657-658. every hour ten] probably, does not know or care what time it is. Related to the proverbs "He can tell ten" (Tilley, T90a), and "To know what it is O'clock" (Tilley, O10).

668. *Utopia*] paradise; literally "no place."

[SCENE III]

A bar set out. Enter the Duke of Verona, Pandulpho,

Spinoso, Jaspro, Jovani, Lorenzo, Philippo,

Abstemia, a guard, and two slaves.

Vero. Call the accus'd to th' bar.

Phil. We appear,
With acknowledg'd reverence to the presence.

Vero. We meet not
To build on circumstances, but to come plainly
To the business that here plac'd us. Cozen *Lorenzo,*
You have free leave to speak your griefs; but this
Desire the senate to observe, and neerly:
I come here not your kinsman; neither, Madam,
Looking unto the greatness of your blood,
As you are sister to the Duke of *Venice;*
But as an equal judge, I come to doom,
As circumstances and proof informs.

Lor. Thus then,
Great sir, grave Lords, and honourable auditors
Of my dishonour, I affirm 'tis known
To th' signorie of *Verona,* the whole city,

---

674. circumstances] formality, ceremony.

681. equal] impartial.

682. circumstances] logical surroundings or adjuncts.

686. signorie] the governing council.

Nay, the great multitude without, that come
This day to hear unwilling truth, can witness,
How since my marriage with that woman (weepst thou! [*Abstemia weeps.*]
Oh truth, who would not look thee in a woman's tears!
But showers that fall too late, produce deer years),
All know that since our marriage, I have perform'd
So fairly all judicial wedlock offices,
That malice knew not how at my whole actions
To make one blow, and to strike home. I did rather
Honour her as a saint, sir, than respect her
As she was my wife. On pilgrimage I sent
All my endeavours to the fair seeming shrine
Of her desires, where they did offer daily
A plenal satisfaction, which she seem'd
Reciprocally to return, paid back
As much obedience as I lent of love.
But then the serpent stings, when like a dove
Opinion feathers him; women's sweet words
As far are from their hearts (though from their brests

---

690. Oh truth . . . tears] from the proverb, "Trust not a woman when she weeps" (Tilley, W638).

695-697. I did rather . . . my wife] Cf. Greene's *Philomela* (p. 164): " . . . yet I did rather honour her as a saint, then regarde her as a wife . . ."

700. plenal] full, complete. *NED* cites l. 1349 as one of its two examples (see also l. 1434).

704. feathers him] i.e., disguises from.

They flie) as lapwings' cries are from their nests.

Pand. Oh you enveigh!

Lor. I would appear no satyre.

And for this man (how fain I would call him friend!)
I appeal to the whole state, if at the fight
Betwixt *Bizerta* gallies and your Grace,
Wherein you pleas'd to send me general there,
That he deserv'd (let me not take from him
His merit's meet confession), but I was there
The man (the erring man) that crown'd his merit
With approbation and reward; brought him home,
Prefer'd him to those graces you heap'd on him;
Wore him a neighbour to my heart, as lovers
Wear jewels, left by their dead friends. I lock'd him

704-706. women's sweet . . . their nests.] Cf. Greene's *Philomela* (p. 137): ". . . so womens wordes are like the cries of Lapwings, farthest from their thoughts, as they are from their nests . . ." B and Olive (p. 337) also cite *Measure for Measure*, I, iv, 31-33:

> . . . 'tis my familiar sin,
> With maids to seem the lapwing, and to jest
> Tongue far from heart . . .

Olive (p. 338) notes that Davenport and Shakespeare have in common the word "heart (s)" which is not in Greene. Tilley (L68) cites numerous examples, including this line from Davenport.

707. enveigh] inveigh, rail loudly.

708. satyre] alternate spelling of satyr, censorious person. The *NED* notes that confusion between the words *satiric* and *satyric* gave rise to the notion that the satyrs who formed the chorus of the Greek satyric drama had to deliver "satirical" speeches. Hence, in the sixteenth and seventeenth centuries, the frequent attribution to the satyrs of censoriousness as a characteristic quality. The usual association, with lechery, does not fit here.

711. *Bizerta* gallies] ships from Bizerta, a seaport in Tunisia at this time under Turkish control.

718-719. as lovers . . . friends] this custom not specifically identified.

Into my heart, and double-bar'd him there
With reason and opinion. His extremities
Fastn'd me more unto him, whilst like an arch
Well built, by how much the more weight I bore,
I stand the stronger under him; so lov'd him,
That in his absence still mine ear became
A sanctuary to his injur'd name.

Vero. And what from hence infer you?

Lor. That 'twas base,
Base in the depth of baseness, for this wife
So honour'd, and this smooth friend so belov'd,
To conspire betwixt them my dishonour.

Vero. How?

Lor. To stain my sheets with lust, a minute's theft;
To brand perpetually three faces: a husband's,
A wife's, and friend's.

Abst. Oh good my Lord.
Cast out this devil from you.

Lor. Oh good my Lady,
Keep not the devil within you, but confess.

Phil. Hear me, great sir. I will confess, *Lorenzo,*
And print thee down the fool of passion.

Spin. Speak, sir.

Phil. 'Tis true, this boasting man did thus erect me
In his opinion, plac'd me in his love,
Grac'd me with courtesies. Oh, the craft of jealousie!

---

741. print] brand. *NED* notes no examples after 1598.

As boys, to take the bird, about the pit
Cast wheat and chaff, contriving a neat train
To intice her to her ruine, so this friend,
Falser than city-oaths, it is not doubted,
Having so far indear'd me, when he came
To enjoy a fair wife, guest it impossible
For me to share with him in all things else,
And not in her; for fair wives oft, we see,
Strike discord in sweet friendship's harmony.
And having no way to insnare me so,
To separate our loves, he seriously
Woo'd me to try his wife.

Lor. 'Tis false.

Phil. 'Tis true,

By all that honest men may be believed by.
Three several witnesses I try'd her, by him urg'd to't,
Yet still my truth not started, kept so constant,
That till this hour this Lady thus much knew not.
I bore her brave reproofs. Oh, when she spake,
The saints sure listen'd, and at every point
She got the 'plause of angels! Now upon this,
This jealous Lord infers (and it may be but
To shun futurity) that I
(His betray'd friend) could not hold the cup,

---

746. pit] trap; or perhaps, the pit-bird, or reed-warbler (then, no comma after bird).

747. train] lure, bait.

761. several witnesses] separate attempts.

768. futurity] future time or events.

But I must drink the poyson. No, *Lorenzo,*
An honest man is still an unmov'd rock,
Wash'd whiter, but not shaken with the shock;
Whose heart conceives no sinister device,
Fearless he playes with flames, and treads on ice.

Vero. Cozen, did you, as your friend here affirms,
Counsel him to these tryals?

Lor. I?

Phil. You did.

Lor. *Philippo,* thou art fallen from a good man,
And hast ta'en leave of modestie. Let these my servants
(That incredulity should be induction
To my more certain shame), let these speak
And relate what they saw. They grew so publick,
My servants could discover them.

Pand. Speak, friends, be fearless;
And what you know, even to a sillable,
Boldly confess.

1 *Slave.* Then know, great sir, as soon
As ere my Lord was gone to meet your Grace,
Signor *Philippo* and my Lady privately
Went up to her bed-chamber. We two suspecting
What afterwards we found, stole softly up,
And through the key-hole (for the door was lock'd)
We saw my Lady and Count *Philippo* there
Upon the bed, and in the very act,

---

781. induction] introduction, preface.

As my Lord before affirm'd.

Abst. Canst thou hear, heaven,
And withhold thy thunder?

Phil. My Lords, one devil, ye know,
May possess three bodies.

Vero. Will you swear this, sir?

1 Slave. I will, my Lord.

Spin. And you?

2 Slave. I will, and dare, sir.

Lor. [*Aside*?] Brave rascals!

Vero. Reach them the book.

Abst. Ye poor deluded men, oh do not swear!

Lor. [*Aside*] Think of the chain of pearl.

1 Slave. Give us the book.
That we affirm the truth, the whole truth,
And nothing but the truth, we swear.

Pand. Believe me, I am sorry for the Lady.

Phil. How soon
Two souls more pretious than a pair of worlds
Are levell'd below death!

Abst. Oh hark! Did you not hear it?

Omn. What, Lady?

797-798. Canst thou . . . thunder?] B parallels with *Othello*, V, ii, 235-236:

> Are there no stones in heaven,
> But what serve for the thunder?

805. Brave] stout-hearted; also, bullying, assassining.

810-811. That we . . . truth] Tilley lists this standard oath as proverbial (T590).

815. levell'd below death] i.e., damned to hell.

Abst. This hour a pair of glorious towers are fallen;
Two goodly buildings beaten with a breath
Beneath the grave. You all have seen this day,
A pair of souls both cast and kist away.

Spin. What censure gives your Grace?

Vero. In that I am kinsman
To the accuser, that I might not appear
Partial in judgement, let it seem no wonder
If unto your gravities I leave
The following sentence. But as *Lorenzo* stands
A kinsman to *Verona,* so forget not,
Abstemia still is sister unto V*enice.*

Phil. Misery of goodness!

Abst. Oh! *Lorenzo Medico,*
Abstemia's lover once, when he did vow
And when I did believe; then when *Abstemia*
Deny'd so many princes for *Lorenzo,*
Then when you swore. Oh maids! How men can weep!
Print protestations on their brests, and sigh,

---

821. both cast and kist away] this proverbial expression, apparently deriving from the throw of dice, is not in Tilley.

822. censure] judgment, sentence.

826. gravities] a title of respect, directed toward one of authority; here, the counselors present.

831-832. Oh! . . . lover once] Cf. Greene's *Philomela* (p. 169): "O *Philippo Medici,* once lover of *Philomela* . . ."

831. *Medico*] D4 notes: A not unusual form of De Medici. In *Philomela* Greene uses both the Medico (p. 115) and Medici (p. 160) spellings.

And look so truly, and then weep again,
And then protest again, and again dissemble!
When once enjoy'd, like strange sights we grow stale,
And find our comforts, like their wonder, fail.

Phil. Oh Lorenzo! [Abstemia weeps.]
Look upon tears, each one of which, well valued,
Is worth the pity of a king; but thou
Art harder far than rocks, and canst not prize
The pretious waters of truth's injur'd eyes.

Lor. Please your Grace, proceed to censure.

Vero. Thus 'tis decreed, as these Lords have set down
Against all contradiction. Signor Philippo,
In that you have thus grosly, sir, dishonour'd
Even our blood it self, in this rude injury
Lights on our kinsman, his prerogative
Implies death on your trespass; but your merit
Of more antiquity than is your trespass,
That death is blotted out, and in the place
Banishment writ, perpetual banishment
(On pain of death, if you return) for ever
From Verona, and her signories.

Phil. Verona is kind.

Vero. Unto you, Madam,
This censure is alotted. Your high blood
Takes off the danger of the law; nay, from
Even banishment it self. This Lord, your husband,
Sues only for a legal fair divorce,
Which we think good to grant, the church allowing.

And, in that the injury
Chiefly reflects on him, he hath free licence
To marry when and whom he pleases.

Abst. I thank ye,
That you are favourable unto my love,
Whom yet I love and weep for.

Phil. Farewel, *Lorenzo.*
This brest did never yet harbour a thought
Of thee, but man was in it, honest man.
There's all the words that thou art worth. Of your Grace
I humbly thus take leave; farewel, my Lords;
And lastly farewel, thou fairest of many,
Yet by far more unfortunate. Look up
And see a crown held for thee; win it, and die
Love's martyr, the sad map of injury.
And so remember, sir, your injur'd Lady
Has a brother yet in *Venice.* *Exit.*

Abst. Farewel, *Lorenzo,*

866-867. he hath free . . . he pleases] Cf. Greene's *Philomela* (p. 167): ". . . and he at free liberty to marry whom he list . . ."

872-873. This brest . . . Of thee] Cf. Greene's *Philomela* (p. 168): "This brest *Philippo,* did never harbour any disloyall thought against thee . . ."

877-878. Look up . . . for thee] This favorite image of Davenport, that of a martyr striving for the crown of heavenly salvation promised by Christ, is the subject of *A Crown for a Conquerour.* Also, cf. *King John and Matilda,* IV, ii (B, p. 62):

> At the end of chastities white race, an Angell
> Holds in his hand (shot through a silver cloud),
> A Crown for Conquerours.

And see ll. 903, 1929, and 2418 for this same imagery.

879. map] a representation in epitome, used figuratively.

Whom my soul doth love. If you ere marry,
May you meet a good wife, so good, that you
May not suspect her, nor may she be worthy
Of your suspition. And if you hear hereafter
That I am dead, enquire but my last words,
And you shall know that to the last I lov'd you;
And when you walk forth with your second choyce
Into the pleasant fields, and by chance talk of me,
Imagine that you see me lean and pale,
Strewing your paths with flowers. And when in bed
You cast your arms about her happy side,
Think you see me stand with a patient look,
Crying, "All hail, you lovers, live and prosper."
But may she never live to pay my debts. *Weeps.*
If but in thought she wrong you, may she die
In the conception of the injury.
Pray make me wealthy with one kiss. Farewel, sir.
Let it not grieve you when you shall remember
That I was innocent. Nor this forget:
Though innocence here suffer, sigh and groan,
She walks but through thorns to finde a throne. *Exit.*

Vero. Break up the court, and cozen, learn this reed:
Who stabs truth's bosom, makes an angel bleed.

883-886. If you are . . . your suspition] Cf. Greene's *Philomela* (pp. 169-170): "I leave thee to the choice of a new love, and the fortune of a faire wife, who if she prove as honestly amorous towards thee as *Philomela,* then wrong her not with suspition . . ."

896. But may . . . my debts] Cf. Greene's *Philomela* (p. 170): " . . . then wrong her [your new wife] not with suspition, as thou hast don me with jelousie: least she prove too liberall, and pay my debts."

904. reed] rede, advice.

Lor. The storm upon my brest, sir. *Exeunt.*

Finis Actus Secundus.

ACTUS TERTIUS.

[SCENE I]

Enter Lodovico, Jaspro, Jovani,

and Clown.

Lod. Did chronicle ever match this couple, gentlemen?

Jasp. You make us wonder,
That both should seem to yeild to the temptation,
And both so meet in one resolved goodness,
Unknown to one another!

Lod. There lyes the jest on't. Sirrah *Pambo*, I do but think, and she had met him in the garden, how she would have rattled him.

Clown. And ruffled him too, sir; the camomile would have been better for it many a day after.

Jov. Such an honest minded servant, where shall one finde?

Lod. Servant? My sworn brother, man; he's too honest for an

---

913. rattled] scolded, railed at.

915. ruffled] discomposed, disordered; with a pun on the second meaning of touzle, or handle with rude familiarity.

915-916. the camomile . . . day after.] Cf. Greene's *Philomela* (p. 199): " . . . the Camomill the more it is troden, the sweeter smell it yeeldeth . . ."

camomile] a creeping herb, popularly thought to grow faster when trampled, hence the proverb: The more camomile is trodden down the more it spreads (Tilley, C34).

office, he'll never thrive in't. Ye have few servants will deal so mercifully with their Lords.

Jasp. A wife! Why she's a saint, one that ever bears a good sound soul about her.

Clown. Yes, when she wears her new shooes.

Jov. Shall we see her, my Lord?

Lod. Where is she, *Pambo*?

Clown. Walking a turn or two i'th' garden with *Francisco*, sir; I'll go call her.

Lod. No, no, no, let her alone; 'tis pity indeed to part them, they are so well match'd. Was he not reading to her?

Clown. No, sir, she was weeping to him. She heard this morning that her confessor, Father *Jacomo*, was dead.

Jasp. Father *Jacomo* dead?

Lod. Why, now shall not we have her eat one bit this five daies.

Clown. She'll munch the more in a corner; that's the Puritan's fast.

Lod. Nay, do but judge of her, my Lords, by one thing; whereas most of our dames go to confession but once a month, some twice a quarter, and some but once a year, and that upon constraint too, she never misses twice a week.

Jasp. 'Tis wonderful.

934-935. Puritan's fast] i.e., in reference to Puritans' notorious hypocrisy. Puritans, in contrast to Anglicans, practiced fasting, not as an end in itself, but to "call people to serious thinking and attendance upon an extra sermon or lecture." See Marshall M. Knappen, *Tudor Puritanism* (1939; rpt. Gloucester, Mass.: Peter Smith, 1963), p. 287. No reference to specific attacks on Puritan fasting practice has been located, although numerous charges of hypocrisy were levelled. William P. Holden, in *Anti-Puritan Satire 1572-1642* (1954; rpt. n.p.: Archon Books, 1968), states that "one of the most persistent and damaging of the Anglican's indictments of the Puritan was that of hypocrisy" (p.41).

Jov. 'Tis a sign she keeps all well at home. They are even With the whole world, that so keep touch with heaven.

Lod. Nay, I told ye, ye should finde no *Philippo* of *Francisco*.

Clown. And I remember I told your honour, ye should finde no *Abstemia* of my Lady.

Lod. Nor no *Lorenzo* of my self; he was ever a melancholy stubborn fellow; he kept her in too much, and see what comes on't; I give my wife her will, and see what comes on't too.

Clown. Nay, sir, there is two come on't, and a man could discover 'em.

Lod. Two what, I prethee?

Clown. It may be two babies, sir, for they come commonly with giving a woman her will.

Lod. I'd laugh at that, yfaith, boy. But who has she now for her confessor?

Clown. She looks for one they call him Father *Antony*, sir, and he's wish'd to her by Madona *Lussuriosa*.

Enter Dorothea [*weeping, and*] *Francisco*.

Lod. There's another modest soul too, never without a holy

---

941. she keeps . . . at home] this proverbial expression not in Tilley.

958. wish'd] D3, D4, B correctly note: recommended.

Lussuriosa] Florio (*Queen Anna's New World of Words*, London, 1611) defines *lussurioso*: "luxurious, letcherous, lustfull, wanton, riotous, ranke" (p. 291). In *The Return from Parnassus, Pt. I*, a *Luxurioso* is a student who has only learned to live beyond his means and to love wine and women. In *The Revenger's Tragedy*, the duke's son is suitably named *Lussurioso*.

man at her elbow. But here comes one out-weighs them all. Why, how now, chick! Weeping so fast? This is the fault of most of our Ladies; painting, weeping for their sins I should say, spoils their faces.

Fran. Sweet Madam! [*Francisco weeps too.*]

Lod. Look, look, look, loving soul, he weeps for company.

Clown. And I shall laugh out-right, by and by.

Dor. Oh that good man!

Lod. Why, bird?

Jasp. Be patient, Lady.

Dor. Would he go to heaven without his zealous pupil?

Clown. It may be he knew not your mind, forsooth.

Dor. He knew my mind well enough.

Clown. Why, then it may be he knew you could not hold out for the journey. Pray, do not set us all a crying. *Weeps.*

Lod. Prethee, sweet birds-nye, be content.

Dor. Yes, yes, content, when you too leave my company?
No one comes neer me; so that were it not
For modest simple *Francis* here------

Clown. [*Aside*] As modest as a gib-cat at midnight.

Dor. That sometimes reads
Vertuous books to me; were it not for him,
I might go look content. But 'tis no matter,
No body cares for me.

---

962. painting] makeup (hence, loose behavior), with pun on "panting" (?).

975. birds-nye] term of endearment. See note for l. 522.

979. gib-cat] male cat.

982. I might go look content] D4 notes: I might go in search of it. B notes: Look for, search after.

Lod. Nay, prethee, *Doll*; pray, gentlemen, comfort her. *Weeps.*

Clown. Now is the devil writing an encomium upon cunning cuckold-makers.

Fran. You have been harsh to her of late, I fear, sir.

Lod. By this hand, I turn'd not from her all last night. What should a man do?

Jasp. Come, this is but a sweet obedient shower,
To bedew the lamented grave of her old father.

Clown. He thinks the devil's dead too.

Dor. But 'tis no matter; were I such a one
As the Count *Lorenzo*'s Lady, were I so graceless
To make you wear a pair of wicked horns,
You would make more reckoning of me-- *Weeps.*

Lod. Weep again? She'll cry out her eyes, gentlemen.

Clown. No, I warrant ye; remember the two lines your Honour read last night:

A woman's eye,
'S April's dust, no sooner wet but dry.

Lod. Good pigs-nye! *Frank*, prethee walk her t'other turn i'th' garden, and get her a stomach to her supper; we'll be with ye presently, wench.

Dor. Nay, when ye please.------But why should I go from ye?

---

992. He thinks the devil's dead too.] D4 notes: A proverbial expression, by which the Clown ironically suggests that the world is going to be good at last. Tilley (D244) cites this line as one example.

1002. pigs-nye] pigsney, commonly used as an endearing form of address. Similar in use to birds-nye (cf. ll. 522, 975).

Lod. Loving soul! Prethee, Frank, take her away.

Dor. Pray let me kiss ye first. Come, Francis, No body cares for us. At the door Francis kisses her. Exeunt.

Lod. Well, there goes a couple; where shall a man match ye indeed? Hark Pambo!

Jasp. [To Jov.] Did you observe?

Jov. [To Jasp.] They kist.

Jasp. [To Jov.] Peace.

Lod. And intreat Madona Lussuriosa to sup with us, as you go; tell her my Lady's never well, but in her company.

Clown. What if your honour invited the Count Lorenzo? He'll be so melancholy now his Lady and he are parted!

Lod. Pray do as you are bid, kind sir, and let him alone; I'll have no cuckold sup in my house to night.

Clown. 'Tis a very hot evening; your honour will sup in the garden then.

Lod. Yes, marry, will I, sir; what's that to you?

Clown. Why, your honour was ever as good as your word. Keep the cuckolds out of door, and lay a cloath for my Lord in the arbour, gentlemen. Exit.

Lod. I have been this three months about a project.

Jov. What is't, my Lord?

Lod. Why, I intend to compose a pamphlet of all my wife's vertues, put them in print, and dedicate them to the Duke, as

---

1029-1030. Why, I . . . in print] Fleay (I, 104) notes this apparent allusion to Thomas Overbury's A Wife, which "had reached its eleventh impression in 1622."

orthodoxal directions against he marries.

<u>Jasp</u>. 'Twill give him apt instructions, when he does marry, to pick out such a woman.

<u>Lod</u>. Pick her! Where will he pick her? As the English proverb says, he may as soon finde a needle in a bottle of hay. Would I know what sins she has committed, I would set them down all one with another; they would serve as foils to her vertues. But I do think she has none; d'ye think she has any, gentlemen?

<u>Jov</u>. Oh none, sir, but has some!

<u>Lod</u>. I, pidling ones it may be, as when a pin pricks her fingers to cry at sight on't, and throw't away; but for other matters------

<u>Jasp</u>. Now I think on't, sir, I have a device newly begotten, that if you be so desirous to be resolv'd of her perfections, 'twill be an apt means for your intelligence.

<u>Lod</u>. That will be excellent; and then my book, grounded upon mine own experience, the report of my judgement in the choyce of a woman, will sell them off faster than the compositor can set the letters together.

<u>Jasp</u>. We will discourse it as we go; mean time, sir, Let this prepare the path to your construction:

1031. against] in preparation for when.

1035. he may . . . of hay] bottle: bundle. A common proverb (Tilley, N97).

1052. construction] i.e., preparation, but with the second meaning of learning, a meaning the <u>NED</u> does not record. (See also l. 1730 for another example of construction to mean instruction.)

Conceit and confidence are juglers born;
One grafts in air, t'other hides the real horn.

Lod. Well, he that believes he has horns, has horns;
And *Crede quod habes, & habes* shall be my motto. *Exeunt.*

[SCENE II]

Enter Pandulpho and Spinoso.

Spin. The powers of *Venice* upon our confines!

Pand. Yes, Signor *Philippo,* it seems, having possest him
With the passages that past upon his sister,
Embassadors were dispatch'd to *Bergamo,*
Where then his forces lay; who thus return'd,
That he came not a publick foe unto *Verona,*
But to require justice against Count *Lorenzo,*
To approve his sister innocent.

Spin. What witness,
Proof or apparent circumstance builds he
His bold attempt upon?

1054. grafts] grows.

1058. possest him] informed him.

1060-1061. Embassadors . . . forces lay] Cf. Greene's *Philomela* (p. 185): "The Ambassadours having their charge, came to the Duke [father of Abstemia], lying then not farre off from *Bergamo* . . ."

Bergamo] a city of Lombardy, and dependency of Venice (1428-1797).

1062-1064. That he . . . innocent] Cf. Greene's *Philomela* (p. 185): ". . . that hee was not come as an enemy against them, but as a private foe to *Philippo,* and therefore required to approove his daughters innocencie . . ."

1064. approve] prove, demonstrate.

Pand. He says, besides
The honour of *Philippo*, he has proof
So unresistable to affirm the plot
Of Count *Lorenzo*, that he only crav'd
(Hostages being tendered for their safe returns)
Here in the senate-chamber, the fair tryal
Might publickly be censur'd. And by this
They are at hand.

Enter at one Door, Duke of Venice, Philippo and Lords;
at the other, Duke of Verona, Jaspro, Jovani,
Lorenzo guarded, [and] the 1st Slave. A bar set out.

Vero. Fair sir, the presence is levell'd for your grevances.
Ven. First summon to the bar the Count *Lorenzo*.
Pand. *Lorenzo Medico*, stand to the bar.
Lor. I do stand to the bar.
Ven. I come not here, witness the good man's comfort, to adde one step
Unto my territories; and though I burthen
The neighbour-bosom of my confines with
The weight of armour, or do wound your brest
(My dukedom's neer next neighbour) with the hoofs
Of war-apparell'd horses, 'tis not to seek
For martial honours, but for civil justice.

1072. tendered] B emends to rendered, but the change is unnecessary, since tendered can mean offered. Cf. *Cymbeline*, III, iv, 11: Why tender'st thou that paper to me . . . .

1076. the presence is levell'd] i.e., the signorie of Verona is ready to listen.

Conceive mine honour wounded; a sister's shame
Is an unpleasant spot upon our arms.
Yet that we come not here to sanctifie
A sister's sin. For if she so be prov'd,
Shame sleep within her epitaph, and brand her;
Let bears and wolves that angel's face confound,
Gives goodness such a foul unfriendly wound.
But if she chaste be prov'd, what balm can cure
A wounded name? As he that not inflicts
The bitter stroak of law upon the strumpet,
Fattens the sad afflictions of a thousand;
So who but stains an honest woman's name,
Plagues are yet kept for him; steel is no defence
For the unclean tongue injures innocence.
I affirm my sister wrong'd, wrong'd by this man,
This that has wrong'd pure judgement, and thrown poyson
Upon the face of truth, and upon him
I seek a satisfaction.

Lor. I reply.
The law must give you satisfaction,
That justly did divorce us. I appeal
To the whole consiliadory, if equal law

1080-1086. I come not here . . . civil justice.] Cf. Greene's *Philomela* (pp. 186-187): "I come not Venetians to enlarge my territories with the sworde, though I have burdened your borders with the waight of armed men: I rise not in armes to seeke martiall honours, but civil justice . . ."

1089-1090. Yet, that . . . sister's sin] Cf. Greene's *Philomela* (p. 187): "For proofe that I come not to sanctifie sinne in my daughter . . ."

1108. consiliadory] counseling body (see note to l. 74).

In her progression went a step astray,
Either by proof or information.
Let the Duke speak (not as he is my kinsman)
If I produc'd not legally in court,
Besides mine own assertion (which even reason
Grounded on probability), two of my servants
That upon oath affirm'd they saw your sister
Even in the very act of sin and shame
With that Philippo there. Blame me not then, sir,
If I return an error to your cause.
Reason (the base whereon we build the laws)
You injure in this action; give her the lye.
Who dares not build his faith upon his eye?
They swore what they did see; and men still fear,
(Reason concludes) what they not see, to swear.

Vero. You hear my kinsman's answer.

Pand. And 'tis requisite
That you produce your authour; it is held
Meer madness on a hill of sand to build.

Phil. The foundation-work is mine, and that I answer.
He builds on truth, the good man's mistris,
And not in the sanctuary

1118. return an error to your cause] i.e., show your cause to be in error.

1121. Who dares . . . eye] proverbial, related to: "I will believe it when I see it" (Tilley, B268), and "seeing is believing" (Tilley, S212).

1126-1127. it is held . . . to build.] Common proverb originating in Matthew vii,26: And every one that heareth these sayings of mine, and doeth them not, shall be likened unto a foolish man, which built his house upon the sand. (Tilley, S88).

Of this injur'd brother's power, but the integrity
And glory of the cause. I throw the pawn
Of my afflicted honour, and on that
I openly affirm your absent Lady
Chastitie's well-knit abstract, snow in the fall
Purely refin'd by the bleak northern blast,
Not freer from a soyl the thoughts of infants,
But little neerer heaven. And if these princes
Please to permit, before their guilty thoughts
Injure another hour upon the Lady,
My right drawn sword shall prove it.

Lor. Upon my knee, sir,
(How my soul dances!) humbly I intreat
Your grant to his request; fight with *Philippo*
I'th' midst of flame, or pestilence, in a cave
Where *Basiliskes* do breed.

Vero. We must take counsel;
The price of blood is pretious.

1132-1138. I throw . . . neerer heaven] *The Shakespeare Allusion-Book* (p. 109) notes the similarity between Davenport's snow metaphor and the one in *The Winter's Tale*, IV, iv, 364-365:

or the fann'd snow that's bolted
By the northern blasts twice o'er.

This was first noted in *I Notes and Queries*, i, 330.

Also, Cf. *Two Noble Kinsman*, V, i, 137: O . . . constant queen . . . as chaste, and as pure as wind-fann'd snow. And cf. Tilley, S 591.

1137. soyl] i.e., soyl [are].

1138. But little] i.e., But [a] little.

1146. *Basiliskes*] a mythological reptile, said to have a fatal look and breath.

Lor. Blood desires burthen:
The price of truth is pretious. For all the fights
I have fought for you on land; the fears at sea,
Where I have tug'd with tempests, stood storms at midnight,
Out-star'd the flaring lightning, and the next morning
Chas'd the unruly stubborn Turk with thunder;
For all the bullets I have bravely shot,
And sent death singing to the slaughter, sir------

Vero. Peace.

Lor. What should a souldier do with peace? Remember,
Mine honour lies a bleeding, and in mine yours;
Her wide wound inward bleeds; and while you cry peace,
Shame wars upon my name. Oh rather kill me,
Than cast me to this scandal.

Spin. The doubtful cause,
With such a dare approv'd, you may permit it.

Vero. Your request is granted, coze'.

Lor. You have now, sir, breath'd
Fresh air in the face of fainting honour.
Rapiers of fair equality.

1149. Blood desires burthen] B adds [?] to indicate unclear meaning. The passage makes better sense if truth were substituted for burthen, but what Davenport most likely means is the burden of truth. It is also possible that Davenport is alluding to the proverb, "Blood will have blood" (Tilley, B458), and then "burthen" should be emended to "brethren."

1153. out-star'd] to look on or stare at without blinking or flinching. In this sense, *NED* records no example before 1646.

1159. lies a bleeding] proverbial; in its original form, "all lies and bleeds" (Tilley, A159).

Ven. Look with what cunning
The spider, when she would snare the fly, doth weave;
With neater art, appearances deceive.
Stay; as you said, sir, blood is a pretious price.
Let me but see the men produc'd, who swore
They saw them in the shameful act; and then
Farewel a sister and her honour.

Pand. Produce your servants, sir. Venice sends off a Lord.

Lor. [Aside] Plague of this change!--Here's one of them; t'other,
In that I threaten'd him for some neglect,
The next day ran away.

Ven. Did you, sir, swear
You saw our sister and this gentleman
In this base act of sin?

Lor. Fear nothing.

1 Slave. To deny truth is more dangerous than to displease
a Duke.
I saw it and did swear it.

Enter Lord and 2 [nd] Slave.

Ven. But here comes one
Will swear you saw it not, and are forsworn.

1 Slave. [Aside] 'Sfoot, Stratzo!

Spin. This is the other fellow took his oath.

Vero. What come you here to say, sir?

2 Slave. That we swore falsely, may it please your Grace,
Hyr'd by my Lord with gifts and promises;
And as I now have spoke the truth, so heaven

Forgive my former perjury.

Vero. Hear you, cozen?

1 Slave. [*To Lor*.] Would you would say something; I have nettles in my breeches.

Lor. Now, now, I hope your eyes are open, Lords,
The bed of snakes is broak, the trick's come about,
And here's the knot i'th' rush. Good heaven, good heaven,
That craft, in seeking to put on disguise,
Should so discover her self!

Vero. Explain your self.

Lor. Now see, sir, where this scorpion lurks to sting
Mine honour unto death. This noble Duke
By nature is ingag'd to defend a sister;
And to this Duke so ingag'd, this malitious Lord
(For sin still hates her scourger) makes repair,
And prepossesses him with that suppos'd innocence
Of an injur'd sister; which he had hyr'd this slave
To follow him, and affirm, and layes the cause
To scruple, and to conscience. They did consent
To steal belief by seeming accident.
Sin, jugler-like, casts sin before our eyes;
Craft sometimes steals the wonder of the wise.

1197-1198. I have nettles in my breeches] probably a proverb, but not in Tilley (but cf. T239, to sit upon thorns).

1201. And here's the knot i'th' rush] Cf. Greene's *Philomela* (p. 128): "*Philomela* who straight found the knot in the *rush* . . . . *Philomela* hearing this, began to finde a knot in the rush . . . ." -- knot i'th' rush: to make difficulties where there are none; alluding to the proverb "to seek a knot in a rush (bulrush)" (Tilley, K168).

With an equal hand now weigh me, and if I want
A grain of honour, tear me from your blood,
And cast me to contempt.

1 Slave. [To Lor.] My Lord would have made an excellent state-sophister.

Vero. In what a strange dilemma judgement sits,
Charm'd to her chair with wonder.

Ven. Shall I have justice?

Pand. Yes, in that this fellow swears for the Duke.
Reach him the book; you shall see him again
Take the former oath.

Vero. This doubt must be so ended;
If it give not satisfaction, send back our hostages,
You have fair regress to your forces. But
The blood remains on you; and still remember,
The price of blood is pretious.

Phil. Let us end it.

Ven. Oh what a combat honour holds with conscience!
Reach him the book; and if thou false dost say,
May thine own tongue, thine own foul heart betray.

1 Slave. Amen, say I.
Give me the book; my oath must end all then.

Spin. It must.

Lor. Now you shall hear him swear
He saw them both in the base act.

1 Slave. Nay, I swear

1226. book] i.e., the Bible.

They are now both seen in the base act.

Omn. How's this?

Pand. 'Tis a strange oath.

1 Slave. 'Tis true, though.

Lor. True, villain! Are both now seen in the base act?

1 Slave. Yes, both.

Lor. Which both?

1 Slave. You and I, sir.

Omn. How?

1 Slave. Both you and I are seen in the base act,
Slandering spotless honour; an act so base,
The barbarous Moor would blush at.

Phil. D'ye hear him now?

Lor. Out, slave, wilt thou give ground too? Fear works upon 'em.
Did you not both here swear i'th' senate-chamber
You saw them both dishonest?

1 Slave. Then we swore true, sir.

Lor. I told you 'twas but fear.

Vero. Swore ye true then, sir, when ye swore
Ye both saw them dishonest?

1 Slave. Yes, marry, did we, sir.
For we were both two villains when we saw them,
So we saw them dishonest.

1253-1254. Slandering . . . blush at.] Olive (p.342) notes a possible allusion to *Othello*, similar to the one in *The Honest Whore*, I, i:

> --thou kill'st her now again
> And art more savage than a barbarous Moor--

Ven. Heaven, thou art equal!

1 Slave. This is a jealous Lord; his Lady chaste,
A rock of christal not more clear; this gentleman
Basely abus'd; this great Prince dishonour'd;
And so we kneel for mercy.

Vero. You have redeem'd it;
Depart, prove honest men. That I should bear
Dishonour in my blood!

Omn. Much injur'd Lady!

Ven. What justice, sir, belongs unto the injur'd?

Vero. First, witness heaven, I tear thee from my blood,
And cast thee off a stranger. Assume you, sir,
(Since the great cause is yours) my seat of justice,
And sentence this foul homicide; it must be,
And suddenly; he will infect the air else.
Proceed, great sir, with rigor, whilst I stand by
And do adore the sentence.

Ven. Answer, Lorenzo,
Art thou not guilty?

Lor. Give me my merit, death;
Princes can build and ruine with one breath.

Ven. The cause may seem to merit death, in that
Two souls were hazarded, a Princess' fame,
A Duke dishonour'd, and a noble Lord

1267. Heaven, thou art equal!] i.e., only heaven (God) is equal to putting up with this double-talk; or, perhaps, heaven, you are just!

1269. A rock . . . clear] "As clear as crystal" is proverbial (Tilley, C875).

Wounded in reputation; but since she lives,
And that no blood was spilt (though something dearer),
Mercy thus far stretches her silver wings
Over your trespass; we do banish you,
Both from our dukedom's limits and your own.
If you but set a daring foot upon them
Whilst life lends you ability to stand,
You fall into the pit of death, unless
You shall finde out our most unfortunate sister,
And bring her to our court.

Lor. You, sir, are merciful!

Vero. This let me adde, in that you have made impartial justice, sir,
Princes should punish vice in their own blood.
Until you finde that excellent injur'd Lady,
Upon this gentleman, who hath suffer'd for you,
We confer your lands, revenues, and your place;
That during three days' stay within our confines
It shall be death to any that relieves you,
But as they do a begger at their door.
So cast him from our presence.

Lor. Your dooms are tust!
Oh love, thy first destruction is distrust!

Exeunt Lorenzo, Jaspro and Jovani.

Vero. For you, fair sir, until we shall hear tydings

1302. sir] i.e., the Duke of Venice. See textual notes.

1309. But] except (contrary to what B suggests; see textual note).

Of your most injur'd sister, please you to call
My court your own, conceive it so. Where live,
Two partners in one passion we will be,
And sweeten sorrow with a sympathy. *Exeunt.*

[SCENE III]

Enter Lodovico like a fryer, Jaspro and Jovani.

Lod. What, am I fitted, gallants? Am I fitted?

Jasp. To th' life, able to cheat suspition, and so like
Father *Antony* the confessor, that I protest
There's not more semblance in a pair of egges.

Jov. An apple cut in half is not so like.

Lod. Well, Lords, you're mad Lords to counsel me to this; but now in this habit shall I know the very core of her heart, all her little pidling sins, which will shew in my book as foils to her giant-bodied vertues.

Jasp. That will be admirable!

Jov. We'll step aside; by this she's upon coming.

Jasp. We shall know all.

Lod. Reveal confession? But go your ways; as much as may lawfully be reveal'd, we'll laugh at, at next meeting.

Jasp. Come, let's be gone. But once upon a time, sir,
A begger found a lark's nest, and o'er-joy'd
At his suddain glut, for he thought 'twas full of young ones;
Looking, they were all gone; he was forc'd again to beg,

1315. Where live] i.e. where [we] live.

1318. fitted] ready.

For he found in the lark's nest a serpent's egge;
So much good d'ye, sir. *Exeunt.*

Enter *Dorothea.*

Lod. [*Aside*] Well, thou surpassest all the courtiers in these pretty ones, if a man had the wit to understand them. Yonder she comes; I can hardly forbear blushing, but that for discovering my self.

Right reverend habit, I honour thee
With a son's obedience, and do but borrow thee,
As men would play with flyes, who i'th' midst of modest mirth
With care preserve themselves.

Dor. Hail, holy father.

Lod. Welcome, my chaste daughter.

Dor. Death having taken good Father *Jacomo,*
Upon the plenal and approv'd report
Of your integrity and upright dealing,-----

Lod. [*Aside*] Delicate *Doll.*

Dor. I have made a modest choyce of you, grave sir,
To be my ghostly father; and to you I fall
For absolution.

Lod. Empty then, my daughter,
That vessel of your flesh of all the dregs,
Which (since your last confession clear'd you) have

1342. habit] the friar's robes.

1349. plenal] complete (see note to l. 700).

Taken a setled habitation in you;
And with a powerful sweet acknowledgment,
Hunt out those spirits which haunt that house of flesh.
Tears make dry branches flourish green and fresh.

Dor. Since last I confest, then I do confess
My first sin w^s, that my taylor bringing home
My last new gown, having made the sleeves too flanting,
In an unchristian passion I did bid
The devil take him.

Lod. That was something harsh, dear daughter,
Yet the more pardonable, for it may be your taylor
Lyes in hell, night by night. Pray, to your second.

Dor. Next, in a more savage rage, my chamber-maid
Putting a little safforn in her starch,
I most unmercifully broak her head.

Lod. 'Twas rashly done too. But are ye sure, dear daughter,
the maid's head was not broak before?

Dor. No, no, sir, she came to me with ne'er a crack about
her.

1364. flanting] flaunting, showy, gaudy.

1369. Lyes in hell] B notes: An allusion to the "tailor's hell"--the hole (under the counter) where purloined scraps of cloth were deposited.

1371. Putting a little safforn in her starch] i.e., making the starch yellow; safforn: saffron, the crushed dryed stigmas of the autumnal crocus, used as yellow and orange coloring. B notes: "The wearing of yellow starched bands and ruffs is said to have been introduced by Mrs. Turner (accomplice in the Overbury murder). She wore them at the gallows in 1615. After her execution the fashion fell temporarily into disrepute, but soon revived." In *A New Tricke to Cheat the Divell*, IV, i (B, p. 252), the devil says: "I was first Father for this yellow Sterch . . ."

Lod. [*Aside*] These will be brave sins to mix with her vertues; why, they will make no more shew than three or four bayliffs amongst a company of honest men. [*To Dor.*] These sins, my dove-like daughter, are out of contradiction venial, trivial and light. Have you none of greater growth?

Dor. Oh yes, sir, one!

Lod. [*Aside*] One? What should that be, I wonder?

Dor. One yet remains behind,
Of weight and consequence. The same order
Heralds prescribe in shews, I now observe
In placing of my sins; as there inferiours
(Because the last lives freshest in our memories)
Fare 'fore the persons of great note, so last
My great sin comes to obliterate those past.

Lod. [*Aside*] Sh'as trod some chicken to death, I warrant her.

Dor. Hear me, and let a blush make you look red,
Unseemly I have abus'd my husband's bed.

Lod. You did ill to drink too hard ere you went to bed.

Dor. Alas, sir, you mistake me; I have lain
With another man, besides my husband.

Lod. How?

Dor. Nay, the same way I use to lye with him,
But not altogether so often.

Lod. [*Aside*] Why then, *Crede quod habes, & habes*; I will believe I

1380. out of contradiction] in contrast. *NED* records no example for this usage between 1597 and 1777.

1389. Fare 'fore] i.e., comes before.

have horns, for I have 'em. 'Sfoot, a woman, I perceive, is a neat herald; she can quarter her husband's coat with butcher's arms at pleasure. But I have a penance for your pure whoreship. [*To Dor.*] You are somewhat broad; are you not with child, daughter?

Dor. Yes, yes, sure 'twas that night's work.

Lod. How know you that?

Dor. Alas, by experience, sir. The kind fool my husband
Wishes all well; but like a light piece of gold,
He's taken for more than he weighs.

Lod. [*Aside*] With child! There's charges too; a't'other side, there should follow
A zealous exhortation. [*To Dor.*] But great affairs
That brook no stay make me be brief, remembring
Lawful necessity may dispence with ceremony.

1401. 'Sfoot] By God's foot (an oath).

1402. neat herald] clever herald (one who regulated the use of armorial bearings and recording of family pedigree).

quarter] in heraldry, to add another's coat (or arms) to one's hereditary arms.

1402-1403. butcher's arms] a pun on quarter (i.e., meat) as B suggests. The butcher (with his skewer) was considered promiscuous and virile (Farmer and Henley, V, 288, 294, cite an example from Dekker and Massinger's *Virgin Martyr*, II, i, 32-34: "Bawdy Priapus, the first schoolmaster that taught butchers to stick pricks in flesh, and make it swell, thou know'st, was the only ningle that I cared for under the moon.").

1409. light piece of gold] a clipped coin, in which part of the gold is clipped or filed off, lessening its weight and value.

1411. charges] i.e., against his wife.

a] on.

You are ingenuously sorry?

Dor. Yes, indeed, sir.

Lod. And resolve to fall no more so?

Dor. No, in truth, sir.

Lod. I then pronounce you here absolv'd. Now for your penance.

Dor. Any thing.

Lod. As the fact in you seems strange, so blame me not
If your penance be as strange. You may wonder at it,
But it is wondrous easie in performance,
But as your penance I enjoyn it. Nay, now I remember,
In an old French authentick author, his book
Titled, *De Satisfactione*, I read the same
Enjoyn'd a Lady of *Dauphin*. 'Tis no holy fast,
No devout prayer, nor no zealous pilgrimage;
'Tis out of the prescrib'd road.

Dor. Let it be
So strange, storie ne'er matcht the injunction, I do vow
The plenal strict performance.

Lod. Listen to me.
Soon at night (so rumour spreads it through the city),
The two great Dukes of *Venice* and *Verona*

1416. ingenuously] sincerely.

1427-1429. In an old . . . *Dauphin*] This title and author have not been identified.

1429. *Dauphin*] or Dauphine, a large province in southeastern France.

1434. plenal] complete (see note to l. 700).

Are feasted by your Lord, where a mask's intended.

Dor. That's true, sir.

Lod. Now, when ye all are set round about the table,
In depth of silence, you shall confess these words
Aloud to your husband: "You are not this
child's father."
And 'cause my orders bar me such inquisition,
You shall say, such a man lay with me, naming the party
Was partner in your sin.

Dor. Good sir!

Lod. This is your penance I enjoyn you; keep it,
You are absolv'd; break it, you know the danger of it. Good-buy.

Dor. Oh good sir, stay; never was penance of more shame than this.

Lod. You know the danger of the breach; as to us,
'Tis the shameful loss of our religious orders, if we reveal.

Dor. For heaven sake,
Enjoyn me first upon my knees to creep
From *Verona* to *Loretto*.

Lod. That's nothing.

Dor. Nothing indeed to this. Is this your penance so wondrous easie in performance?

Lod. 'Tis irrevocable.

Dor. I am silent. Your new penance may meet a new performance. Farewel, sir.

1456. *Loretto*] or Loreto, a shrine for pilgrimage to the Virgin Mary, about 200 miles from Verona. This line cited in Sugden, *A Topographical Dictionary* . . . (p. 318).

You are the cruelst e're confest me before.

Lod. [*Aside*] And this the trick to catch a neat pure whore.

Exeunt.

Finis Actus Tertius.

ACTUS QUARTUS.

[SCENE I]

Enter Abstemia.

Abst. Here, miserable despis'd *Abstemia,*
In *Millain* let thy misery take breath,
Wearied with many sufferings. Oh *Lorenzo!*
How far in love I am with my affliction,
Because it calls thee father! Unto this house,
Where gentlewomen lodge, I was directed;
But I here discover
Strange actions closely carried in this house.
Great persons (but not good) here nightly revel
In surfets, and in riots, yet so carried,
That the next day the place appears a sanctuary,
Rather than sin's foul receptable. These ways
Have to me still been strangers; but, *Lorenzo,*

1464. neat] skillful, cleverly contriving.

1474. surfets] surfeits, excesses.

Thou couldst not though believe it. Oh jealousie!
Love's eclipse, thou art in thy disease
A wild mad patient, wondrous hard to please.

Enter Timpanina and Morbo.

Mor. [*To Tim.*] Yonder she walks mumbling to her self; the Prince *Antonio* has blest her with's observation; and ye win her but to him, your house bears the bell away. Accost her quaintly.

Tim. [*To Mor.*] I warrant thee, *Morbo*, Madona *Timpanina* has effect'd wonders of more weight than a maiden-head. Have I ruin'd so many city-citadels, to let in court-martialists, and shall this country-cottage hold out? I were more fit for a cart than a coach then, yfaith. [*To Abst.*] How now, *Millicent*, how d'ye this morning?

Abst. Well, I do thank so good a landlady.

Tim. But hark you, *Mill*. Is the door close, *Morbo*?

Mor. As a usurer's conscience. *Grace* was coming in, till she

---

1480a. *Timpanina*] to have a two-legged tympany is to be got with a bastard child (Farmer and Henley, VII, 246). Also, any swelling, as inflated style or bombast, which is one of Timpanina's characteristics.

1483. bears the bell away] a proverb meaning to carry away the prize (Tilley, B275).

1484. quaintly] craftily, skillfully; also, elegantly.

1485. *Morbo*] Florio (*Queen Anna's New World of Words*, London, 1611) defines as "any evill, disease, or contagion" (p. 322). *Morbus* (Latin): disease, vice, sorrow.

1489. cart] a vehicle for conveying prisoners to the gallows, or for public exposure of offenders, especially prostitutes. Earliest recorded use in *NED* is Heywood's *Captives* (1624).

saw the door shut upon her.

Tim. I'll set *Grace* about her business, and I come to her. Is here any work for *Grace*, with a wannion to her? We shall have eaves-droppers, shall we?

Abst. [*Aside*] Chastity guard me, how I tremble!

Tim. Come hither, mistris *Millicent*. Fie, how you let your hair hang about your ears too? How do you like my house, *Mill*?

Abst. Well, indeed well.

Tim. Nay, I know a woman may rise here in one month, and she will her self. But truth's truth, I know you see something, as they say, and so forth. Did you see the gallant was here last [night] till 12?

Abst. Which of them mean you? Here was many.

Tim. Which? He in the white feather that supp'd in the gallery; was't not white, *Morbo*?

Mor. As a lady's hand, by these five fingers.

Tim. White? No, no, 'twas a tawny, now I remember.

Mor. As a gipsie, by this hand; it look'd white by candle-light though.

1493-1494. *Grace* . . . upon her] with a pun on the name Grace, referring to the proverb, "whoredom and grace can never bide in one place" (Tilley, W328).

1496. with a wannion] may a curse or plague light on. *NED* cites this line as one example.

1510. by these five fingers] see note to l. 622.

1511. tawny] applied to various shades of brown, yellow-brown, or orange-brown.

Tim. That lusty springal, *Millicent,* is no worse man than the Duke of *Millain*'s son.

Abst. His excellent carriage spoke him of noble birth.

Tim. And this same Duke's son loves you, *Millicent.*

Abst. Now heaven defend me!

Tim. What, from a Duke's son? Marry, come up with a murren; from whence came you tro, ha?

Mor. Thus nice *Grace* was at first, and you remember.

Tim. I would have ye know, houswife, I could have taken my coach and fetch'd him one of the best pieces in *Millain,* and her husband should have look'd after me, that's neighbours might have noted, and cry'd, "Farewel, naunt, commend me to mine uncle."

Mor. And yet from these perfum'd fortunes heaven defend you.

Abst. Perfum'd indeed.

Mor. Perfum'd! I am a pander, a rogue, that hangs together

1514. lusty] pleasing, vigorous.

springal] young man.

1519-1520. murren] murrain, plague; hence, may a plague fall upon you. *NED* cites this line as one example.

1520. tro] trow, used parenthetically or at the end of a sentence (often merely expletive); *NED* cites *Merry Wives of Windsor,* I, iv, 127: "Who's there, I thoa?"

1525. naunt] i.e., mine aunt; slang for prostitute or procuress.

1527. perfum'd] sweet.

1529-1530. Perfum'd . . . pander] perfume was associated with prostitutes and panders. Cf. *King John and Matilda,* IV, ii (B, p. 63):

> . . . wilt thou play the Court Camelion,
> The perfum'd Pander?

like a begger's rags, by geometry, if there were not three ladies swore yesterday that my mistris perfum'd the coach! So they were fain to unbrace all the side-parts, to take in fresh air.

Tim. He tells you true, I keep no common company, I warrant ye; we vent no breath'd ware here.

Abst. But have ye so many several women to answer so many men that come?

Mor. I'll answer that by demonstration. Have ye not observ'd the variation of a cloud? Sometimes 'twill be like a lyon, sometimes like a horse, sometimes a castle, and yet still a cloud.

Abst. True.

Mor. Why, so can we make one wench one day look like a country-wench, another day like a citizen's wife, another day like a lady, and yet still be a punk.

Abst. What shall become of me? Oh, the curse
Of goodness, to leave one wo for a worse!

Enter Philippo [disguised]:

Phil. Morrow, sweet madam. Oh, look how like the sun

1533. side parts] i.e., coach sides.

1535. vent] vend.

breath'd ware] tarnished goods.

1538-1540. Have ye not . . . a cloud] Both B and Olive (p. 341) compare with Antony and Cleopatra, IV, xiv, 2-4:

> Sometimes we see a cloud that's dragonish,
> A vapour sometime, like a bear, or lion,
> A tower'd citadel, a pendent rock . . .

The Arden edition notes, however, cite nine similar passages, many of which parallel Davenport's lines as closely as Shakespeare's.

1544. punk] strumpet.

behind a cloud, the beams do give intelligence it is there.

Tim. You're reciprocal welcome, sir.

Phil. What, have ye not brought this young wild haggard to the lure yet?

Tim. Faith, sir, she's a little irregular yet; but time, that turns citizens' caps into court-periwigs, will bring the wonder about.

Phil. Bless you, sweet mistris.

Enter Antonio and Slave.

Mor. 'Sfoot, here's the Prince; I smell thunder.

Tim. Your Grace is most methodically welcome. You must pardon my variety of phrase; the courtiers e'en cloy us with good words.

Anto. What's he?

Mor. A gentleman of *Ferrara*, sir, one *Pedro Sebastiano*.

Anto. And do ye set her out to sale? I charg'd ye reserve for me alone.

Tim. Indeed, sir.

Anto. Pox of your deeds. *Kicks her.*

Tim. Oh my sciatica!

1547-1548. Oh, look . . . is there.] Olive (p. 343) suggests that Davenport seems to be imitating *The Rape of Lucrece*, 372-373:

Look as the fair and fiery-pointed sun
Rushing from forth a cloud, bereaves our sight.

1550-1554. have ye . . . wonder about] referring to the proverb, "In time all haggard hawks will stoop to lure" (Tilley, T298). wild haggard] untrained female hawk.

1566. sciatica] oftentimes associated with bawds. Cf. *Measure for Measure*, I, ii, 55.

Anto. Sirrah, you perfum'd rascal. *Kicks Philippo; they draw.*

Tim. Nay, good my Lord.

Mor. Good sir, 'tis one of the Duke's chamber.

Phil. Let him be of the devil's chamber.

Anto. Sirrah, leave the house, or I will send thee out with thunder.

Slave. Good sir, 'tis madness here to stand him.

Phil. 'Sfoot, kickt? Pray that we meet no more again, sir.
[*To Abst.*] Still keep heaven about you. [*Exit.*]

Abst. What ere thou art, a good man still go with thee.

Anto. Will you bestow a cast of your professions?

Mor. We are vanish'd, sir.

Tim. This 'tis to dream of rotten glasses, *Morbo.* [*Exeunt.*]

Abst. Oh what shall become of me? In his eye
Murder and lust contends.

Anto. Nay, flie not, you sweet,
I am not angry with you, indeed I am not.
Do you know me?

Abst. Yes, sir, report hath given intelligence
You are the Prince, the Duke's son.

Anto. Both in one.

Abst. Report sure

1577. cast] shadow.

1579. rotten glasses] perhaps, glasses of spoiled wine; or, rotten (smelly) chamber-pots (Farmer and Henley, IV, 233). Perhaps also, Davenport is playing on "eye" of l. 1580, the rotten eye of the prince, glass also meaning a seeing instrument.

1588-1589. Report . . . language] referring to the proverb, "Report is a liar" (Tilley, F44).

Spoke but her native language; you are none of either.

Anto. How?

Abst. Were you the Prince, you would not sure be slav'd
To your blood's passion. I do crave your pardon
For my rough language; truth hath a forehead free,
And in the tower of her integrity,
Sits an unvanquish'd virgin. Can you imagine
'Twill appear possible you are the Prince?
Why, when you set your foot first in this house,
You crush'd obedient duty unto death,
And even then fell from you your respect.
Honour is like a goodly old house, which
If we repair not still with vertue's hand,
Like a citadel being madly rais'd on sand,
It falls, is swallow'd and not found.

Anto. If you rail upon the place, prethee, how cam'st thou hither?

Abst. By treacherous intelligence. Honest men so
In the way ignorant, through theeves' purlewes go.
Are you son to such a noble father?
Send him to's grave then,
Like a white almond-tree, full of glad daies,

1602-1603. Like a citadel . . . falls] referring to the same proverb as ll. 1126-1127.

1607. purlewes] purlieus, haunts. *NED* records no use of this meaning before 1643.

1610. white almond-tree] having greyish-white flowers, hence used figuratively to mean grey or white hair. *NED* cites only one example (1590: *Pasquil's Apol.* 1. E b): "Upon whose silver heads the Almond-tree hath blossomde."

With joy that he begot so good a son.
Oh sir, methinks I see sweet majesty
Sit with a mourning sad face full of sorrows
To see you in this place. This is a cave
Of scorpions and of dragons. Oh turn back!
Toads here ingender, 'tis the stream of death;
The very air poysons a good man's breath.

Enter Timpanina and Morbo.

Anto. Within there!

Mor. Sir.

Anto. Is my caroach at door?

Tim. And your horses too, sir; ye found her pliant.

Anto. Y'are rotten hospitals hung with greasie sattin.

Tim. Ah!

Mor. Came this nice piece from *Naples*, with a pox to her?

1620. caroach] caroche.

1622. Y'are rotten hospitals hung with greasie sattin] Olive (p. 335) parallels with a similar situation in *Pericles*, IV, vi, 118-120:

> Avaunt thou damned door-keeper! Your house,
> But for this virgin that doth propit,
> Would sink and overwhelm you. Away!

hospitals] hotels, in this case in the sense of brothels. *NED* gives Greene's *Groat's Worth of Wit* (1617) as an example: "The house where Lamilia (for so we call the Curtezan) kept her Hospitall." A pun on a place of treatment (i.e., for veneral disease).

greasie] indecent, in a smutty way.

sattin] cheap, gaudy material; also, woman. Cf. *A New Tricke to Cheat the Divell*, II, iii (B, p. 225):

> Canst not endure his name, yet com'st thy selfe
> To tempt me with his Sattin?

In a note, Bullen (p. 225) suggests a play on sattin and satan, possible in this instance as well.

Tim. And she has not Neapolitanis'd him, I'll be flead for't.

Exeunt Baud and Pander.

Anto. Let me borrow goodness from thy lip. Farewel.
Here's a new wonder, I have met heaven in hell. *Exeunt.*

[SCENE II]

Enter Venice, Verona, Lodovico, Pandulpho, and Jaspro.

Vero. Is this your chaste religious Lady?

Lod. Nay, good my Lord, let it be carried with a silent reputation, for the credit of the conclusion; as all here are privy to the passage, I do desire not to be laugh'd at, till after the mask and we are all ready. I have made bold with some of your Grace's gentlemen, that are good dancers.

Vero. 'Tis one of my greatest wonders, credit me,
To think what way she will devise, here openly,
To perform her so strict penance.

Ven. It busies me, believe me, too.

Jasp. Ye may see now, sir, how possible 'tis for a cunning Lady to make an ass of a Lord too confident.

Lod. An ass! I will prove a contented cuckold, the wisest

1624-1625. Came this . . . Neapolitanis'd him] Sugden (p. 359) notes that it was widely believed syphilis made its first appearance in Europe at Naples, about 1494, and cites numerous examples associating Naples and veneral disease, including these lines from Davenport.

1625. flead] flayed.

1629-1630. reputation] opinion, account of something. *NED* records no use with this meaning after 1613.

man in's company.

Vero. How prove you that, sir?

Lod. Because he knows himself.

Vero. Very well brought in.
Is all our furniture fit, against the morning,
To go for *Millain*?

Jasp. Ready, and like your Grace.

Vero. We are given to understand, the injur'd Princess,
Whom Count *Lorenzo* and noble *Philippo*
Are (unknown to one another) gone in search of,
Hath been seen there disguis'd. Strict inquisition
From the Duke himself shall ere many daies
Give our hopes a satisfaction.

Enter Dorothea, ladies, Francisco and Clown.

Jasp. The ladies, sir; *Francisco* keeps before, sir,
And *Pambo* keeps all well behind.

Lod. Yes, there's devout lechery between hawk and buzzard.
But please ye set the ladies. The mask attends your Grace.

Exit.

Vero. Come, Ladies, sit. Madona *Dorothea*,

1640-1641, 1643. wisest man in's company. Because he knows himself] a proverb, deriving ultimately from Plato (Tilley, K175).

1645. furniture] provision.

1656. between hawk and buzzard] proverbial; the earliest example recorded by Tilley is 1638 (H223).

Your ingenious Lord hath suddenly prepar'd us
For a conceited mask, and himself it seems
Playes the presenter.

Dor. Now fie upon this vanity.
A profane mask! Chastity keep us, Ladies.

Ven. What, from a mask? Whereon grounds your wish?

Dor. Marry, my Lord, upon experience.
I heard of one, once brought his wife to a mask,
As chaste as a cold night; but, poor unfortunate fellow,
He lost her in the throng, and she, poor soul,
Came home so crush'd next morning!

Ven. 'Las, that was ill.
But women will be lost against their will?

Vero. Silence, the masquers enter.

Enter Lodovico, Clown and masquers: a stag, a ram, a bull and a goat.

Clown. Look to me, master.

Lod. Do not shake, they'll think th'art out. ---------A mask-------

---

1660. conceited] clever, witty.

1671. But women . . . will] referring to the same proverb as l. 253 (Tilley, W723).

1674. out] out of practice, or out of one's part. Cf. *Coriolanus*, V, iii, 40-41: "Like a dull actor now, I have forgot my part, and I am out . . . ."

A mask] D3, D4, and B note: Lodovico stands by and prompts the Clown as he speaks the prologues.

Clown. A mask, or no mask; no mask but a by-clap;
And yet a mask yclep'd a "City-Night-Cap."

Lod. And conve------

Clown. And conveniently for to keep off scorns,
Considerately the cap is hedg'd with horns.

Lod. We insinuate------

Clown. Speak a little louder.

Lod. We insinuate------

Clown. We insinuate by this stag and ram so pritty,
With goat and bull, court, country, camp and city.

Lod. Cuckold------

Clown. Cuckold, my Lord?

Lod. 'Tis the first word of your next line.

Clown. Oh.------Cuckold begins with C. And is't not sport?
Then C. begins with country, camp and court.
But here's the fine figary of our poet,
That one may wear this night-cap, and not know it.

Dor. Why, chicken, shall they make such an ass of thee? Good your Grace, can a woman indure to see her loving husband wear horns in's own house?

Vero. Pray, Lady, 'tis but in jest.

Dor. In jest? Nay, for the jest sake, keep then on, sweet bird.

1675. by-clap] beclap; NED records no use of this word as a noun. Perhaps Davenport means a performance of small merit, from by (little) and clap (chatter, or applause). There is a pun intended with yclep'd, in the next line.

1676. yclep'd] called, named.

1690. figary] fegary, a corruption of vagary.

Clown. Now to our mask's name. But first, be it known-a,
When I name a city, I only mean Verona.
Those two lines are extempore, I protest, sir; I brought them in because here are some of other cities in the room that might snuff pepper else.

Ven. You have fairly ta'en that fear off; pray, proceed.

Lod. Your kindest men------

Clown. Your kindest men most cuckolds are, oh pity!
And where have women most their will, oh city!
Seek for a night-cap, go to cuckolds' luck;
Who thrives like him, who hath the daintiest duck
To deck his stall? Nay, at the time of rapping,
When you may take the watch at corners napping;
Take it forsooth, it is a wondrous hap
If you finde master constable without his cap.
So a city-night-cap; for whilst he doth rome

1697-1698. But first . . . Verona] Fleay (I, 104) states that the clown's disclaimers "plainly show the play to have been a personal satire."

1701. snuff pepper] get angry, become quickly offended; from the proverbs "to take pepper in the nose" (Tilley, P231) and "to take in snuff" (Tilley, S598).

1705. And where . . . will] another reference to the same proverb as ll. 253 and 1671 (Tilley, W723).

1708. rapping] either seizing, or uttering an oath; reference to the early hours of morning, when the watch has fallen asleep.

1709. take . . . napping] to "take one napping" is proverbial (Tilley, N36-7).

1711. master constable] as one of the watch, he must remain out all night, giving his wife a chance to give him his city-night cap; also, with a possible reference to the proverbial lack of wit of the constable (cf. Tilley, C616).

And frights abroad, his wife commits at home.

Ven. A *Verona*-constable.

Clown. A constable of *Verona*; we will not meddle with your City of *Venice*, sir.

Therefore 'tis fit the city, wise men say,
Should have a cap call'd *cornucopia*.

Lod. To con------

Clown. To conclude our cap, and stretch it on the tenter,
'Tis known a city is the whole land's center;
So that a city-night-cap, ours we call,
By a conclusion philosophical.
Heavie bodies tend to th' center, so (the more the pity)
The heaviest heads do butt upon the city.
And to our dance this title doth redound,
A "City-Night-Cap", *alias* "Cuckolds' Round."

Dor. Cuckolds' round! And my sweet bird leads the dance!

Vero. Be patient, Madam, 'tis but honest mirth;
From good construction pleasure findes full birth. *Dance.*

1713. frights] perhaps: is ridiculous. D emends to "fights", which is possible. However, *NED* suggests that frights may sometimes have been misused for "frets" (worries), which also makes sense here.

1718. *cornucopia*] literally, horn of plenty, but also suggesting horn of cuckoldry. The long poem, *Cornucopiae, Pasquil's Night-Cap* (1612, 1623?) uses both the cornucopia and the night-cap as cuckold's horns. *NED* cites only one example with this meaning (1600).

1720. tenter] a wooden framework on which cloth is stretched after being milled, so that it may set or dry evenly and without shrinking; hence, to conclude or complete the last step, continuing the cloth "cap" image.

1727. round] dance.

1730. construction] structure, instruction (see note to l. 1052).

Vero. *Jaspro,* fill some wine.

Jasp. 'Tis here, sir.

Vero. Count *Lodovico!*

Lod. Sir.

Vero. [*To Lod.*] I'll instantly give you a fair occasion to produce
The performance of her penance.

Lod. [*To Vero.*] I'll catch occasion by the lock, sir.

Vero. Here, a health to all; it shall go round.

Lod. 'Tis a general health, and leads the rest into the field.

Clown. Your honour breaks jests as serving-men do glasses--by chance.

Vero. As I was drinking, I was thinking--[*Aside, to Lod.*] trust me--
How fortunate our kind host was to meet
With so chaste a wife. Troth, tell me, good Count *Lodovico,*
Admit heaven had her.

Lod. [*To Vero.*] Oh, good your Grace, do not wound me.
Admit heaven had her! 'Las, what should heaven do with her?

Vero. [*To Lod.*] Your love makes you thus passionate; but admit so.
Faith, what wife would you chuse?

Lod. Were I to chuse then, as I would I were, so this were

1737. I'll catch occasion by the lock] Emblem writers of the sixteenth and seventeenth centuries depicted occasion (or opportunity) as a young woman with a large forelock of hair. E.g. Geffrey Whitney, *A Choice of Emblemes* (London, 1586), p. 181:

> What meanes longe lockes before? that suche as meete,
> Maye houlde at firste, when they occasion finde. (ll. 9-10)

To catch time or occasion by the forelock is proverbial (Tilley, T311).

1746. had] bore; with a pun in l. 1748.

at *Japan*,
I would wish, my Lord, a wife so like my Lady,
That once a week she should go to confession;
And to perform the penance she should run,
Nay, should do nought but dream on't, till 'twere done.

Jasp. [*Aside*] A delicate memento, to put her in mind of her penance.

Dor. Now you talk of dreams, sweet heart, I'll tell ye a very unhappy one; I was a dream'd last night of *Francis* there.

Lod. Of *Frank*?

Dor. Nay, I have done with him.

Lod. [*To Vero*.] Now your Grace shall see the devil out-done.

Vero. Pray let us hear your dream?

Dor. Bless me! I am e'en asham'd to tell it; but 'tis no matter, chick,
A dream is a dream, and this it was.
Me thought, sweet husband, *Francis* lay with me.

Lod. The best friend still at home, *Francisco*.
[*To Vero*.] Could the devil, sir, perform a penance neater,
And save his credit better? [*To Dor*.] On, chick, a dream is but a dream.

Dor. Me thought I prov'd with child, sweet heart.

Lod. I, bird?

Fran. [*Aside*] Pox of these dreams.

1752. at Japan] Sugden (p. 282) explains this passage as meaning "a very remote place." So Lodovico means that he would choose a wife that is like Dorothea, assuming his present wife were in Japan.

1769. The best friend still at home] alluding to the same proverb as ll. 325-326.

Dor. Me thought I was brought to bed. And one day sitting
I'th' gallery, where your masking suits and vizards hang,
Having the child me thought upon my knee,
Who should come thither as to play at foils,
But thou, sweet heart, and *Francis*?

Lod. *Frank* and I!--[*To* *Vero.*] Does your Grace mark that?

Vero. [*To* *Lod.*] I do, and wonder at her neat conveyance on't.

Dor. Ye had not play'd three venies, but me thought
He hot thee such a blow upon the forehead,
It swel'd so that thou couldst not see.

Lod. See, see!

Dor. At which the child cry'd, so that I could not still it;
Whereat, me thought, I pray'd thee to put on
The hat thou wor'st but now before the Duke, thinking thereby
To still the child. But being frighted with't,
He cry'd the more.

Lod. He? *Frank*, thou get'st boys.

Fran. In dreams it seems, sir.

Dor. Whereat I cry'd, me thought, pointing to thee,
Away you naughty man, you are not this child's father.

Lod. Meaning the child *Francisco* got.

Dor. The same. And then I wak'd and kist thee.

1776. vizards] face protectors.

1781. conveyance] legal term for transference of property; also, trickery or cunning.

1782. venies] bouts (*venue*).

1783. hot] past tense of hit.

Omn. A pretty merry dream!

Enter Jaspro.

Jasp. Your servant tells me,
Count *Lodovico,* that one Father *Antony,*
A holy man, stays without to speak with you.

Lod. With me, or my Lady?

Jasp. Nay, with you, and about earnest business.

Lod. I'll go send him up, and he shall interpret my Lady's
dream. [*To Jasp.*] Pist, *Jaspro.* *Exeunt.*

Dor. Why, husband, my Lord.

Fran. [*Aside*] Didst mark? I must interpret.

Clown. [*Aside*] I smell worm-wood and vineger.

Ven. [*Aside*] She changes colour.

Dor. [*Aside*] He will not sure reveal confession.

Vero. We'll rise and to our lodgings. I think your Highness
Keeps better hours in *Venice*?

Ven. As all do, sir,
We many times make modest mirth, a necessity
To produce Ladies' dreams.

Fran. [*Aside*] How they shoot at us! Would I were in *Millain.*
These passages frye me.

Enter Jaspro and Lodovico [*disguised as Father Antony*].

Jasp. Here's strange jugling come to light.

1804. Pist] *NED* records no examples after 1622.

1807. wormwood] a plant most noted for its bitter taste.

Vero. Ha, jugling!

Jasp. This fryer hath confest unto Count Lodovico,
That his Lady here, being absolv'd,
Confess'd this morning to him here, in her own house,
Her man Francisco here had lain with her.
At which her Lord runs up and down the garden
Like one distracted, crying, "Ware horns, ho."

Dor. [To Lod.] Art mad? Deny it yet, I am undone else.

Clown. Father Tony.

Lod. I confess it, I deny it, I any thing, I do every thing, I do nothing.

Vero. The fryer's fallen frantick; and being mad,
Depraves a Lady of so chaste a brest;
A bad thought never bred there.

Dor. 'Tis my misfortune still to suffer, sir.

Lod. Did you not see one slip out of a cloak-bag i'th' fashion of a flitch of bacon, and run under the table amongst the hogs?

Ven. He's mad, he's mad.

Clown. I, I, a tythe-pig 'twas overlaid last night, and he speaks nonsence all the day after.

Dor. Shall I, sir, suffer this, in mine own house, too?

1833-1837. Did you not see . . . last night] obscure, but perhaps a reference to St. Anthony, considered the patron of hogs. Hence, the friar has gone mad because a "tythe-pig" was lost, which he should have protected, and which also represented a future meal.

1837. tythe-pig] a pig due as a tithe to the church.

overlaid] smothered, or perhaps stolen (?).

Clown. I'd scratch out's eyes first.

Vero. Since, Lady, you and your man Francisco
Are the two injur'd persons, here disrobe
This irregular son of his religious mother,
Expose him to the apparent blush of shame,
And tear those holy weeds off.

Fran. [To Lod.] Now you, my frantick brother,
Had you not been better spar'd your breath?

Dor. [To Lod.] And ye keep counsel, sir, no better?
We'll ease you of your orders.

Clown. Nay, let me have a hand in't. I'll tear his coat with more zeal than a Puritan would tear a surplis.

Fran. See what 'tis to accuse when you're mad.

Dor. [To Lod] I confess again to you now, sir, this man did lye with me.

Clown. [To Lod.] And I brought him to her chamber too. But come, turn out here.

Dukes. Who's this?

Omn. 'Tis Count Lodovico.

Lod. How dreams, sweet wife, do fall out true!

Clown. I was a dream'd, now I remember, I was whipt through Verona.

Lod. I was your confessor.
Did not I enjoyn your chaste nice Ladyship
A dainty penance?

Jasp. And she perform'd it as daintily, sir, we'll be sworn for

---

1851. surplis] surplice.

that.

Dor. Oh good sir, I crave your pardon!

Lod. And what say you, *Francis*?

Fran. You have run best, sir, vain 'tis to defend,
Craft sets forth swift, but still fails in the end.

Lod. You brought him to her chamber, *Pambo*.

Clown. Good my Lord, I was merely inveagled to't.

Lod. I have nothing to do with ye, I take no notice of ye; I have play'd my part off to th' life, and your Grace promis'd to perform yours.

Vero. And publickly we will still raise their fame.
Who ere knew private sin 'scape publick shame?
You, sir, that do appear a gentleman,
Yet are within slave to dishonest passion;
You shall through *Verona* ride upon an ass
With your face towards his back-parts, and in your hand his
tail 'stead of a bridle.

Clown. 'Snailes, upon an ass! And 't had been upon an horse, it had been worthy, gramercy.

Vero. Peace, sirrah.
After that, you shall be branded in the forehead,
And after banish'd. Away with him!

Fran. Lust is still

1883. 'Snailes] by God's nails (an oath).

1884. worthy, gramercy.] worthy of thanks; with a pun on god-a-mercy (gramercy) horse (l. 1883), an ironic expression of thanks (see Tilley, G276).

Like a midnight-meal; after our violent drinkings,
'Tis swallowed greedily. But the course being kept,
We are sicker when we wake than ere we slept. *Exit.*

Clown. He must be branded; if the whore-master be burnt, what shall become of the procurer?

Vero. You, Madam, in that you have cosen'd sanctity,
To promise her the vows you never paid,
You shall unto the monasterie of matrons,
And spend your daies reclusive. For we conceive it
Her greatest plague, who her daies in lust hath past
And soil'd, against her will to be kept chaste.

Dor. Your doom is just, no sentence can be given
Too hard for her plays fast and loose with heaven.

Lod. I will buss thee, and bid fair weather after thee. But for you, sirrah------

Clown. Nay, sir, 'tis but *Crede quod habes, & habes* at most; believe I have a halter, and I have one.

Vero. You, sirrah, we are possest, were their pander.

Clown. I brought but flesh to flesh, sir, and your Grace does as much when you bring your meat to your mouth.

1901. plays fast and loose] i.e., cheats. A trick used to cheat people in which a leather strap was folded, with a skewer thrust through the middle. The strap was "fast" or "loose" as the holder wished, since he could control it by the ends. See Scot's *Discoverie of Witchcraft* (1584), chapter 29, for a complete description of this trick. Tilley (P401) cites numerous examples.

1902. buss] ship (*NED* records only as a noun, meaning a vessel of burden); also, pun on meaning of kiss.

1906. possest] informed, given to understand.

Vero. You, sirrah, at a cart's tail shall be whipt
Through the city.

Clown. There's my dream out already; but since there is no
remedy but that whipping-chear must close up my stomach,
I would request a note from your Grace to the carman,
to intreat him to drive apace; I shall never indure it
else.

Vero. I hope, Count *Lodovico*, we have satisfied ye.

Lod. To th' full; and I think the cuckold catch'd the
cuckold-makers.

Vero. 'Twas a neat penance; but oh! The art of woman in
the performance.

Lod. Pshew, sir, 'tis nothing. Had she been in her great
granam's place,
Had not the devil first began the sin,
And cheated her, she would have cheated him.

Vero. Let all to rest; and, noble sir, i'th' morning,
With a small private train, we are for *Millain*.
Vice for a time may shine, and vertue sigh;
But truth, like heaven's sun, plainly doth reveal,

1909. cart's tail] the hinder most part of a cart, to which offenders were tied to be whipped through the streets.

1912. whipping-chear] whipping chair.

1921. Pshew] Pshaw; see note for l. 253.

1921-1924. her great granam's place] i.e.,Eve.

And scourge or crown, what darkness did conceal.

Finis Actus Quarti.

ACTUS QUINTUS.

[SCENE I]

Enter Antonio and a slave, one in the other's habit.

Slave. But faith, sir, what's your device in this? This change
Insinuates some project.

Anto. Shall I tell thee?
Thou art my slave, I took thee (then a Turk)
In the fight thou knowest we made before *Palermo.*
Thou art not in stricter bondage unto me
Than I am unto *Cupid.*

Slave. Oh, then you are going, sir,
To your old rendevow; there are brave rogues there.
But the Duke observes you narrowly, and sets spies
To watch if you step that way.

Anto. Why therefore, man,
Thus many times I have chang'd habits with thee,
To cheat suspition, and prejudicate nature

1934. *Palermo*] In *Philomela* Palermo is where Abstemia stays after the trial, and where her husband is accused of killing the ruling Duke's son.

1938. rendevow] rendezvous.

1943. prejudicate] prejudicial.

(Mistris of inclinations) sure intended
To knit thee up so like me, for this purpose,
For th'ast been taken in my habit for me.

Slave. Yes, and have had many a French cringe
As I have walk'd i'th' park; and for fear of discovery,
I have crown'd it only with a nod.

Enter a Lord [*unobserved*].

Anto. Th'art a mad villain.
But, sirrah, I am wondrously taken
With a sweet face I saw yonder; thou know'st where.

Slave. At *Venus* colledge, the court-baudy-house.

Anto. But this, man, howsoever she came there,
Is acquainted so with heaven, that when I thought
To have quench'd my frantick blood, and to have pluck'd
The fruit a king would leap at, even then she beat me
With such brave thunder off, as if heaven had lent her
The artillery of angels.

Slave. She was coy then.

Anto. Coy, man! She was honest; left coyness to court-ladies.
She spake the language of the saints, me thought.
Holy spectators sate on silver clouds,

1947. French] i.e., French-like, referring to the court-manner of bowing.

1949. crown'd] honored, acknowledged.

1953. colledge] school.

1963. sate] past tense of sit.

And clapt their white wings at her well-plac'd words.
She piecemeal pull'd the frame of my intentions,
And so joyn'd it again, that all the tempest
Of blood can never move it.

Slave. Some rare Phoenix. What's her name?

Anto. 'Tis Millecenta, and wondrous aptly,
For she is mistris of a hundred thousand holy heavenly thoughts.
Chastly I love her now, and she must know it.
Such wondrous wealth is vertue, it makes the woman
Wears it about her worthy of a king,
Since kings can be but vertuous. Farewel.
A crown is but the care of deceiv'd life;
He's king of men, is crown'd with such a wife.

Exit Antonio, and the Lord after him.

Slave. Are your thoughts levell'd at that white, then?
This shall to th' Duke your dad, sir. He can never talk with me,
But he twits me still with, "I took thee at that fight
We made before Palermo." I did command
Men as he did there, Turks and valiant men.

1963-1964. Holy spectators . . . words] Olive (p. 335) parallels these lines with Pericles, IV, vi, 132-133: "she has here spoken holy words to the Lord Lysimachus." He also cites l. 1970, but leaves out "heavenly" in his quotation. He concludes: "In each case the wonder of the situation is remarked."

1969. Millecenta] Latin for hundred thousand.

1975. A crown . . . life] perhaps referring to the proverb, "crowns have cares" (Tilley, C863).

1977. levell'd at that white] i.e., aimed at that target (the white bullseye).

And though to wind my self up for his ruine,
That I may fall and crush him, I appear
To renounce Mahomet, and seem a Christian;
'Tis but conveniently to stab this Christian,
Or any way confound him, and 'scape cleanly.
And one expects the deed. To hasten it,
This letter came even now, which like wise certifies
He waits me three leagues off, with a horse for flight,
Of a Turkish captain, commander of a gally.
He keeps me as his slave, because indeed
I play'd the devil at sea with him; but having
Thus wrought my self into him, I intend
To give him but this day to take his leave
Of the whole world. He will come back by twilight;
I'll wait him with a pistol. Oh sweet revenge!
Laugh, our great prophet; he shall understand,
When we think death farthest off, he's neerest hand.

Enter Philippo.

Phil. You and I must meet no more, sir; there's your kick again. *Kicks him.*

Slave. Hold, hold, what mean you, sir?

Phil. I have brought your kick back, sir. *Shoots him.*

Slave. Hold, man, I am not------ *Falls.*

Phil. Thou hast spoken true, thou art not. What art thou?------ But I am for *Verona.* *Exit.*

Slave. Mine own words catch me, 'tis I now understand,
When we think death farthest off, he's neerest hand. *Dies.*

Enter Lorenzo.

Lor. She lives not sure in *Millain.* Report but wore
Her usual habit, when she told in *Verona,*
She met *Abstemia* here. Oh *Abstemia*!
How lovely thou look'st now? Now thou appearest
Chaster than is the morning's modestie
That rises with a blush, over whose bosom
The western wind creeps softly. Now I remember
How, when she sat at table, her obedient eye
Would dwell on mine, as if it were not well,
Unless it look'd where I look'd. Oh how proud
She was, when she could cross her self to please me!
But where now is this fair soul? Like a silver cloud
She hath wept her self, I fear, into th' dead sea,
And will be found no more. This makes me mad,
To rave and call on death; but the slave shrinks,
And is as far to finde as she. *Abstemia,*
If thou not answer or appear to knowledg,

2006. I now] i.e., I who now.

2008-2009. report . . . usual habit] "Report is a liar" is a common proverb (Tilley, F44). (Cf. ll. 1588-1589.)

2021-2023. This makes . . . as she.] D2, D3, D4 and Olive (p. 340) parallel with *Cymbeline*, V, iii, 68-71:

I, in mine own woe charm'd,
Could not find death where I did hear him groan,
Nor feel him where he struck. Being an ugly monster,
'Tis strange he hides him . . .

That here with shame I sought thee in this wood,
I'll leave the blushing witness of my blood. *Exit*.

Enter the Duke of Millain, Sebastian, Sanchio,

and the Lord.

Mill. Followed you him thus far?

Lord. Just to this place, sir.
The slave he loves left him; here they parted.

Mill. Certain he has some private haunt this way.

Seb. Ha------private indeed, sir. Oh behold and see
Where he lyes full of wounds!

Lords. My Lord.

Mill. My son *Antonio*! Who hath done this deed?

Sanch. My Lord *Antonio*!

Mill. He's gone, he's gone; warm yet, bleeds fresh, and whilst
We here hold passion play, we but advantage
The flying murderer. Bear his body gently
Unto the lodge. Oh what hand hath so hid
That sunlike face, behind a crimson cloud!
Use all means possible for life, but I fear
Charity will arrive too late. To horse,
Disperse through the wood, run, ride, make way,
The sun in *Millain* is eclips'd this day.

Omn. To horse, and raise more pursuit. *Exeunt*.

[SCENE II]

Enter Lorenzo, with his sword drawn.

Lor. *Abstemia!* Oh take her name, you winds, upon your wings,
And through the wanton region of the air,
Softly convey it to her. There's no sweet sufferance,
Which bravely she past through, but is a thorn
Now to my sides. My will the center stood
To all her chaste endeavours, all her actions,
With a perfection perpendicular,
Pointed upon. She is lost. Oh she,
The well-built fort of vertue's victory!
For still she conquer'd. Since she is lost, then,
My friendly sword finde thou my heart. *Within,* [*shouts*]. Follow, follow.

Enter Millain, Sanchio, Sebastiano.

Mill. This way. What's he? Lay hands on him.

Seb. The murderer, on my life, my Lord, here in the wood
Was close beset; he would have slain himself.

Mill. Speak, villain, art thou the bloody murderer?

Lor. Of whom?

Sanch. His dissembled ignorance speaks him the man.

Seb. Of the Duke's son, the Prince *Antonio*, sir; 'twas your
hand that kill'd him.

Lor. Your Lordship lyes, it was my sword.

Mill. Out slave!
Ravens shall feast upon thee. Speak, what cause

2067. Ravens shall feast upon thee] Cf. *King John and Matilda,* V, ii (B, p. 79): "And every Raven that should feast upon't [a body] . . ."

Hadst thou with one unhappy wound, to cloud
That star of *Millain*?

Lor. Because he was an erring star,
Not fix'd nor regular; I will resolve nothing.
I did it, do not repent it; and were it
To do again, I'd do't.

Omn. Blood-thirsty villain!

Mill. Lead him to swift destruction, tortures and death.
Oh my *Antonio*! How did thy youth stray,
To meet wild winter in the midst of May?

Lor. Oh my *Abstemia*! Who cast thy fate so bad,
To clip affliction, like a husband clad? *Exeunt.*

[SCENE III]

Enter Antonio [disguised as the slave] and Abstemia.

Abst. Good sir, the Prince makes known his wisdom,
To make you speaker in his cause.

Anto. Me? Know, mistris,
I have felt love's passions equal with himself,
And can discourse of love's cause. Had you seen him
When he sent me to ye, how truly he did look;
And when your name slip'd through his trembling lips,

2070-2071. erring star, Not fix'd nor regular] The heavens, according to the Ptolemaic system, were fixed and unchanging, and erring (or moving) stars such as comets were supposed to occur near earth (below the moon) and be a portent of evil.

2079. clip] clasp, clutch.

A lover's lovely paleness straight possest him.

Abst. Fie, fie.

Anto. Go, says he, to that something more than woman,
(And he look'd as if by something he meant saint)
Tell her I saw heaven's army in her eyes,
And that from her chaste heart, such excellent goodness
Came like full rivers flowing; that there wants nothing
But her soft yeilding will, to make her wife
Unto the Prince Antonio. Oh will you flie
A fortune which great ladies would pursue
Upon their knees with prayers?

Abst. [Aside] No, Lorenzo.
Had law to this new love made no denial,
A chaste wife's truth shines through the greatest tryal.

Enter Morbo.

Mor. How now, what makes you i'th' wood here? Where's my old lady?

Abst. I know not.

Mor. All the countrie's in an uprore yonder, the Prince Antonio's slain.

Ambo. How?

Mor. Nay, no man can tell how; but the murderer with's sword in's hand is [taken.

Anto. Is he of Millain?

Mor. No, of Verona. I heard his name, and I have forgot it.

Anto. [Aside] I am all wonder; 'tis the slave, sure.

Mor. Lor, Lor, Lorenzo.

Abst. Ha, Lorenzo! What, I pray?

Mor. *Lorenzo* *Me*-----*Medico* has run him in the eye, some thirty three inches, two barly corns. They could scarce know him for the blood, but by his apparel. I must find out my Lady. He us'd our house, intelligence has been given of his pilgrimage thither. I am affraid I shall be sing'd to death with torches, and my Lady stew'd between two dishes. [*Exit.*]

Anto. Why hath this thus amaz'd you, mistris?

Abst. Oh leave me, leave me, I am all distraction,
Struck to the soul with sorrow.

Enter Millain, Lords and Lorenzo guarded.

Anto. [*Aside*] See where they come.
My father full of tears too? I'll stand by;
Strange changes must have strange discovery.

Abst. [*Aside*] 'Tis he. Heart, how thou leap'st! [*To Omn.*] Oh ye [deluded,
And full of false rash judgement! Why do ye lead
Innocence like a sacrifice to slaughter?
Get garlands rather, let palm and lawrel round
Those temples, where such wedlock-truth is found.

Lor. Ha?

Omn. Wedlock!

Abst. Oh *Lorenzo*! Thou hast suffer'd bravely,
And wondrous far. Look on me, here I come,

2112. two barly corns] approximately two-thirds of an inch, supposedly the length of two grains of barley.

2116. stew'd] confined; with a pun on, soaked in a steam bath, a common treatment for veneral disease.

2126. round] D4: surround, crown.

Hurried by conscience to confess the deed.
Thy innocent blood will be too great a burthen
Upon the judge's soul.

Lor. *Abstemia!*

Abst. Look, look, how he will blind ye; by and by, he'll tell ye
We saw not one another many a day,
In love's cause we dare make our lives away.
He would redeem mine; 'tis my husband, sir,
Dearly we love together. But I being often
By the dead Prince your son solicited
To wrong my husband's bed, and still resisting,
Where you found him dead, he met me, and the place
Presenting oportunity, he would there
Have forc'd me to his will; but prizing honesty
Far above proffer'd honour, with my knife
In my resistance, most unfortunately
I struck him in the eye. He fell, was found,
The pursuit rais'd, and ere I could get home
My husband met me; I confest all to him.
He excellent in love as the sea-inhabitant,
Of whom 'tis writ, that when the flattering hook
Has struck his female, he will help her off
Although he desperately put on himself;
But if he fail, and see her leave his eye,

2151ff. He, excellent . . .] This story has not been traced to any source.

He swims to land, will languish and there dye.
Such is his love to me; for pursu'd closely,
He bid me save my self, and he would stay
With his drawn sword, there about the place, on purpose
To requite my loyalty, though with his death.
Fear forc'd my acceptance then, but conscience
Hath brought me back to preserve innocence.

Seb. The circumstances produce probability.

Lor. By truth her self, she slanders truth. She and I
Have not met these many months. Oh my *Abstemia*!
Thou wouldst be now too excellent.

Anto. [*Aside*] These are strange turns.

Mill. Let not love strangle justice; speak, on thy soul,
Was it her hand that slew the Prince?

Lor. Not, on my life;
'Tis I have deserv'd death.

Abst. Love makes him desperate,
Conscience is my accuser. Oh *Lorenzo*!

The Duke and Lords whisper.

Live thou and feed on my remembrance,
When thou shalt think how ardently I lov'd thee;
Drop but a pair of tears, from those fair eyes,
Thou offer'st truth a wealthy sacrifice.

2156. will languish and there dye] Robert Burton, in *The Anatomy of Melancholy* (London: Dent, Everyman's Library, 1968), cites Gomesius who says, "Fishes pine away for love and wax lean" (III,p. 44).

Lor. Did ye hear her, sir?

Mill. No, what said she?

Lor. She ask'd me why I would cast my self away thus,
When she in love devis'd this trick to save me.

Sanch. There may be jugling, sir, in this; it may be
They have both hands i'th' deed, and one in love
Would suffer for't.

Enter a Lord.

Mill. What newes?

Lord. The Dukes of Venice and Verona,
With some small train of gentlemen, are privately
This hour come to th' court.

Mill. Bear them to prison
Until we have given such entertainment sorrow
Will give us leave to shew. Until that time,
The satisfaction of my lost son's life
Must hover 'twixt a husband and a wife.

Exeunt; manet Antonio.

Anto. How strangely chance to day runs! The slave kill'd
In my apparel, and this fellow taken for't,
Whom to my knowledg I ne'er saw. She loves him
Past all expression dearly. I have a trick,
In that so infinitely dear she loves him,
Has seal'd her mine already; and I'll put

This wondrous love of woman to such a nonplus,
Time hath produc'd none stranger. I will set
Honour and love to fight for life and death.
Beautie (as castles built of cards) with a breath
Is levell'd and laid flat.

Enter Philippo, putting on a disguise, lays down a pistol [without seeing Antonio].

Phil. Misery of ignorance!
It was the Prince *Antonio* I have slain.

Anto. [*Aside*] Ha! The clew of all this error is unravell'd;
This is the valiant gentleman so threaten'd me;
He met the slave doubtless in my habit,
And seal'd upon him his mistaken spleen.
If it be so, there hangs some strange intent
In those accuse themselves for't.

Phil. It seems some other had laid the plot to kill him;
This paper I found with him speaks as much,
And, sent to the intended murderer,
Happen'd it seems to his hands. It concurs;
For they say, there is one taken for the fact,
And will do me the courtesie to be hang'd for me.

Antonio takes up the pistol.

2200. nonplus] utmost limit; also, perplexity.

2217. fact] deed.

There's comfort yet in that. So, so, I am fitted, And will set forward.

Anto. Goose, there's a fox in your way.

Phil. Betray'd!

Anto. Come, I have other business afoot; I have no time to discover 'em now, sir; see, I can inforce ye. But by this hand, go but with me, and keep your own counsel; garden-houses are not truer bawds to cuckold-making, than I will be to thee and thy stratagem.

Phil. Th'art a mad knave. Art serious?

Anto. As a usurer when he's telling interest-mony.

Phil. Whatere thou art, thy bluntness begets belief. Go on, I trust thee.

Anto. But I have more wit than to trust you behind me, sir. Pray, get you before; I have a private friend shall keep you in custody, till I have past a project; and if you can keep your own counsel, I will not injure you. And this for your comfort, the Prince lives.

Phil. Living! Thou mak'st my blood dance. But prethee, let's be honest one to another.

Anto. Oh sir, as the justice's clarke and the constable, when they share the crowns that drunkards pay to the poor. Pray, keep fair distance, and take no great strides. *Exeunt.*

2225. garden-houses] often considered a place of intrigue, as in *Measure for Measure*, V, i, 211 and 228.

2239. clarke] clerk.

2240. crowns . . . to the poor] apparently a fine which was supposed to go to charity; no example of this practice has been found.

[SCENE IV]

Enter Lorenzo and Abstemia, as in prison.

Lor. Can then *Abstemia* forgive *Lorenzo*?

Abst. Yes, if *Lorenzo* can but love *Abstemia*,
She can thus hang upon his neck, and call
This prison true love's palace.

Lor. Oh let kings
Forget their crowns, that know what 'tis to enjoy
The wondrous wealth of one so good. Now
Thou art lovely as a young spring, and comly
As is the well-spread cedar; the fair fruit,
Kist by the sun so daily, that it wears
The lovely blush of maids, seems but to mock
Thy soul's integrity. Here let me fall,
And with pleading sighs beg pardon.

Enter Antonio.

Abst. Sir, it meets you,
Like a glad pilgrim, whose desiring eye
Longs for the long-wish'd altar of his vow;
But you are far too prodigall in praise,
And crown me with the garlands of your merit.
As we meet barks on rivers, the strong gale
(Being best friends to us), our own swift motion
Makes us believe that t'other nimbler rows,

Swift vertue thinks small goodness fastest goes.

Lor. Sorrow hath bravely sweetned thee. [*To Anto.*] What are you?

Anto. A displeasant black cloud. Though I appear dismal,
I am wondrous fruitful. What cause soever
Mov'd you to take this murder on your self,
Or you to strike your self in to the hazard
For his redemption, 'tis to me a stranger,
But I conceive you are both innocent.

Lor. As new-born vertue. I did accuse
My innocence to rid me of a life
Look'd uglier than death, upon an injury
I had done this vertuous wife.

Abst. And I accus'd
My innocence to save the belov'd life
Of my most noble husband.

Anto. Why, then, now 'twould grieve you,
Death should unkindly part ye.

Lor. Oh but that, sir,
We have no sorrow. Now to part from her
(Since heaven hath new married, and new made us),
I had rather leap into a den of lyons,
Snatch from a hungry bear her bleeding prey;
I would attempt desperate impossibilities
With hope, rather than now to leave her.

Anto. [*Aside*] This makes for me.

Abst. And rather than leave you, sir, I would eat

2265. displeasant] unpleasant.

Hot coals with *Portia*, or attempt a terrour
Nature would snail-like shrink her head in at,
And tremble but to think on.

Anto. [*Aside*] Better and better!------
If you so love him, what can you confess?
The greatest kindness can express that love.

Abst. To save his life? Since there is no hope,
Seeing he so strongly has confest the murder,
We shall meet the happiness to dye together.

Anto. Fire casts the bravest heat in coldest weather,
I'll try how ardently you burn; for know
Upon my faith, and as I am a gentleman,
I have (in the next room, and in the custody
Of a true friend) the man that did the deed
You stand accus'd for.

Abst. Hark there, *Lorenzo*.

Lor. You will not let him go, sir?

Anto. That's in suspence; but, mistris, you did say
You durst eat coals with *Portia*, to redeem
The infinitely loved life of your husband.

2288-2289. I would . . . *Portia*] Cf. Greene's *Philomela* (p. 132): " . . . she [Abstemia] will eate coales with *Portia* before she prove unchaste . . ." And (p. 198): "Why did *Portia* eate coales for the love of Brutus, if it were not that wives ought to end their lives with their loves." The ultimate source of this incident is Plutarch's life of Marcus Brutus.

2298. Fire casts . . . weather] i.e., [Since] fire------ This proverbial expression not in Tilley.

2307. You durst eat coals with *Portia*] See note for ll. 2288-2289.

Abst. And still strongly protest it.

Lor. Oh my *Abstemia*!

Anto. You shall redeem him at an easier rate.
I have the murderer, you see, in hold.

Lor. And we are blest in your discovery of him.

Anto. If you will give consent that I shall taste
That sence-bereaving pleasure so familiar
Unto your happy husband------

Abst. How?

Anto. Pray hear me.
Then I will give this fellow up to th' law.
If you deny, horses stand ready for us,
A bark for transportation, where we will live
Till law by death hath sever'd ye.

Lor. But we will call for present witness.

Anto. Look ye. *Shews the pistol.*
Experienc'd navigators still are fitted
For every weather. 'Tis almost past call
To reach the nimblest ear. Yet but offer it,
I part ye presently for ever.
Consider it;
The enjoying him thou so intirely lov'st
All thy life after; that when mirth-spent time
Hath crown'd your heads with honour, you may sit
And tell delightful stories of your loves.
And when ye come to that poor minute's scape

2334. scape] sin.

Crowns my desire, ye may let that slip by,
Like water that ne'er meets the miller's eye.
Compare but this, to th' soon-forgotten pleasure
Of a pair of wealthy minutes. The thriftiest lapidarie
Knows the most curious jewel takes no harm,
For one daie's wearing. Could you, sir, (did your eye
Not see it worne) your wife having lent your cloak,
(If secretly return'd and folded up)
Could you conceive, when you next look'd upon't,
It had neatly furnish'd out a poor friend's want?
Be charitable, and think on't.

Lor. Dost hear, *Abstemia*?
Oh shall we part for ever, when a price
So poor might be our freedome?

Abst. Now goodness guard ye!
Where learnt you, sir, this language?

Lor. Of true love.
You did but now profess, that you would dye
To save my life, and now like a forward chapman,
Catch'd at thy word, thou giv'st back, asham'd

2335-2336. ye may . . . miller's eye] Cf. Greene's *Philomela* (p. 141): ". . . they may let much water slippe by the Mill that the Miller knoweth not of . . ." A common proverb (Tilley, W99).

2338-2339. The thriftiest lapidarie . .. no harm] Cf. Greene's *Philomela* (p. 153): "The *Lapidaries* value the stones no longer than they hold their vertues . . ."

2339. curious] exquisite, fine.

2353. forward chapman] presumptuous merchant.

To stand this easie proffer.

Abst. Could you live,

And know your self a cuckold?

Anto. What a question's that?

Many men cannot live without the knowledge.

How can ye tell,

Whether she seems thus to respect your honour,

But to stay till the law has choak'd ye? It may be then

She will do't, with less intreaty.

Lor. I, there, there 'tis.

Abst. 'Tis your old fit of jealousie, so judges.

A foul devil talks within him.

Lor. Oh the art,

The wondrous art of woman! Ye would do it daintily,

You would juggle me to death, you would perswade me

I should dye nobly to preserve your honour;

That dead, ignobly you might prove dishonourable,

Forget me in a day, and wed another.

Abst. Why then would I have dy'd for you?

Anto. That was but a proffer, that dying, you might idolize her love;

'Twould have put her off the better.

Lor. Oh you have builded

A golden palace, strew'd with palm and roses,

To let me bleed to death in! How sweetly

You would have lost me! Abstemia, you have learn'd

The cunning fowler's art, who pleasantly
Whistles the bird into the snare. Good heaven!
How you had strew'd the inticing top o'th' cup
With *Arabian* spices! But you had laid i'th' bottom
Ephesian aconite. You are love's hypocrite;
A rotten stick in the night's darkness born,
And a fair poppie in a field of corn.

Abst. Oh sir! hear me------ *Kneels.*

Lor. Away, I will no more
Look pearl in mud. Oh slie hypocrisie!
Durst ye but now dye for me? Good heaven! Dye for me!
The greatest act of pain, and dare not buy me
With a poor minute's pleasure?

Abst. No sir, I dare not; there is little pain in death,
But a great death in very little pleasure.

2385. *Ephesian*] the inhabitants of Ephesus were notorious for their devotion to the black arts (Sugden, p. 180).

aconite] deadly poison, from several plants, variously known as Monk's-hood or Wolf's-bane.

2386. stick] weed (?); no definition in *NED* fits Davenport's usage.

2387. a fair poppie . . . corn] poppie: corn-cockle. So Milton, in *Reason of Church-Government*, says, "[Anselme] little dreamt then that the weeding-hook of reformation would after two ages pluck up his glorious poppy from insulting over the good corne." [*The Works of John Milton* (New York: Columbia University Press, 1931) III, 208.] Related to the proverb: "cockle and corn grow in the same field" (Tilley, C497).

2390. I will . . . in mud] i.e., I will not look for precious objects in the mud. Related to the proverb, "cast not pearls before swine" (Tilley, P165).

2391. dye] Davenport puns even in the most serious situations (Cf. l. 2044, the pun on son-sun).

I had rather, trust me, bear your death with honour,
Than buy your life with baseness. As I am expos'd
To th' greatest battery beauty ever fought,
Oh blame me not, if I be covetous
To come off with greatest honour. If I do this
To let you live, I kill your name, and give
My soul a wound; I crush her from sweet grace,
And change her angel's to a furie's face.
Try me no more then; but, if you must bleed, boast,
To preserve honour, life is nobly lost.

Lor. Thou wealth worth more than kingdoms, I am now confirm'd,
Past all suspition; thou that art far sweeter
In thy sincere truth, than a sacrifice
Deck'd up for death with garlands. The *Indian* winds
That blow off from the coast, and cheer the saylor
With the sweet savour of their spices, want
The delight flowes in thee. Look here, look here,
Oh man of wilde desires; we will dye the martyrs
Of marriage, and 'stead of the loose ditties
With which they stab sweet modestie, and ingender
Desires in the hot room, thy noble storie
Shall lawrel-like crown honest ears with glory.

2396-2397. I had rather . . . with baseness] Olive (p. 337) parallels with *Measure for Measure*, III, i, 87-88:

Thou art too noble to conserve a life
In base appliances.

2405. To preserve honour, life is nobly lost.] Cf. *Measure for Measure*, II, iv, 184: "More than our brother is our chastity." And *I Promos and Cassandra*, III, ii: "Honor farre dearer is then life . . . ." Earlier Cassandra says: "my selfe wyll dye, ere I my honor staine . . . ."

Anto. [Shouts] Murder, murder, murder!

Enter the three Dukes, with Lords [and Phillippo].

Mill. Ha, who cries murder?

Phil. As y'are a gentleman, now be true to me.

Abst. Sir!

Ven. Sister?

Vero. My shame, art thou there?

Ven. Oh sister, can it be
A Prince's blood should stain that white hand?

Ambo. Hear us.

Anto. No, no, no, hear me, 'twas I cry'd murder.
Because I have found them both stain'd with the deed,
They would have throtled me.

Lor. Hear us, by all------

Mill. Upon your lives be silent! Speak on, sir,
Had they both hands in our son's blood?

Anto. Two hands apiece, sir.
I have sifted it, they both have kill'd the Prince;
But this is the chief murderer. Please you give me audience,
Ye shall wonder at the manner how they kill'd him.

Mill. Silence.

Anto. He came first to this woman, and, truth's truth,
He would have lain with her.

Mill. Her own confession.

Anto. Nay, good your Grace.

Mill. We are silent.

Anto. Coming to seise upon her, with the first blow
She struck his base intent so brave a buffet,
That there it bled to death. She said his horse
Would teach him better manners. There he dy'd once.

Vero. What does this fellow talk?

Abst. I understand him.

Anto. He met her next i'th' wood, where he was found dead.
Then he came noblier up to her, and told her
Marriage was his intent; but she as nobly,
(Belike to let him know she was married)
Told him in an intelligible denial,
A chaste wife's truth shin'd through the greatest tryal.
There the Prince dy'd again.

Lor. There's twice; beware the third time.

Anto. The third time, he came here to them both in prison,
Brought a pistol with him, would have forc'd her again;
But had ye seen how fairly then she slew him,
You would have shot applauses from your eyes.
Oh she came up so bravely to that Prince,
Hot potent lust, (for she slew no Prince else)
With such a valiant discipline she destroy'd
That debosh'd Prince, Bad Desire; and then by him
So bravely too fetch'd off, that (to conclude)
Betwixt them they this wonder did contrive,
They kill'd the Prince, but kept your son alive. *Discovers himself.*

2443. seise] seize.

2464. debosh'd] debauched.

Mill. *Antonio*?

Omn. The Prince!

Ven. Come home, my sister, to my heart.

Vero. And now *Lorenzo* is again my belov'd kinsman.

Anto. Oh sir, here dwells vertue epitomiz'd,
Even to an abstract, and yet that so large,
'Twill swell a book in folio.

Lod. She swells beyond my wife then.
A pocket-book bound in *decimo sexto*
Will hold her vertues, and as much spare paper left
As will furnish five tobacco-shops.

Mill. But here's the wonder; who is it was slain
In your apparel?

Phil. [*Aside*] I will give them all the slip. *Offers to go.*

Anto. Here's a gentleman of *Ferrara*------

Phil. [*To Anto.*] As you are noble.

Anto. That saw them fight. It was the slave was slain, sir,
I took before *Palermo*; he that kill'd him,
Took him but for a gentleman his equal.
And as this eye-witness says, he in my apparel
Did kick t'other first.

Phil. Nay, upon my life, sir,
He in your apparel gave the first kick; I saw them fight,
And I dare swear t'other honest gentleman
Little thought he had slain any thing like the Prince;

2476. *decimo sexto*] a book in which each leaf is one-sixteenth of the original printed sheet; hence, small.

For I heard him swear but half an hour before,
He never saw your Grace.
Mill. Then he kill'd him fairly.
Phil. Upon my life, my Lord.
Ven. T'other had but his merit then; who dyes,
And seeks his death, seldom wets others' eyes.
Anto. Let this perswade you, I believe you noble;
I have kept my word with you.
Phil. You have out-done me, sir,
In this brave exercise of honour. But let me
In mine own person thank you. [*Discovers himself.*]
Omn. *Philippo!*
Phil. Unwittingly I did an ill (as 't happen'd)
To a good end. That slave I for you kill'd,
Wanted but time to kill you. Read that paper
Which I found with him, I thinking by accident
You had intercepted it. We all have happily
Been well deceiv'd; you are noble, just and true;
My hate was at your cloaths, my heart at you.
Vero. An accident more strange hath seldom happen'd.
Lor. *Philippo*, my best friend, 'twixt shame and love
Here let me lay thee now for ever.
Abst. Heaven
Hath now plain'd all our rough woes smooth and even.
Mill. At court, large relation in apt form
Shall tender past proceedings; but to distinguish,

2518. tender] present for approval and acceptance.

Excellent Lady, your unparallel'd praises
From those but seem, let this serve: bad women
Are nature's clouds eclipsing her fair shine;
The good, all gracious, saint-like and divine. [*Exeunt.*]

FINIS.

TEXTUAL NOTES

Drammatis Personae:

Lords of Venice] The S.D. call for no Lords of Verona other than Pandulpho, Spinoso, Jaspro, and Jovani, but does call for "Lords" of Venice at l. 1075a.

Senators of Verona] No senators of Venice are called for.

ACTUS PRIMUS] D1 adds "Scene I" to Act I, and D2 adds "Scene I" at the beginning of each act, with no further division of scenes; "scene" is dropped by D3 with explanatory note. B divides into scenes and numbers each one, as does this edition.

2. fie.] D: fie!

3. do't.] D2,D3,D4,B; 1661,D1: do't:

8. ones] D: ones,

9. point,] D2,D3,D4: point

10. Young sir,] 1661,D,B: (Young Sir)

11. precedent. Pray,] D2,D3,D4; 1661,D1,B: precedent: pray

do't?] D; 1661,B: do't.

12. Pray, fool] D2,D3,D4; 1661,D1,B: Pray fool

farther;] D: farther:

13. me,] D2,D3,D4: me;

14. reconciliation.] D2,D3,D4; 1661,D1,B: reconciliation:

15. you] D: you,

16. Duke,] D2,D3: duke; D4: duke?

22. And] D: And,

white] D4: white,

26. Pish.] D4: Pish!

27. truth.] D2,D3,D4; 1661,D1,B: Truth:

28. vertue;] D1; 1661,B: Vertue, D2,D3,D4: virtue:

29. storie,] D3,D4: story.

31. detraction] D; 1661,B: Detraction,

32. sullen,] D2,D3,D4; 1661,D1,B: sullen;

silence;] D2,D3,D4; 1661,D1,B: silence,

33. words (for] D4: words, for,

34. wonder)] D4: wonder;

36. chaste,] D: chaste;

38. (Though...young)] D4: Though...young,

to expose] D4: t'expose

39. eyes;] 1661,D1,B: eyes: D2,D3,D4: eyes.

40. company,] D2,D3,D4: company;

44. fields;] D: fields:

45. time,] D: time

character.] D2,D3,D4; 1661,D1,B: character:

48. friend,] B: friend

50. stomack;] 1661,D1,B: stomack: D2,D3,D4: stomach.

51. friend,] D3,D4: friend.

53. infectious;] 1661,D,B,: infectious:

54. vertue;] 1661,D,B,: Vertue:

55. comb.] D; 1661,B: comb:

57. Oh!] D4: O,

58. bitter;] 1661,D1,B: bitter: D2,D3,D4: bitter.

59. instance;] D: instance:

holy,] D4: holy

60. hollow.——] D4: hollow.

comes.] D4: comes,

62. again] D: again,

65. conference,] D3,D4: conference;

66. ear] D2,D3,D4; 1661,D1,B: ear,

68. S.D.] not in 1661 or D; B notes this and other asides with a dash between the speaker and the line of dialogue.

69. horns.] D3,D4; 1661,D1,D2: Horns: B: Horns!

S.D.] not in 1661 or D.

will;] D2,D3,D4: will.

70. occasion.] 1661,D,B,: occasion:

74. certifie] D,B; 1661: certifie,

75. kinsman] D: kinsman,

79. with't.] 1661,D,B: with't---

S.D.] B adds after Exit: Lorenzo conceals himself.

80. Oh] D1,D2,D3: Oh,

81. confess,] D: confess

83. more] D2,D4: more,

84. assailant;] D2,D3,D4: assailant.

85. fountains] D4: fountains,

86. streams.] D4; 1661,D1,D2,D3,B: streams:

87. quench,] D4: quench

fire:] D2,D3: fire.

89. love;] D2,D3,D4: love.

94. friend] 1661,D1,D2,D3,B: friend, D4: friend;

cause;] D2,D3,D4: cause:

97. hath, but me.] 1661,D1,D2,B: hath, but me; D3: hath, but me: D4: hath but me:

Oh] D: Oh,

counterfeit.] D3,D4: counterfeit!

99. dust;] D2,D3,D4: dust:

102. opinion.] D; 1661,B: Opinion:

Oh] D1,D2,D3: Oh,

104. painted] D,B; 1661: pointed NED lists no possible meaning for "pointed" which makes sense here.

105. S.D.] not in 1661. D3,D4, and B indicate Lorenzo's lines following are all asides.

106. wagtail;] D3,D4: wagtail:

109. S.D.] not in 1661.

110. seeks;] D2; 1661,D1,D3,B: seeks, D4: seeks:

111. fits,] D4: fits

strumpet;] D2,D3,D4; 1661,D1,B: Strumpet,

112. one.] D2; 1661,D1,D3,D4,B: one:

115. calumny.] D; 1661,B: Calumny:

him.] D3; 1661,D1: him; D2: him: D4,B: him!

116. him;] D2,D3,D4: him:

118. horns.] D2,D3,D4; 1661,D1,B: Horns:

120. strangers] D2,D3,D4; 1661,B: strangers, D1: strangers.

121. scent,] D2,D3,D4; 1661,D1: scent; B: scent:

inhabitants] D2,D3,D4; 1661,D1,B: inhabitants,

122. quality.] D2,D3,D4; 1661,D1: quality: B: quality

125. through] 1661,B: thorow

127. made.] B; 1661: made: D: made?

129. you] D; 1661,B: you,

131. them,] D3,D4; 1661,D1,D2,B: them;

133. S.D.] not in 1661,D,B.

134. S.D.] not in 1661,D,B.

'Has] D2,D3: H'as D4: H'has

135. see] D4: see,

137. mead.] D2,D3,D4; 1661,D1,B: Mead:

139. S.D.] not in 1661,D,B.

brave,] D,B; 1661: brave

141. sorrows.] D2,D3,D4; 1661,D1,B: sorrows:

Read] D2,D3,D4: Read,

finde] D4: find,

142. death;] 1661,D,B: death:

144. calms,] D4: calms

145. 'larum] D3 (suggested in a note),D4,B; 1661: Alarm The meter makes "'larum" more likely, a form Davenport uses both in King John and Matilda and A New Tricke to Cheat the Divell.

147. blackness.] 1661,D1: blackness: D2,D3,D4: blackness! B: darkness:

151. And] D2,D3,D4: And,

you:] 1661,D1,D2,B: you; D3,D4: you:---

153. desire;] D3,D4: desire,

155. feathers;] D2,D3,D4: feathers:

pass,] D2,D3,D4: pass

156. than] D; 1661,B: then

157. seems] D1 and D2 emend to "is" (without note), while D3 and D4 emend with note. B reads "seems", but with a note that it cannot be correct. Although "seems" appears inappropiate, it has parallels in ll. 541-545 and 2520. For Abstemia, "seems" is the same as reality.

157a. S.D.] first indicated in D4.

160. sir,] 1661,D,B: sir;

161. Duke.] D3,D4; 1661,D1,D2,B: Duke:

162. Farewel.] D2,D3,D4; 1661,D1,B: Farewel:

164. off!] D3,D4: off?

rogues.] D3,D4: rogues!

166. conster] D: construe

168. Francisco.] D2,D3,D4; 1661,B: Francisco; D1: Francisco:

169. him;] D; 1661,B: him:

170. musick.] 1661,B: musick: D2,D3,D4: music.

172. sometimes,] D,B: sometimes

straight,] D2,D3,D4: straight

173. look.] D2,D3,D4; 1661,D1,B: look:

177. Oh, sir...requisite] This line is apparently set as verse, but the next line is prose. It is possible that this entire scene should be set as prose, and therefore ll. 169-177 are incorrectly set.

crown;] D2,D3,D4: crown:

178. sociable.] D2,D3,D4; 1661,D1,B: sociable;

179. window;] D2,D3,D4: window!

183. so.] D2,D3,D4; 1661,D1,B: so:

185. him;] D2,D3,D4: him:

189. forbear,] D: forbear

cause;] 1661,D1,B: cause: D2,D3,D4: cause.

191. indeed;] D2,D3,D4: indeed:

then] D4: then,

192. penny.] D2,D3,D4; 1661,D1,B: penny:

193. sir;] D2,D3,D4: sir.

195. pence,] D4; 1661,D1,D2,D3,B: pence;

202. Why] D2,D3,D4: Why,

to her] D omits.

205. here] D: there

212. stand,] D2,D3,D4: stand;

215. Pray,] D2,D3,D4; 1661,D1,B: Pray

216. S.D.] not in 1661,D,B.

217. findes,] D4: finds

219. Yes,] D,B; 1661: Yes

220. sirrah;] D3,D4: sirrah!

221. S.D.] not in 1661,D,B.

224. S.D.] not in 1661, D,B.

226. Francis;] D3,D4: Francis:

228. vertuous] D2,D3,D4: virtuous!

231. thee.] 1661,D,B: thee:

already!] D3,D4: already? B: already.

233. Venice.] D4; 1661,D1,D2,D3,B: Venice:

234. Lady.] D,B; 1661: Lady

235. 'Las,] D: Alas!

239. walk] so all editions. Perhaps should be emended to "talk" (see clown's reply in l. 240).

240. Why,] D3,D4; 1661,D1,D2,B: Why

242. delay'd] D1,D2: allay'd. D3 retains and notes change. D4: delayed (with the note: Allayed, diluted. Mr. Collier altered the word to allayed [sic].).

243. Why,] D3,D4; 1661,D1,D2,B: Why

246. Why,] D4,B; 1661,D1,D2,D3: Why

248. S.D.] not in 1661,D,B.

said;] 1661,D1,D2,B: said, D3,D4: said:

249. not;] 1661,D,B: not:

251. Why,] D4; 1661,D1,D2,D3,B: Why

252. will] D3,D4: will,

be] D4: be,

256. Lords,] D2: lords; D3,D4: lords:

256. order.] 1661,D,B: order;

259. Nay,] D2,D3,D4; 1661,B: Nay D1: Nay good,

260. nations.] 1661,D,B: Nations:

262. too,] D2,D3,D4; 1661,D1,B: too

264. fie.] D4: fie!

265. now.] D2,D3,D4: now!

266. Lady.] D,B; 1661: Lady

271. No,] 1661,B: no; D1,D2,D3: no: D4: no.

still;] D3: still: D4: still.

273. sir;] D3,D4: sir,

275. prethee,] D4; 1661,D1,D2,D3,B: prethee

lady.] D3,D4; 1661,D1,D2,B: Lady:

276. her.] 1661,D,B: her:

277. gone----] D,B; 1661: gone.

279. Pish,] D3: Pish; D4: Pish!

286. ha't] D,B: ha't,

yfaith,] 1661: yfaith D: i'faith, B: y faith

288. farewel,] D,B; 1661: farewel

289. Doll.] D3,D4; 1661,D1,D2,B: Doll:

290. again.] D3,D4; 1661,D1,D2,B: again:

Farewel,] D,B; 1661: farewel

291. Adieu,] D,B; 1661: Adieu

mistris.] 1661,D,B: mistris:

292. than] D; 1661,B: then

are.] D4: are!

300. now,] D4,B; 1661,D1,D2,D3: now

Francis?] D: Francis!

302. Why,] D,B; 1661: Why

Francis!] B; 1661: *Francis*. D: Francis---

304. Nay, but *Francis*!] 1661: Nay but *Francis*. D1: Nay but Francis--- D2,D3: Nay, but Francis--- D4: Nay, but, Francis--- B: Nay but, *Francis*---

305. *Francis*.] 1661,D1,B: *Francis*: D2,D3,D4: Francis!

310. which,] D4,B: which

311. service.] 1661,D,B: service:

313. *Francis*.] D2,D3,D4: Francis?

lately:] D4: lately---

314. ye,] D4: ye

315-316. Extreams...nice.] The typography of the 1661 edition suggests that these lines possibly could have been sung.

315. vice;] D3,D4; 1661,D1,D2,B: vice:

317. Indeed,] 1661,D,B: Indeed

319. again;] D3,D4: again.

habes,] D; 1661,B: habes

320-321. can believe...none,] D4: [and] can believe himself none, B changes back to original, notes the D4 emendation, and explains that the "omission of the relative who is very common," so the meaning is "holds it impossible for any man to be cuckolded who believes that he cannot be cuckolded."

320. cuckold] B; 1661,D: Cuckold,

321. none,] D3,D4; 1661, D1,D2,B: none:

323. And truly,] D4,B; 1661: And truly D1,D2,D3: And, truly

324. with,] D,B: with

325. than] D; 1661,B: then

327. plaister.] D3,D4; 1661,D1,D2,B: plaister:

328. is.] 1661,D,B: is:

But and] D4: but, and

more,] B: more

334. Possible?] D: Possible!

335. Francis.] 1661,D,B: Francis:

night,] D2,B; 1661,D1,D3,D4: night

336. journey,] D4: journey

338. still,] D4: still

drinking),] 1661,D,B: drinking)

341. slumbers;] D; 1661,B: slumbers:

though] D1,D2: and tho' D3,D4: and though

344. out,] D3,D4: out

347. he,] D; 1661,B: he

348. 'Sfoot,] D; 1661,B: 'Sfoot

brave;] 1661,D,B: brave,

349. fool] D4,B; 1661,D1,D2,D3: fool,

knave.] D3,D4; 1661,D1,D2,B: knave:

350. But pray,] 1661,D1,D2,D3,B: But pray D4: But, pray

353. chamber.] 1661,D,B: chamber:

truly,] D4; 1661,D1,D2,D3,B: truly

356. maid,] D4: maid:

357. mistris.] D3,D4; 1661,D1,D2,B: Mistris:

358. strick] D: strike

359. kiss.] D2,D3,D4: kiss?

360. so;] D3,D4; 1661,D1,D2,B: so:

364. Why then] D4: Why, then,

Adieu,] D,B; 1661: Adieu

365. Farewel,] D,B; 1661: Farwel

366. all,] D3,D4; 1661,D1,D2,B: all;

367. them.] D3,D4; 1661,D1,D2,B: them:

368. so.] B; 1661,D: so:

370. Than] D; 1661,B: Then

beside.] D3,D4,B; 1661,D1,D2: beside:

372. horns.] 1661,D,B: horns:

375. affliction!] D3,D4: affliction;

376. And] D2,D3,D4: And,

378a. S.D.] D4 adds: Lorenzo aside.

379. apparent,] D3,D4,B: apparent;

too;] D3: too: D4,B: too!

380. meet;] 1661,D1,D2,D3,B: meet, D4: meet:

bastard.] D3,D4,B: bastard!

381. hand] D4: hand,

382. S.D.] not in 1661 or D; B indicates with a dash.

ye.] D2,D3,D4: ye!

384. S.D.] not in 1661 or D.

385. murder,] D4: murder

stay;] 1661, D,B: stay:

386. Oh] D4: O,

388. wife,] D4: wife

389. faith, then,] D2,D3,D4: faith then

gentleman,] D3,D4; 1661,D1,D2,B: gentleman;

390-391. a great oath; ... good)] D3: a great oath, ... good) D4: (a great oath, ... good),

391. (For...you)] D4: For...you---

it self,] D4: itself;

392. (For still...you)] D4: For still...you---

393. first,] D: first

her] D,B: your

chastity] D: chastity,

394. storie.] 1661,D,B: storie:

401. you,] D3,D4; 1661,D1,D2,B: you;

402b. S.D.] Officers are needed to escort Philippo away (ll. 417-419), since all the lords remain on stage.

405. hypocrite,] D2,D3,D4: hypocrite

406. behold,] D4: behold

407. There,] D3,D4; 1661,D1,D2,B: there

them] D4,B: thee Hazlitt and Bullen assume that Lorenzo is still addressing only Abstemia, but it is as likely that he is referring to both his wife and Philippo, since he casts them both to the law.

408. heart,] D4: heart

409. saint.] D4: saint?

411. what's] B: what [i]s

done] D2,D3,D4: done,

412. Duke,] D2,D3,D4: duke;

morning,] 1661,D,B: morning

413. Grace,] D: grace

415. Why] D2,D3,D4: Why,

417. gentlemen,] D; 1661,B: gentlemen

419. fool.] D2,D3,D4,B: fool!

Exeunt.] 1661,D,B: *Exit.*

422. her,] D4; 1661,D1,D2,D3,B: her

wonder.] 1661,D,B: wonder:

425. grain] D4; 1661,D1,D2,D3,B: grain,

428. whore.] D2,D3,D4: whore!

430. her!] 1661,D,B: her:

432. S.D.] Abstemia and her guards apparently exit here.

435. woman's] D: women's

laps.] D: laps!

439. Why,] D2,D3,D4; 1661,D1,B: why

442. horn-mad.] 1661,D,B: horn-mad:

443. Oh] D1,D2,D3: Oh! D4: O,

444. friend?] D4: friend,

445. Than] D; 1661,B: Then

446. afflictions;] D3,D4: affliction:

447. calumny.] 1661,D,B: calumny:

449. And, in betraying, tears] D2,D3,D4,B; 1661: And in betraying teares,
D1: And, in betraying tears,

still] D3,D4: 'stil

450. Oh!] D4: O,

451. oaths] D: oath

wife's] D; 1661,B: wives

453. late,] D4: late;

453d. out.] D3,D4; 1661,D1,D2,B: out:

cloaths;] D3,D4; 1661,D1,D2,B: cloaths:

Dorothea] 1661: Dorathea

453e. bed.] D; 1661,B: bed:

454. Softly,] D,B; 1661: Softly

Pambo.] 1661,D,B: Pambo:

457. not,] D3,D4: not;

458. then,] D,B; 1661: then

459. Ha, ha, ha,] D4: Ha, ha, ha!

see,] D,B: see

460. catching.] D3,D4; 1661,D1,D2,B: catching:

462. wonder,] D4: wonder

463. desperate] D4: desperate,

466. sleep in my talk] While this does make sense, perhaps should be emended to: talk in my sleep

467. ever.] 1661,D1,D2,B: ever: D3,D4: ever!

469. broath.] 1661,B: broath: D1,D2: broth: D3,D4: broth.

470. page.] 1661,D,B: page:

Sea-sick] D4: sea-sick,

471. salt-water?] D2,D3,D4: salt water!

472. venter] D: venture

between,] D; 1661,B: between

476. fear] D4,B; 1661,D1,D2,D3: fear,

delight.] D; 1661,B: delight:

477. devil,] D4,B: devil---

479. Let me four] D: Let me [see]: Four B: Let me [see], four

hand.] D2,D3,D4; 1661,D1,B: hand:

480. lyes.] D2,D3,D4; 1661,D1,B: lies:

'Sfoot,] D; 1661,B: 'Sfoot

a] D3 omits.

beard?] D: beard!

481. side] D4: side,

sure.] D2,D3,D4; 1661,D1,B: sure:

482. her,] D2,D3,D4: her:

touch;] 1661,D1,B: touch: D2,D3,D4: touch.

483. passion.] D2,D3,D4; 1661,D1,B: passion;

484. desires;] 1661,D1,B: desires: D2,D3,D4: desires.

485. lock'd,] D2,D3,D4,B; 1661,D1: lock'd;

veynes,] D1,D2,D4: veins D3: veins. B: veynes

491. hand,] D,B; 1661: hand

492. 'tis;] 1661,D1,B: 'tis: D2,D3,D4: 'tis.

already.] D2,D3,D4: already!

493. Lord,] D3,D4: lord!

awake.] D3,D4,B: awake!

495. Lord,] D2,D3,D4: lord!

496. S.D.] not in 1661,D,B.

499. S.D.] not in 1661,D,B.

500. Pray hear me, sir,] B; 1661: Pray hear me sir, D1: Pray hear me, sir, D2,D3,D4: Pray, hear me, sir;

sleep] D4: sleep,

504. mid-night.] 1661: mid-night; D1: mid-night: D2,D3,D4,B: mid-night!

506. tempted] D,B; 1661: temped

507. S.D.] not in 1661,D,B.

thus?] D2,D3,D4: thus!

509. Nay,] D; 1661,B: Nay

510. S.D.] not in 1661,D,B.

511. seem'd,] D1,D2,D4; 1661,D3,B: seem'd

heart,] D; 1661,B: heart

him.] D: him----

512. S.D.] not in 1661,D,B.

seemings.] D3,D4; 1661,D1,B: seemings; D2: seemings:

515. purpose----] D,B; 1661: purpose.

516. S.D.] not in 1661,D,B.

518. S.D.] not in 1661,D,B.

519. Now, sweet-heart,] D1,D2,D4; 1661: Now sweet-heart. D3,B: Now sweet-heart,

522-529. D2,D3,D4 set this speech as verse.

522. thee?] D: thee!

523. still;] D3,D4: still.

524. cuckolded.] D; 1661,B: cuckolded:

525. sirrah;] D; 1661,B: sirrah:

526. villain] 1661: Villian

528. Lady.] D2,D3,D4; 1661,D1,B: Lady:

531. than] D,B; 1661: then

goose;] D2,D3,D4: goose.

farewel,] D2,D3,D4,B; 1661,D1: farewel

532. chaste] D4: chaste,

Doll.] D2,D3,D4; 1661,D1,B: Doll:

533. to,] D4: to

wife?] D2,D3,D4: wife!

534. Pish,] D,B; 1661: Pish

Pambo.] D4,B: Pambo!

535. Here,] D2,D3,D4,B; 1661,D1: Here

539. Well,] D; 1661,B: Well

place,] D2,D3,D4: place;

541. Well,] D; 1661,B: Well

see,] B: see:

542. it,] D2,D3,D4; 1661,D1: it; B: it

543. and can be what she seems;] D: but not be what she seems: (D4 substituting a period for the colon). B returns to the original reading and notes that the change in Dodsley "makes the whole passage absolutely unintelligible." 1661,B: seems:

545. seems.] D2,D3,D4; 1661,D1,B: seems:

547. dainty smooth-fac'd] D4: dainty, smooth-fac'd,

Exeunt.] 1661,D,B: *Exit.* However, Francisco and Dorothea both exit here.

550. Why right, man;] 1661: Why right man: D1,D2: Why, right man: D3: Why, right man; D4: Why, right, man; B: Why, right, man:

horns,] B: horns

553. Oh!] D4: O

husbands,] D,B; 1661: husband's

554. ye full] D4,B: ye, fall

wives!] D3,D4: wives.

556. Sirrah] D2,D3,D4; 1661,D1,B: Sirra

559. No, no,] D2,D3,D4: No, no;

fortunes.] D2,D3,D4; 1661,D1,B: fortunes;

560. *Lorenzo*] D4: Lorenzo,

example] D4: example,

now,] D2,D3,D4: now;

561. wife.] D2,D3,D4; 1661,D1,B: wife:

562. servants] D2,D3; 1661,D1,D4,B: servants,

563. Philippo,] D2,D3,D4: Philippo; B: Philippo

564. Nay,] D2,D3,D4; 1661,D1,B: Nay

act.] D2,D3,D4; 1661,D1,B: act:

566. Nay,] D; 1661,B: Nay

568. head,] D4: head

569. I,] 1661,B: I D: Ay,

570. heads,] D2,D3,D4: heads

than] D; 1661,B: then

they] D3,D4: those

573. horns.] 1661,D1,D2,B: horns; D3,D4: horns:

574. 'Has] D2,D3: H'as D4: H'has B: has

576. 'has] D2,D3: h'as D4: h'has

580. hark,] D2,D3,D4: hark!

581. he sure,] D2,D3: he sure; D4: he, sure;

'has] D2,D3: h'as D4: h'has B: has

pace;] D2,D3,D4: pace.

pray] D2,D3,D4: pray,

584. S.D.] not in 1661 or D; B sets off with a dash.

585. S.D.] not in 1661,D,B.

586. Pray] D2,D3,D4: Pray,

then,] D; 1661,B: then

588. S.D.] not in 1661,D.B.

589. bravely.] D; 1661: bravely: B: bravely.——

S.D.] not in 1661,D,B.

Who's there] D4,B: Who's there?

593. S.D.] indicated only in D4.

594. night;] D2,D3,D4; 1661,D1,B: night,

596. S.D.] indicated only in D4.

597. Come,] D; 1661,B: Come

598. rushes;] D2: rushes: D3,D4: rushes,

600. S.D.] indicated only in D4.

601. Lady,] D2,B: Lady; D3,D4: lady:

602. enough] D,B: enough,

604. S.D.] not in 1661,D,B.

605. Nay] D: Nay,

thy] B: my

606. S.D.] not in 1661,D,B.

Out,] D2,D3,D4; 1661,D1,B: Out

607. so.] D2,D3,D4; 1661,D1: so: B: so

609. him,] D4: him

610. penions] D,B: pinions

612. neighbour,] D; 1661,B: neighbour

613. S.D.] not in 1661,D,B.

I,] B; 1661: I D: Ay,

hand] D4: hand,

615. S.D.] not in 1661,D,B.

617. woman.] D2,D3,D4; 1661,D1,B: woman:

618. absence,] D: absence

tryal,] D,B; 1661: tryal

Lady,] D3,D4: lady.

619. than] D; 1661,B: then

620. sought,] D4: sought [her]

sped;] D2,D3,D4: sped:

I would] D4: I'd

621. loving----] D,B; 1661: loving.---- This sentence continues after Lodovico's aside.

622. S.D.] not in 1661,D,B.

624. Back,] D,B; 1661: Back

bed;] D3,D4: bed:

625. Lord's calf's head] D: lord's-----calf's head. [suggesting an aside. But this final comment would make no sense as an aside.] 1661: Lords Calves head. B: Lord's-----calves head.

626. Well,] D,B; 1661: Well

better.] 1661,B: better: D: better----

628. S.D.] not in 1661,D,B.

629. ever,] D2,D3,D4: ever:

634. hold, man.] D2,D3; 1661,D1: hold man. D4,B: hold, man!

S.D.] not in 1661,D,B.

636. than] D; 1661,B: then

637. thee.] D2,D3,D4; 1661,D1,B: thee:

man,] D2,D3,D4: man:

639. Lady,] D4: lady B: Lady

641. than] D; 1661,B: then

642. me] D2,D3,D4; 1661,D1,B: me,

643. Nay,] D2,D3,D4; 1661,D1,B: Nay

sh'as] D4: sh'has

bravely;] D2,D3,D4: bravely.

sh'as] D4: Sh'has

644. yfaith,] 1661,B: yfaith D1: i'faith D2,D3,D4: i'faith,

man;] D2,D3,D4: man:

645. thee.] D2,D3,D4; 1661,D1,B: thee:

leases,] D4: leases

646. th'ast] D4: th'hast

648. them.] D2,D3,D4; 1661,D1,B: them:

650. Nay,] D2,D3,D4; 1661,D1,B: Nay

friend.] D2,D3,D4; 1661,D1,B: friend;

651. servant.] D2,D3,D4; 1661,D1,B: servant:

654. necessity;] D2,B: necessity: D3,D4: necessity.

pray] D2,D3,D4: pray,

655. Pambo;] D2,D3,D4: Pambo:

656. too;] D2,D3,D4: too:

I'll to bed.] D3,D4: I'll go to bed. B changes back to the original reading, with a note that it was "Needlessly altered in Dodsley..." 1661: bed:

657. see;] D2,D3,D4: see.

rascal] D2,D3,D4: rascal,

658. night,] D,B; 1661: night

Frank;] D2,D3,D4: Frank.

bed,] D,B; 1661: bed

661. So,] D; 1661,B: So

662. thee.----] D2,D3: thee---- D4: thee!

663. on,] D2,D3,D4: on

664. Oh] D4: O,

667. Nothing] D4: Nothing,

mean;] 1661,D1,B: mean: D2,D3,D4: mean.

669. nimble,] D2,D3,D4,B; 1661,D1: nimble

sir;] D2; 1661,D1: sir, D3,D4,B: sir:

671. appear,] D4: appear

675. us.] D; 1661,B: us:

677. neerly:] B: neerly;

678. kinsman;] D,B; 1661: kinsman

682. circumstances] D4: circumstance

684-685. Great...dishonour,] 1661,D,B: (Great...dishonour)

686. city,] D3,D4,B: city;

687. Nay,] D2,D3,D4; 1661,D1,B: Nay

689. How] D4: How,

woman (weepst] D4: woman---weep'st

thou!] D: thou?

S.D.] not in 1661, D,B.

691. deer] D: dear

years),] 1661,D1,D2,D3,B: years) D4: years---

692. that] D4: that,

693. offices,] B: offices

695. blow,] D3,D4,B; 1661,D1,D2: blow:

home.] D3,D4; 1661,D1,D2: home, B: home:

696. than] D; 1661,B: then

her] D4: her,

697. wife.] D4; 1661,D1,D2,D3,B: wife:

699. her] D3,D4: their

702. lent] B: sent

love.] 1661,D,B: love:

703. dove] D,B; 1661: dove.

704. him;] 1661,D,B: him:

705. hearts (though] D4: hearts, though

706. flie)] D4: fly,

707. Oh] D4: O,

enveigh!] D3,D4: inveigh.

708. satyre] D1,D2: satyr D3,D4: satire

714. confession),] 1661,D,B: confession)

there] D3,D4: there,

717. him;] 1661,D,B: him:

719. jewels] 1661: Jewls

friends.] D3,D4; 1661,D1,D2,B: friends;

721. opinion.] 1661,D,B: opinion:

722. whilst] D4: whilst,

724. stand] D4: stood

727. hence] B: hence,

730. honour'd,] D4: honour'd

belov'd,] D4: belov'd

733. theft;] D3,D4; 1661,D1,D2: theft: B: theft

734. faces:] D4; 1661,D1,D2,D3,B: faces;

736. Oh] D2,D3: Oh,

737. you.] B: you!

738. Oh] D2,D3: Oh,

740. sir.] 1661,D,B: sir;

745. courtesies.] 1661,D,B: courtesies:

Oh,] 1661,D,B: Oh

746. boys,] D2,D3,D4,B; 1661,D1: boys

bird,] D2,D3,D4,B; 1661,D1: bird

pit] D2,D3,D4,B; 1661,D1: pit,

748. ruine,] 1661,D1,D2,B: ruine: D3: ruin; D4: ruin---

friend,] D4,B; 1661,D1,D2,D3: friend

749. than] D,B; 1661: then

753. for] D1,D2,D3: (for

oft,] D4,B; 1661,D1,D2,D3: oft

see,] D4,B; 1661,D1,D2,D3: see

754. Strike discord] D3,D4: strike the discord

harmony.] 1661,D4,B: harmony: D1,D2,D3: harmony:)

760. by.] D2,D3,D4,B; 1661,D1: by,

761. witnesses] 1661: witnesses, D,B: times

to't,] B: to't;

763. not.] D,B; 1661: not

764. reproofs.] D3,D4; 1661,D1,D2,B: reproofs:

Oh,] D4; 1661,D1,D2,D3,B: Oh

765. sure] D4: (sure)

766. the 'plause] 1661,D1,D2,B: the plause D3,D4: th'applause

Now] D4: Now,

768. I] D4: I,

769. (His betray'd friend)] D4: His betray'd friend,

770. poyson.] D; 1661,B: poyson:

772. shock;] D3,D4,B: shock.

773. device,] D1,D2,D3,B; 1661,D4: device:

780. modestie.] D3,D4; 1661,D1,D2,B: modestie:

servants] D4: servants---

781. (That] D4: That

782. shame),] 1661,D1,D2,D3,B: shame) D4: shame---

783. saw.] 1661,D,B: saw:

788. great] D2,D3,D4,B; 1661,D1: great,

791. chamber.] 1661,D,B: chamber:

two] D4,B: two,

799. Lords,] D,B; 1661: Lords

805 and 808. S.D.] B notes: "An 'aside,' of course." However, l. 805 need not be an aside; Lorenzo could be complimenting the servants' courage as if they were being brave to step forward and testify, and "rascal" could be either an endearing term (as at l. 657) or simply a reference to their low station in life. Since l. 808 is an obvious aside, l. 805 could be too. D4 has l. 808 only as an aside.

807. oh] 1661: Oh D4: O,

809. book.] 1661,D,B: book:

814. souls] D: souls,

than] D; 1661,B: then

worlds] D: worlds,

816. Oh] D4: O,

820. grave.] D3,D4; 1661,D1,D2,B: grave:

823. kinsman] D3,D4: a kinsman

827. sentence.] 1661,D,B: sentence:

831. Oh! *Lorenzo Medico,*] D4: O Lorenzo Medico!

835. weep!] D3,D4: weep,

836. brests,] D4: breasts

sigh,] B: sigh

840. comforts,] D4; 1661,D1,D2,D3,B: comforts

841. S.D.] not in 1661,D,B.

842. which,] D4; 1661,D1,D2,D3,B: which

843. which,] D4; 1661,D1,D2,D3,B: which

844. than] D; 1661,B: then

846. Grace,] D4,B; 1661,D1,D2,D3: Grace

848. contradiction.] D3,D4; 1661,D1,D2,B: contradiction:

850. self,] D3,D4: self

852. but] B: but,

merit] D2,D3,D4: merit,

853. than is] D1,D2,D3; 1661,B: then is D4: is than

854. That death is blotted out] In a note, D3 suggests: "That death has blotted out". D4 retains the original reading, but notes incorrectly that original reads: "than is" [an error for l. 853?].

856. (On pain of death, if you return) for ever] 1661,D1,D2: (On pain of death (if you return) for ever) D3: (On pain of death, if you return, for ever) D4: (On pain of death, if you return) for ever, B: (On pain of death if you return) for ever

859. *Vero.*] 1661,D,B: *Pan.*

860. alotted.] 1661,B: alotted: D1,D2: allotted: D3,D4: allotted.

861. law;] D3,D4: law,

nay,] D4; 1661,D1,D2,D3,B: nay

862. self.] D3,D4; 1661,D1,D2,B: self:

Lord,] 1661,D,B: Lord

husband,] 1661,D,B: husband

864. allowing.] 1661,D,B: allowing:

865. And,] 1661,D,B: And

866. licence] 1661: lience

867. marry] D4: marry,

868. ye,] B: ye

871. Farewel,] D,B; 1661: Farewell

Lorenzo.] B: *Lorenzo*:

873. man.] 1661,D1,D3,D4,B: man: D2: man;

874. worth.] D3,D4,B; 1661,D1: worth; D2: worth:

Grace] D3: grace. D4: grace,

875. leave;] D2,D3,D4,B: leave:

farewel,] D,B; 1661: farewel

Lords;] B; 1661,D1: Lords, D2,D3,D4: lords:

876. farewel, thou] D3,D4,B: farewell thou,

877. unfortunate.] D4; 1661,D1,D2,D3,B: unfortunate:

879. Love's] D2,D3,D4,B; 1661,D1: Lovers

injury.] 1661,D,B: injury:

882. Farewel,] D,B; 1661: Farewell

883. doth] D4: doth [yet] B: [yet] doth

love.] 1661,D,B: love:

884. wife,] D3: wife; D4: wife:

886. suspition.] 1661,D,B: suspition:

hereafter] D4: hereafter,

887. last] D,B; 1661: lasts

888. you;] D3,D4: you:

889. choyce] D4,B; 1661,D1,D2,D3: choyce,

892. flowers.] 1661,D,B: flowers:

893. side,] D4: side[s], B notes: It is hard to say why "side" should be altered to "side[s]" in Dodsley.

895. prosper.] D3,D4,B; 1661,D1: prosper; D2: prosper:

896. debts.] D4,B; 1661,D1,D2,D3: debts:

S.D.] D3 and D4 omits.

899. Pray] D4: Pray,

kiss.] D3,D4; 1661,D1,D2,B: kiss:

sir.] D4; 1661,D1,D2,D3,B: sir:

900. grieve you] D4: grieve you,

901. innocent.] 1661,D,B: innocent:

forget:] 1661,D1,D2,D3: forget, D4: forget--- B: forget,---

902. sigh] D4: sigh,

903. through] 1661: thorow

904. court,] D2,D3,D4: court;

and] D2,D3,D4: and,

cozen,] D2,D3,D4; 1661,D1,B: Cosen

reed:] 1661,D1,D2,B: reed; D3,D4: rede;

906. Lor.] D; 1661,B: Lod.

906d. Lodovico,] 1661: Lodovico

Jovani,] 1661: Jovani

907. Lod.] D,B; 1661: Lor.

908. make] D,B; 1661: maks

909. yeild] D,B: yield However, the 1661 spelling is an acceptable alternate in NED, and Davenport's apparent preferred form.

912. Sirrah] D1,D2,D3: Sirrah,

think,] D,B; 1661: think

913. and] D: an'

garden] 1661: gardon

915. sir;] D: sir:

917. servant,] D,B: servant

918. Servant?] D,B: Servant!

man;] D,B; 1661: man,

919. office,] D,B; 1661: office

in't.] 1661,D,B: in't:

921. Why] D4: Why,

saint,] D3,D4: saint;

922. a] D3,D4; 1661,D1,D2,B: A

about] B: above

926. sir;] D3,D4; 1661,D1,D2,B: sir:

927. I'll go] D,B; 1661: I go

928. no, no,] B; 1661,D: no, no;

alone;] D1,D2,B; 1661: alone, D3,D4: alone:

929. match'd.] D; 1661,B: match'd:

930. him.] 1661,D,B: him:

931. confessor,] D; 1661,B: confessor

Jacomo,] D; 1661,B: *Jacomo*

933. Why,] D4; 1661,D1,D2,D3,B: Why

934. corner;] D1,D2; 1661,B: corner, D3,D4: corner:

936. Nay,] D,B; 1661: Nay

her,] D; 1661,B: her

Lords,] D; 1661: Lords B: Lord

thing;] D: thing:

939. too,] D; 1661,B: too;

940. wonderful.] D: wonderful!

941. home.] 1661,D,B: home:

they] MS,D,B; 1661: thy

945. honour,] D: honour

ye] 1661,D,B: you The clown, however, is paralleling what was said in l. 943.

947. my self;] D: myself:

948. fellow;] D1,D2; 1661,B: fellow, D3,D4: fellow.

on't;] D2,D3,D4,B: on't!

949. too.] D2,D3,D4,B: too!

950. Nay,] D; 1661,B: Nay

and] D: an'

951. 'em.] B:'em!

953. sir,] D1,D2: sir; D3,D4: sir:

955. yfaith,] 1661,B: yfaith D1,D2: 'faith, D3,D4: i'faith,

boy.] D4; 1661,D1,B: boy: D2,D3: boy---

957. sir,] D: sir;

958. he's wish'd] D3: he wish'd

958a. weeping] not in 1661,D,B.

960. elbow.] D1; 1661,B: elbow: D2,D3,D4: elbow!

all.] D4; 1661,B: all: D1,D2,D3: all---

961. Why,] D2,D3,D4,B; 1661,D1: Why

now,] D; 1661,B: now

chick!] D: chick,

962. Ladies;] D2,D3,D4,B; 1661,D1: Ladies,

painting, weeping] D4: painting---weeping B: painting,---weeping

964. Madam!] D3,D4: madam.

S.D.] not in 1661,D,B.

965. look, look,] D4: look, look!

company.] D: company!

966. right,] 1661,D,B: right

968. Why,] D2,D3,D4,B; 1661,D1: Why

bird?] B: bird!

973. Why, then] 1661,D1,D2,D3,B: Why then D4: Why then,

be] D4: be,

974. journey.] D3,D4; 1661,B: journey; D1,D2: journey:

Pray,] D4; 1661,D1,D2,D3,B: pray

crying.] D; 1661,B: crying---

975. Prethee,] D,B; 1661: Prethee

nye,] D,B; 1661: nye

976. content,] D,B: content!

when you too leave] D4: when you two leave B: when you, too, leave

company?] D: company!

978. here---] D,B; 1661: here.---

979. S.D.] indicated in D4 and B.

981. me;] B: me:

982. content.] D3,D4; 1661,B: content: D1,D2: content;

983. me.] B: me

984. Nay,] D; 1661,B: Nay

prethee,] D2,D3,D4; 1661,D1,B: prethee

Doll;] D1,D2,D3: Doll--- D4: Doll.

pray,] D; 1661,B: pray

gentlemen,] D; 1661,B: gentlemen

985. S.D.] B suggests an aside with a dash.

988. night.] D4; 1661,D1,D2,D3,B: night:

992. S.D.] B suggests another aside.

993. matter;] D; 1661,B: matter,

997. again?] B: again!

998. No,] D,B; 1661: No

ye;] 1661,B: yee; D: you:

999. night:] D1,D2,D3; 1661: night. D4,B: night---

1002. prethee] D4: prythee,

1003. supper;] D1: supper: D2,D3,D4: supper.

1005. Nay,] D; 1661,B: Nay

please.---] 1661,D1,D2,D3,B: please--- D4: please;

1007. Prethee, Frank,] D,B; 1661: prethee Frank

1008. Pray] D4: Pray,

first.] D,B; 1661: first

Come,] D2,D3,D4,B; 1661,D1: Come

1009. us.] D3,D4; 1661,B: us--- D1,D2: us.---

1010. couple;] D2,D3,D4: couple:

ye] D: you,

1011. Hark] D,B: Hark,

1012-1014. S.D.] not in 1661 or D; B notes asides with dashes.

1013. kist.] D: kiss'd!

1015. us,] D1,D2,B: us; D3,D4: us:

1016. go;] 1661,D,B: go,

well,] D,B: well

1017. What] D4: What,

1018. melancholy] D2,D3,D4: melancholy,

parted!] D3,D4: parted.

1019. alone;] D: alone:

1021. evening;] D,B; 1661: evening,

1023. marry,] D2,D3,D4,B; 1661,D1: marry

1024. word.] D4; 1661,D1,D2,D3,B: word:

1029. Why,] D2,D3,D4; 1661,D1,B: Why

1034. her!] D,B; 1661: her,

1035. hay.] D; 1661,B: hay:

1038. vertues.] 1661,D,B: vertues:

none;] D2,D3,D4: none:

1040. Oh none, sir,] B; 1661: Oh none sir D: Oh, none, sir,

some!] D3,D4,B: some.

1041. I] D1,D2,D4: Ay, D3: Aye,

ones] D: ones,

be,] D,B: be;

1042. fingers] D: finger

1043. matters---] D,B; 1661: matters.---

1044-1045. begotten, that] D1,D2,D3: begotten, that, D4: begotten that,

1047. excellent] D,B; 1661: excellent,

book,] D; 1661,B: book

1051. go;] D: go:

1052. construction:] 1661,D1,D2,B: construction. D3,D4: construction,

1053. Conceit] 1661: Conceipt

born;] D; 1661,B: born:

1056. *habes,*] D3,D4; 1661,D1,D2,B: *habes*

habes] 1661,D,B: *habes,*

1057. confines!] D3,D4: confines?

1058. Yes,] D2: Yes; D3,D4,B: Yes:

1059. sister,] D; 1661,B: sister;

1066. Proof] D: Proof,

circumstance] D,B: circumstance,

1072. tendered] D: render'd B: rendered See annotations.

returns] 1661: returrs

1073. chamber,] D2,D3,D4: chamber

1074. censur'd.] D3,D4; 1661,D1,D2,B: censur'd:

1075a. Lords;] 1661,D3,D4,B: Lords: D1,D2: lords.

1081. territories;] D; 1661,B: territories:

1085. horses,] D; 1661,B: horses;

1086. justice.] D1,D2: justice:

1087. wounded;] D1,D2; 1661,B: wounded, D3,D4: wounded:

1088. arms.] 1661,B: arms: D: arms;

1090. sin.] 1661,D,B: sin;

1091. her;] D1: her,

1093. wound.] 1661,D,B: wound:

1096. stroak] 1661: straok

strumpet,] D4: strumpet

1097. thousand;] D4; 1661,D1,D2,D3,B: thousand:

1098. name,] D4: name

1099. him;] 1661,D1,D2: him, D3,D4,B: him:

1101. man,] D4: man---

1102. This] D4,B: This,

1103. truth,] D2,D3,D4,B: truth;

1104. seek] 1661: seeek

1105. reply] 1661,B: reply: D1,D2:reply; D3,D4: reply,

1107. us.] 1661,D,B: us:

1110. information.] D; 1661,B: information:

1113. assertion (which] D1,D2,D3: assertion, (which D4: assertion, which

1114. probability),] 1661,D1,D2,D3,B: probability) D4: probability,

servants] D: servants,

1117. there.] D3,D4; 1661,D1,D2,B: there:

1119. Reason (the] D4: Reason, the

laws)] D4: laws

1120. action;] D: action,

give] D4: gives

lye.] D3,D4,B; 1661,D1,D2: lye:

1122. fear,] D4: fear

1124. answer.] D4: answer?

1126. authour;] 1661,D,B: authour:

1128. answer.] 1661,D,B: answer:

1132. cause.] D3,D4; 1661,D1,D2,B: cause:

1135. abstract,] D1,D2,B: abstract; D3,D4: abstract:

fall] 1661,D: fall, B: fall.

1137. soyl] 1661: soyl, D: soil; B: soyl;

infants,] 1661: infants; D,B: infants

1138. heaven.] 1661,D3,D4,B: heaven: D1,D2: heaven;

1144. request;] D: request:

Philippo] B: Philippo.

1145. flame,] D4: flame

pestilence,] 1661: pestilence D1,D2: pestilence: D3,D4,B: pestilence;

cave] 1661,D,B: cave,

1147. counsel;] 1661,B: counsell, D: counsel:

1150. pretious.] D; 1661,B: pretious:

1151. land;] D4: land:

fears] D4: feats B notes: " 'fears' cannot be the true reading. 'Feats' is the correction in Dodsley. Perhaps we should read 'scars'." However, each of the incidents at sea involves fearful action, and "fears" does make sense.

1153. lightning,] D; 1661,B: lightning;

1154. thunder;] D,B; 1661: thunder:

1156. sir---] D,B; 1661: Sir.

1157. Peace.] D4: Peace!

1158. *Lor.*] D,B; 1661: *Lod.*

Remember,] 1661,D,B: remember

1160. peace,] B: peace

1161. name.] D3,D4; 1661,D1,D2,B: name:

Oh] D1: oh! D2,D3,D4: oh,

1162. Than] D,B; 1661: Th n

scandal.] D3,D4: scandal!

1167. honour.] D2,D3,D4; 1661,D1: Honour: B: Honour.---

1168. equality.] B: equality!

1169. *Ven.*] 1661 ascribes this speech to *Ver.*, an obvious error for *Ven.* because of the sense and because Verona is referred to as *Vero.* throughout. D1 and D2, however, follow the 1661 reading; D3 first corrects to Venice.

1170. weave;] D1,D2: weave! D3,D4,B: weave

1171. art,] 1661,D,B: Art

appearances deceive.] D3: appearance deceive. D4: appearance [to] deceive. B retains the original, substituting an exclamation point for the period, and noting: I.e. appearances *which* deceive.

1172. Stay;] 1661,D1,D2: Stay, D3: Stay! D4: Stay!--- B: Stay:

price.] D: price:

1173. produc'd,] D4: produc'd

1174. act;] D1,D2; 1661,B: act: D3,D4: act,

1177. S.D.] First suggested in B with a dash. The first four words are an obvious aside.

change!] D; 1661: change, B: change;

t'other,] 1661: the t'other D,B: the t'other,

1180. you,] D; 1661,B: you

1184. truth] D4; 1661,D1,D2,D3,B: truth,

than] D,B; 1661: then

1185. Duke.] D3,D4; 1661,D1,D2,B: Duke:

1186. it] D: it,

1187. one] D,B; 1661: one,

1189. S.D.] not in 1661,D,B.

1192. Grace,] D,B: Grace;

1193. promises;] 1661,D,B: promises:

1195. perjury.] D4: perjury!

1197. S.D.] not in 1661 or D; B sets as an aside.

something;] D: something:

1199. hope] D: hope,

Lords,] D: lords;

1200. come about] B; 1661: comes about D: come out

1201. rush.] D; 1661,B: rush:

good heaven,] D: good heaven!

1202. craft,] D; 1661,B: craft

1204. self.] D2,D3,D4: self!

1205. see,] D,B; 1661: see

lurks] D: lurks,

1206. death.] D3,D4; 1661,D1,D2,B: death:

1207. sister;] D; 1661,B: sister:

1208. ingag'd,] D4: engag'd B: ingag'd

1208-1209. Lord (For] D4: Lord--For

1209. scourger)] D4: scourger--

1211. sister;] D: sister,

1212. him,] D: him

1213. scruple,] D4: scruple

conscience.] 1661,D,B: conscience:

1215. Sin,] D,B; 1661: Sin

eyes;] D3,D4: eyes:

1220. S.D.] indicated in D4 and B.

1223. wonder.] D,B: wonder!

1225. Duke.] 1661,D,B: Duke:

1226. book;] D; 1661: book, B: Book,

1228. ended;] D: ended:

1229. hostages,] 1661,D,B: hostage, [but see l. 1072]. D2,D3,D4 punctuate with a semi-colon instead of a comma.

1230. forces.] 1661,D,B: forces:

1231. remember,] D4; 1661,D1,D2,D3,B: remember

1234. Oh] D: Oh,

1235. dost] B: doth

1236. tongue,] D,B: tongue

1237. I.] 1661,D,B: I:

1238. book;] D1,D2,B; 1661: book, D3,D4: book.

all then.] D2,D3: all then? D4,B: all, then?

1240. swear] D,B; 1661: swear,

1242. Nay,] D; 1661,B: Nay

1246. true,] D,B; 1661: true

1248. both.] D,B; 1661: both

1253. honour;] D3,D4: honour,

base,] D3,D4,B: base

1256. Out,] D,B; 1661: Out

slave,] D3,D4,B: slave!

1257. 'em.] D: 'em:

1258. swear] D1,D2,D3: swear,

chamber] D: chamber,

1264. Yes, marry,] D2,D3,D4,B; 1661,D1: Yes marry

sir.] 1661,B: sir: D: sir;

1268. Lord;] D1,D2,D3; 1661,D4,B: Lord,

chaste,] D4: chaste.

1269. clear;] D1,D2,D3; 1661,B: clear: D4: clear,

1270. abus'd;] D; 1661,B: abus'd:

1272. it;] 1661,D,B: it:

1273. men.] D; 1661,B: men:

1278. stranger.] D3,D4,B; 1661,D1,D2: stranger:

1279. (Since] D4: Since

yours)] D4: yours,

1280. homicide;] D: homicide:

1281. else.] D; 1661,B: else:

1282. by] D: by,

1286. merit,] D4: merit---

death;] D3,D4: death.

1291. reputation;] D; 1661,B: reputation.

1292. spilt] D1,D2,D3: spilt,

dearer),] 1661,D,B: dearer)

1294. trespass;] D3,D4: trespass. B: trespass:

you,] D4,B: you

1295. own.] 1661,D,B: own:

1296. them] D: them,

1299. sister,] B: sister

1301. You, sir,] D,B; 1661: You sir

1302. adde,] B: adde:

made] D4: had This emendation assumes Verona is talking to Lorenzo, but ll. 1302-1303 are addressed to Venice, who "made" the justice.

1303. blood.] 1661,D,B: blood:

1306. place;] D: place:

1307. That] D: That,

confines] D: confines,

1308. death] D,B; 1661: death,

you,] B: you

1309-1310. But as . . . our presence.] D4: But, as they do a beggar at their door, So cast you from their presence. B retains the original, with the note: "(An unnecessary change, for the meaning is: 'It shall be a capital offence for any to give you even such scanty relief as they would offer to a beggar at their door.'"

1309. door.] D1,D2,D3: door: D4: door,

1312a. Lorenzo] D,B; 1661: Lord

1315. own, conceive it so.] 1661: own, conceive it so: D1: own; conceive it so: D2,D3: own; conceive it so; D4: own---conceive it so--- B: own, conceive it so,

live,] D2,B: live: D3,D4: live.

1319. life,] D1,D2: life;

suspition,] D3,D4: suspicion;

1322. half] D4,B; 1661,D1,D2,D3: half,

1323. Well, Lords,] D4; 1661,B: Well, of Lords D1,D2,D3: Well, of lords,

this;] D3,D4: this.

1324. now] D: now,

habit] D: habit,

heart,] D1,D2,D3: heart, and D4: heart and

1328. aside;] 1661,D,B: aside:

1330. Reveal confession?] 1661: Reveal confession: D1,D2,D3,B: Reveal confession! D4: Reveal, confession!

ways;] D3,D4: ways:

1331. at,] D4: at

1332. gone.] D; 1661,B: gone:

1333. nest,] D: nest;

and] D4: and,

1334. ones;] 1661,D,B: ones,

1335. gone;] D3,D4: gone:

1336. egge;] D3,D4,B: egge.

1337. d'ye,] D,B; 1661: d'ye

1338. S.D.] not in 1661 or D; B sets off with a dash.

1339. ones,] D; 1661,B: ones;

them.] D4; 1661,D1,D2,D3: them--- B: them.---

1340. comes;] D: comes:

1342. I honour] B: I [do] honour

1343. thee,] B: thee;

1344. flyes, who] D1,D2,D3: flies, who, D4: flies who,

1346. Hail,] D,B; 1661: Hail

father,] D,B: father!

1347. Welcome,] D,B; 1661: Welcome

daughter.] D,B: daughter!

1350. dealing,---] 1661: dealing.--- MS: Dealings D,B: dealing---

1351. S.D.] indicated in D4 and B only.

Doll.] D,B: Doll!

1353. father;] D1,D2,D3; 1661,D4,B: father:

1356. flesh] D,B; 1661: flesh,

dregs,] D2,D3,D4: dregs

1357. Which (since] D4: Which, since

you)] D4: you,

1359. And] D1,D2,D3: And,

acknowledgment,] D4: acknowledgment

1360. flesh.] D1,D2,D3,B; 1661: flesh: D4: flesh;

1361. make] MS,D,B; 1661: makes

1362. confess] D2,D3,D4,B; 1661,D1: confess,

1364. flanting,] D,B; 1661: flanting;

1367. daughter,] D2: daughter;

1368. pardonable,] D2: pardonable;

1369. hell,] D4: hell

night.] D; 1661,B: night:

Pray,] D; 1661,B: pray

1373. too.] D2,D3,D4; 1661,B: too: D1: too;

1375. sir,] D2,D3,D4: sir;

1377. S.D.] indicated in D4 and B only.

vertues;] D: virtues!

why,] D4; 1661,D1,D2,D3,B: why

1378. than] D,B; 1661: then

1379. S.D.] not in 1661,D,B.

1380. light.] D2,D3,D4; 1661,D1,B: light:

1382. Oh] D2,D3,B: Oh,

1383. S.D.] not in 1661,D,B.

One?] D: One!

1384. behind,] D: behind

1385. consequence.] D3,D4; 1661,D1,D2,B: consequence:

1387. there] Perhaps should be emended to: their

1388. (Because the last lives freshest in our memories)] D4 removes the parentheses, and switches this line with the next, to make the meaning clearer. B notes that although D4 is better than the original, it breaks up the intended couplet.

memories)] 1661,D2,D3: memories)---

1389. Fare 'fore] D4,B; 1661: Far more MS: ffar more D1,D2,D3: Far 'fore

last] D4: last,

1391. S.D.] indicated in D4 and B only.

Sh'as] D4: Sh'has

1392. red,] D2: red; D3,D4: red.

1395. sir,] D4: sir!

me;] D2,D3,D4: me:

1396. man,] D4: man

1398. Nay,] D; 1661,B: Nay

1400. S.D. indicated in D4 and B only.

then,] D; 1661,B: then

habes;] D: *habes,*

1401. 'em.] D2,D3,D4; 1661,D1,B: 'em:

1402. herald;] D; 1661,B: Herald,

butcher's] D4: another's B, after noting this emendation, says: but the word 'quarter' suggests that some poor quibble was intended.

1403. pleasure;] D2,D3,D4; 1661,D1,B: pleasure:

1403-1404. whoreship.] D,B; 1661: whoreship:

1404. S.D.] not in 1661; indicated with a dash in D and B.

broad;] D1; 1661: broad, D2,D3,D4,B: broad:

1406. Yes, yes,] D2,D3,D4: Yes, yes;

sure] D4: sure,

1408. Alas,] D4: Alas!

sir.] D2,D3,D4; 1661,D1,B: sir:

1409. but] D4: but,

1410. than] D,B; 1661: then

1411. S.D.] not in 1661 or D; B indicates with a dash.

charges] B: charges,

too;] 1661,D: too: B: too,

a t'other] D3,D4: o' th'other

side,] D1,D2,D3: side   B: side!--- [ending the aside here and not after exhortation.]

1413. exhortation.] 1661,D,B: exhortation:

S.D.] not in 1661,D,B.

1414. stay] D4;   1661,D1,D2,D3,B: stay,

1415. ceremony.] D;   1661,B: ceremony:

1417. Yes, indeed,] D,B;   1661: Yes indeed

1419. No,] D,B;   1661: No

truth,] D,B;   1661: truth

1420. absolv'd.] D;   1661,B: absolv'd:

1424. strange.] D2,D3,D4;   1661,D1,B: strange:

at it,] D;   1661: it;   B: at it;

1425. performance,] D2,D3,D4: performance;

1426. it.] D2,D3,D4;   1661,D1,B: it:

Nay,] D;   1661,B: nay

remember,] D2,D3,D4: remember

1433. strange,] D1,D2,D3: strange   D4: strange [that]

1436. city),] 1661,D,B: city)

1440. Now,] D2,D3,D4;   1661,D1,B: Now

table,] D,B;   1661: Table

1442. husband:] D1,D2,D3: husband;   D4: husband,

1443. father.] 1661,B: FATHER;   D: father:

1444. And] D: And,

orders bar] D3 (in a note),D4: order bars

1448. penance] D2,D3,D4,B;   1661,D1: penance,

you;] D2,D3,D4: you:

1449. it.] D2,D3,D4;   1661,D1,B: it:

Good-buy.] D4: Good-bye!   1661: god-buy.

1450. Oh] D1,D2,D3: Oh,

sir,] D,B; 1661: sir

stay;] B; 1661: stay, D: stay!

than] D; 1661,B: then

1452. breach;] B; 1661,D: breach

us,] D2,D3,D4: us:

1453. orders,] D,B; 1661: orders

1454. heaven] D1: heaven's D2,D3,D4: Heaven's

1458. this.] D; 1661,B: this:

penance] D,B: penance,

1461. silent.] 1661,D,B: silent:

1461-1462. performance.] D2,D3,D4; 1661,D1,B: performance:

1462. sir.] B: sir,

1463. e're] D; 1661: ere B: ere [e're]

before.] B: before;

1464. S.D.] not in 1661,D,B.

neat] D4: right

1465. Here,] D2,D3,D4; 1661,D1,B: Here

miserable] D2,D3,D4: miserable,

1474. surfets,] D4: surfeits B: surfets

1475. sanctuary,] D2,D3,D4: sanctuary

1476. than] D; 1661,B: then

receptable.] D2,D3,D4; 1661,D1,B: receptable;

1477. but,] D2,D3,D4; 1661,D1,B: but

1478. not though] D4: not, though,

it.] D2,D3,D4; 1661,D1,B: it:

1479. Love's] D4: [O] love's

eclipse,] D4,B: eclipse!

art] D2,D4: art, D3: art;

disease] B; 1661,D: disease,

1481. S.D.] not in 1661, D,B.

walks] D4: walks,

self;] D2,D3,D4: self.

1483. away.] D2,D3,D4; 1661: away; D1,B: away:

1485. S.D.] not in 1661,D,B.

Morbo, Madona] D2; 1661,D1: Morbo Madona, D3,D4,B: Morbo; Madona

Timpanina] 1661: Timpania

effect'd] 1661: effe D,B: effected

1486. than] D,B; 1661: then

head.] D2,D3,D4; 1661,D1,B: head:

1487. citadels,] D3,D4: citadels

1489. than] D; 1661,B: then

coach then,] D2,D3,D4,B; 1661,D1: Coach, then

yfaith.] 1661: yfaith: D1: i'faith--- D2,D3,D4: i'faith.
B: yfaith:---

S.D.] indicated with dashes in D1,D2,D3 and B.

now,] D,B; 1661: now

1492. Mill.] D4; 1661,D1: Mill, D2: Mill; D3: Mill--- B: Mill:---

1493. conscience.] D3: conscience:

1495. her.] D2,D3,D4; 1661,D1,B: her:

1498. S.D.] not in 1661,D,B.

me,] D2,D3,D4,B: me!

tremble!] D3,D4: tremble.

1499. hither,] D,B; 1661: hither

Millicent.] D2,D3,D4; 1661,D1,B: Millicent;

1500. too?] D2,D3,D4,B: too!

1502. Well, indeed] D: Well indeed,

1503. Nay,] D2,D3,D4,B; 1661,D1: Nay

1504. self.] D2,D3,D4; 1661,D1,B: self:

truth's truth,] D1; 1661,B: truths truth, D2,D3,D4: truth's truth:

you] 1661: yoo

1505-1506. last [night] till 12?] 1661,D,B: last till 12?

1508. feather] D2,D3,D4: feather,

1508-1509. gallery;] 1661,D1,D2: gallery, D3,D4,B: gallery:

1510. white,] D,B; 1661: white

1512. hand;] D2: hand. D3,D4: hand:

1513. light] D2,D3,D4,B: light,

1514. springal,] D,B; 1661: springal

1515. than] 1661,B: Then D: Than

1517. son] D2,D3,D4,B; 1661,D1: son,

1519. What,] D2,D3,D4; 1661,D1,B: What

Marry,] D4; 1661,D1,D2,D3,B: marry

1520. murren;] 1661,B: murren, D: murrain,

you] D4,B: you,

tro] D3,D4: trow

1523. coach] D2,D3,D4: coach,

1525. cry'd,] B; 1661,D1,D2,D3: cry'd D4: cried,

Farewel,] D4,B; 1661,D1,D2,D3: farewel

1527. fortunes] D4,B; 1661,D1,D2,D3: fortunes,

1528. you.] D,B: you!

1529. Perfum'd] D4,B: Perfum'd,

1531. rags,] D2,D3: rags

geometry,] D,B; 1661: geometry:

1534. true,] D2,D3,D4: true;

1535. ye;] D2,D3,D4: ye.

1536. women] D2,D3: women,

1538. demonstration.] D2,D3,D4; 1661,D1,B: demonstration:

1539. 'twill] D: it will

1542. Why,] D2,D3,D4,B; 1661,D1: Why

1544. lady,] D3,D4; 1661,D1,D2,B: Lady;

1545. Oh,] D4,B; 1661,D1,D2,D3: Oh

1546a. Enter Philippo] He is, of course, disguised as Pedro Sebastiano of Ferrara.

1547. Morrow,] D,B; 1661: Morrow

madam.] D2,D3,D4; 1661,D1,B: Madam;

Oh,] D4,B; 1661,D1,D2,D3: Oh

how] D4: how,

1548. there.] D2,D3,D4,B: there!

1550. What,] D,B; 1661: What

1552. Faith,] D2,D3,D4; 1661,D1,B: Faith

yet;] D2,D3,D4: yet:

1555. mistris.] D2,D3,D4: mistress!

1556. 'Sfoot,] D1,D2,D3; 1661,B: 'Sfoot D4: 'Sfoot!

Prince;] D2; 1661,D1,B: Prince, D3: prince! D4: prince:

1557. welcome.] D2,D3,D4; 1661,D1,B: welcome:

1558. phrase;] D2; 1661,D1,B: phrase, D3,D4: phrase:

1561. sir,] D2,D3,D4,B: sir;

1562. sale?] D,B; 1661: sale,

1563. alone.] D,B; 1661: alone?

1564. Indeed,] D,B; 1661: Indeed

sir.] D3,D4: sir---

1565. deeds.] D4: deeds!

1567. rascal.] D2,D3,D4: rascal!

1568. Nay,] D,B; 1661: Nay

1574. 'Sfoot,] D,B; 1661: 'Sfoot

kickt?] D3,D4: kicked!

sir.] B; 1661,D1,D2: sir; D3,D4: sir:

1575. To Abst.] not in 1661,D,B.

Exit.] not in 1661, D1, D2. D3 notes: Philippo here makes his exit which is not marked in the old copy, and, under the circumstances, is not very creditable to him.

1578. vanish'd,] B: vanish'd

1579. S.D.] Morbo and Timpanina's exit indicated in B only. But apparently the slave exits too, since he does not hear the ensuing conversation (see l. 1960).

1580. Oh] D4: O,

1581. contends] D: contend

1582. Nay,] D; 1661,B: Nay

1583. you,] D2,D3,D4,B: you;

indeed] D2,D3,D4: indeed,

not.] D2,D3,D4; 1661,D1,B: not:

1588. Report sure] D4,B: Report, sure,

1589. language;] D2,D3,D4: language:

1591. not sure] D4: not, sure,

1592. passion.] D2,D3,D4; 1661,B: passion: D1: passion;

1593. language;] D2: language. D3,D4: language:

1594. tower] D2,D3,D4: tow'r

integrity,] D4,B: integrity

1595. virgin.] D2,D3,D4; 1661,D1,B: virgin:

1597. Why,] D4; 1661,D1,D2,D3,B: Why

1599. respect.] D2,D3,D4; 1661,D1,B: respect:

1603. swallow'd] D2,D3,D4,B: swallow'd,

found.] D4: found [again].

1604. prethee,] 1661,B: prethee D1,D2,D3: pr'ythee D4: prythee,

1606. intelligence.] D2,D3,D4; 1661,D1,B: intelligence:

so] B: so,

1608. son] D4,B: [the] son

1609. Send him] D4: [And would you] send him B notes this emendation is "to the destruction of the sense."

then,] D4; 1661,D1,D2,D3,B: then

1612. Oh] D2,D3: Oh,

1613. sorrows] D2,D3,D4: sorrows,

1614. place.] D2,D3,D4; 1661,D1,B: place:

1615. dragons.] D2,D3,D4; 1661,D1,B: Dragons;

Oh] D4: O,

back!] 1661,D,B: back:

1616. ingender,] D2,D3: ingender; D4: engender;

stream] D,B: steam Toads,however, do breed in a stream, so the 1661 reading could be correct. D2,D3, and D4 punctuate to make "steam" refer to the poison air of l. 1617.

death;] D: death:

1617a. S.D.] D3,D4 place after l. 1618.

1621. sir;] D2,D3,D4: sir.

pliant.] D4: pliant?

1622. sattin.] D2: sattin! D3,D4: satin!

1625. flead] D4: flea'd

1626. lip.] D2,D3,D4; 1661,D1,B: lip:

Farewel.] D2,D3,D4; 1661,D1,B: farewel:

1627. wonder,] D2: wonder; D3,D4: wonder:

1627a. S.D.] Jovani and Spinoso apparently do not appear at all in the remainder of the play. Perhaps this indicates some doubling of roles by the actors.

1628. chaste] D2,D3,D4: chaste,

1629. Nay,] D2,D3,D4; 1661,D1,B: Nay

1630. conclusion;] D2,D3,D4: conclusion.

1631. at,] D4: at

mask] D1,D2,D3: mask, D4: masque,

1632. ready.] D2,D3,D4; 1661,D1,B: ready:

1633. gentlemen,] D2,D3: gentlemen

1635. devise,] 1661,D,B: devise

openly,] D2,D3,D4: openly

1637. me,] D2,D3,D4; 1661,D1,B: me

1638. 'tis] D: it is

1639. Lady] D,B; 1661: Lady,

1640. cuckold,] 1661,D,B: Cuckold

1650. Are (unknown] D1,D2,D3,B; 1661: Are (unknow D4: Are, unknown

another)] D4: another,

1651. disguis'd.] D2,D3,D4; 1661,D1,B: disguis'd:

1652. shall] D2,D3,D4: shall,

daies] D2,D3,D4: days,

1653. hopes a satisfaction.] D: hopes satisfaction.

1654. sir;] D2,D3,D4: sir.

sir,] D2,D3,D4; 1661,D1,B: sir;

1656. buzzard.] D2,D3,D4; 1661,D1,B: buzzard:

1657. But] D4: But,

ye] D4: ye,

ladies.] D2; 1661,D1,D3,D4,B: Ladies:

1658. Come,] D2,D3,D4; 1661,D1,B: Come

Ladies,] D2,D3,D4,B; 1661,D1: Ladies

sit.] D2,D3,D4; 1661,D1,B: sit:

1660. himself it seems] D4: himself, it seems,

1662. Now] D2,D3,D4: Now,

vanity.] 1661,D1,D2,B: vanity: D3,D4: vanity!

1663. mask!] D3,D4: masque?

Ladies.] B: Ladies!

1665. Marry, my Lord,] D,B; 1661: Marry my Lord

1666. one,] D3,D4: one

mask,] D4: masque

1667. but,] D,B; 1661: but

fellow,] D,B; 1661: fellow

1668. throng,] D2,D3,D4: throng;

she, poor soul,] D2,D3,D4,B; 1661,D1: she poor soul

1670. 'Las,] D3,D4; 1661,D1,D2,B: 'Las

ill.] 1661,D,B: ill:

1671. will?] 1661,D,B: will.

1672. masquers] D3: masker's

1672a. masquers:] D2,D3,D4; 1661,D1,B: Masquers;

1674. shake,] D4: shake:

mask——] D4,B; 1661,D1,D2,D3: Mask.

1678. scorns,] D4: scorns.

1680 and 1682. insinuate——] B; 1661,D: insinuate.

1683. insinuate] D4: insinuate,

pritty] Though Davenport prefers the "pretty" spelling, here "pritty" is used to further the rhyme with "city."

1685. Cuckold——] B; 1661,D: Cuckold.

1686. Cuckold,] D,B; 1661: Cuckold

Lord?] D3,D4,B; 1661,D1,D2: Lord.

1688. Oh.] 1661,D,B: O

1689. Then] D3,D4: The

camp] D4: camp,

court.] 1661,D,B: Court:

1692. Why,] D2,D3,D4; 1661,D1,B: Why

1695. Pray,] D,B; 1661: Pray

1696. Nay,] D4; 1661,D1,D2,D3,B: Nay

keep then on] While this line makes sense, perhaps it should be emended to: keep them on

on,] D,B; 1661: on

1697. name.] 1661,D,B: name:

known-a,] D4: known-a

1699. protest,] D1,D2,D3: protest

in] D: in,

1700. room] D4: room,

1702. pray,] D4; 1661,D1,D2,D3,B: pray

1703. men----] D4,B; 1661,D1,D2,D3: men.

1705. will, oh city!] D4,B: will? i'th'city!

1706. Seek] D4,B; 1661,D1,D2,D3: Sick

1707. him,] D4: him

1708. Nay,] D4; 1661,D1,D2,D3,B: nay

1710. forsooth,] D4: forsooth--- B: forsooth,---

hap] D: hap,

1711. cap.] 1661,D,B: cap:

1712. cap;] D3,D4: cap,

1713. frights] D: fights

1721. center;] 1661,D1,D2,D3,B: center: D4: centre:

1722. cap,] D4,B: cap

call,] D4,B: call

1724. center,] D4; 1661,D1,D2,D3,B: center

1725. butt] D; 1661,B: but

city.] 1661,D,B: City:

1727. alias] D4: alias,

1729. mirth;] 1661,D,B: mirth:

1733-1737. B marks these lines as asides between Lodovico and Verona.

1735 and 1737. S.D.] not in 1661 or D.

1738. all;] D2,D3,D4; 1661,D1,B: all,

1741. glasses---] D4,B; 1661,D1,D2,D3: glasses,

1743. thinking---] 1661,D,B: thinking,

S.D.] not in 1661, D,B.

me---] 1661,D,B: me,

1745. wife.] D3,D4; 1661,D1,D2,B: wife;

Troth,] D3,D4; 1661,D1,D2,B: troth

Lodovico] 1661: Lodowick Throughout the rest of this scene, Lodovico is referred to only as Lodowick. D and B follow 1661 with no explanation. Apparently Lodowick and Lodovico were both forms used interchangeably (as in Beaumont and Fletcher's The Captain, where one of the characters, Lodowick, is also spelled Lodovico).

1746. her.] D4,B: her---

1747. S.D.] not in 1661,D,B.

Oh,] D2,D3; 1661,D1,D4,B: Oh

good] B: good,

me.] D4: me---

1748. 'Las,] D4; 1661,D1,D2,D3,B: 'las

1749. S.D.] not in 1661,D,B.

so.] 1661,D,B: so:

1756. Nay,] D; 1661,B: Nay

nought] D; 1661,B: nought,

on't,] D4,B; 1661,D1,D2,D3: on't

1757. S.D.] indicated in D4 and B only.

memento,] D3,D4: memento

1760. one;] D3,D4,B: one:

1763. S.D.] not in 1661 or D; B indicates with a dash.

1764. Pray] D4: Pray,

dream?] D: dream.

1765. it;] D: it:

1767. was.] D3,D4; 1661,D1,D2,B: was:

1769. home,] B: home;

Francisco.] B: Francisco?

1770 and 1771. S.D.] not in 1661 or D; B indicates with a dash.

1771. chick,] D2,D3,D4: chick;

1773. I] D: Ay

1774. S.D.] Not in 1661, D,B.

dreams.] D4: dreams!

1775. bed.] 1661,D1,D2,B: bed, D3,D4: bed;

1777. child] D4: child,

me thought] D4: methought,

1780. I!] B: I?

S.D.] not in 1661 or D; B indicates with a dash.

1781. S.D.] not in 1661 or D; B indicates with a dash.

1783. hot] MS: hitt D: hit B: hot [sic]

1784. so] D: so,

1789. child.] 1661,D,B: child:

1791. He?] D2,D3,D4: He!

Frank,] D2,D3,D4; 1661,D1,B: Frank

1792. dreams] D2,D3: dreams,

1793. thee,] D4: thee---

1794. Away you] D2: Away, you D3,D4: Away, thou

father.] D4: father!

1796. same.] 1661,D,B: same:

1797a. Enter Jaspro.] As B notes, "Jaspro's previous 'exit' is not marked in the old edition." Jaspro last speaks at ll. 1757-1758, and when he enters it is at the right moment dramatically, but there is no specific line at which he seems to exit. He merely slips away unnoticed, perhaps only for a few lines.

1799. Lodovico] 1661: Lodowick See note for l. 1745.

1803. send him up] D3,D4: send up

1804. S.D.] not in 1661,D,B.

Pist,] B; 1661: Pist D: Hist,

1805. Why,] D2,D3,D4,B; 1661,D1: Why

husband, my Lord.] D2,D3,D4,B: husband! my Lord!

1806. S.D.] not in 1661 or D; B indicates this and following asides with a dash.

I] D1: He D2,D3, D4 all retain emendation, and note: "Francisco seems to allude to Lodovico's last words." B retains, noting change without explanation. But seeing the situation, Francisco may as well be noting that he must interpret the direction events are taking.

1807. S.D.] not in 1661,D1,D2,D3.

1808. S.D.] not in 1661 or D.

1809. S.D.] not in 1661 or D.

not sure] D4: not, sure,

confession.] D2,D3,D4: confession!

1810. rise] D4: rise,

lodgings.] 1661,D,B: lodgings:

1812. sir,] D2,D3,D4,B: sir:

1813. mirth,] D2,D3,D4,B: mirth

1815. S.D.] not in 1661 or D.

Millain.] 1661,D1,B: *Millain:* D2,D3,D4: Milan!

1816a. S.D.] D3 first notes the disguise, which is evident throughout the scene.

1819. *Lodovico,*] 1661: *Lodowick.* D: Lodowick, B: *Lodowick*

1820. here,] D2,D3,D4,B; 1661,D1: here

1822. here] D2,D3: here,

her.] B: her:

1824. horns,] D2,D3,D4,B; 1661,D1: hornes

ho.] D3,D4: ho!

1825. S.D.] not in 1661,D,B.

yet,] D2,D3,D4: yet;

1826. *Tony.*] D2,D3,D4: Tony!

1827. I any thing,] D1,D2: ay anything, D3: ay anything; D4: ---ay, anything.

every thing,] D4: everything;

1830. brest;] 1661,D1,B: brest D2,D3,D4: brest,

1837. I, I,] D1,D2,D4: Ay, Ay, D3: Aye, Aye,

pig] D1,D2,B: pig; D3,D4: pig:

1838. after.] 1661,B: after.--- D: after---

1839. this,] D1,D2,D3; 1661: this D4,B: this---

house,] B; 1661,D: house

1840. out's eyes] D1,D2,B; 1661: out's his eyes MS: out's Eyes D3,D4: out his eyes

1841. Since, Lady,] D,B; 1661: Since Lady

man] B: man [there]

1844. the apparent] D1,D2,D3: apparent D4: th'apparent

1846. S.D.] not in 1661,D,B.

you,] D,B; 1661: you

1848. S.D.] not in 1661,D,B.

counsel, sir,] D,B; 1661: counsel sir

better?] D,B: better,

1850. in't.] 1661,D,B: in't:

his] D: the

1851. than] D; 1661,B: then

1853 and 1855. S.D.] not in 1661 or D; B indicates with dashes.

1853. now,] D,B; 1661: now

1855. too.] 1661,D,B: too:

1858. Lodovico] 1661: Lodowick See note for l. 1745.

1862. confessor.] 1661,D,B: confessor:

1867. Oh] D1,D2,D3: Oh,

1869. best,] D,B; 1661: best

sir,] D: sir:

defend,] D2,D3,D4: defend; B: defend:

1872. Good] D1,D2,D3: Good,

1873. ye,] D4: ye;

ye;] D2,D3,D4,B; 1661,D1: ye,

1876. fame.] 1661,D,B: fame:

1877. 'scape] D; 1661,B: scape

1878. You, sir,] D; 1661,B: You sir

1879. passions;] D: passions,

1881. parts] D: part

1883. 'Snailes,] D4: Snails!

an ass!] D1,D2,D3; 1661: and Asse! D4: an ass? B: an Asse!

And 't had] 1661: an'th ad MS: and it had D1: an th'ad D2,D3,D4: an't'ad B: an't had

horse,] D; 1661,B: horse

1884. worthy,] D,B; 1661: worthy

1885. sirrah.] 1661,D,B: sirrah:

1887. banish'd.] D2,D3,D4; 1661,D1,B: banish'd:

1889. meal;] B; 1661,D1: meal, D2,D3,D4: meal:

1890. greedily.] 1661,D1,B: greedily: D2,D3,D4: greedily;

But] D4: but,

1891. than] D; 1661,B: then

1892. branded;] 1661,D1: branded, D2,D3,D4,B: branded!

burnt,] D2,D3,D4,B; 1661,D1: burnt:

1894. You,] D,B; 1661: You

1897. reclusive.] 1661,D,B: reclusive:

1899. against] D4 notes 1661 reads "is against", but that is not true in any copies I have examined, and B notes the same for the copies he has seen.

1900. just,] D3.D4: just:

1902. thee.] D2,D3,D4; 1661,D1,B: thee:

1903. sirrah——] D,B; 1661: sirrah.——

1904. Nay,] D,B; 1661: Nay

habes,] D,B; 1661: habes

habes] 1661,D,B: habes,

1906. You,] D2,D3,D4,B; 1661,D1: You

1907. flesh,] D,B; 1661: flesh

1909. You, sirrah,] D,B; 1661: You sirrah

1911. already;] D3,D4: already!

but] D4: But,

1912. whipping-chear] D: whipping-cheer

1913. note] 1661: noat

Grace] D,B; 1661: Grace,

1914. apace;] D1,D2: apace:

1916. Lodovico] 1661: Lodowick See note for l. 1745.

1919. but oh!] D4: but, O

1920. performance.] D: performance!

1921. Pshew,] D,B; 1661: Pshew

nothing.] 1661: nothing, D,B: nothing:

great] D omits.

1922. place,] D1,D2,D3; 1661: place. D4,B: place——

1923. began] D4: begun

1925. rest;] D3,D4: rest:

and,] D2,D3,D4,B; 1661,D1: and

morning,] D4: morning

1926. train,] D4: train

1928. truth,] D,B; 1661: truth

sun,] D,B; 1661: Sun

1929. crown,] D3,B: crown

1933. slave,] D3,D4: slave;

1933-1934. (then a Turk) . . . _Palermo_.] 1661,D1: (then a Turk, . . . _Palermo_) D2,D3,D4: (then a Turk) . . . Palermo: B: (then a Turk, . . . _Palermo_):

1936. Than] D; 1661,B: Then

1937. Oh,] 1661,D1,D2,D3,B: Oh D4: O,

1938. rendevow;] B; 1661: rendevow, D1: rendezvous, D2,D3,D4: rendezvous;

there.] 1661,D,B: there:

1941. therefore,] D,B; 1661: therefore

1942. times] D,B; 1661: times,

1943. suspition,] D2: suspicion; D3,D4: suspicion: B: suspition;

1944. inclinations)] D4: inclinations),

sure intended] D2,D3; 1661,D1,B: sure intended, D4: sure, intended

1945. me,] D4: me

purpose,] D2,D3,D4: purpose;

1947. cringe] D4: cringe,

1948. and] D2,D3,D4: and,

1949a. S.D.] B adds: "[unobserved]." The Lord, obviously asked to watch Antonio, exits following Antonio disguised as the slave, a switch of identities he did not recognize (ll. 2027 ff.). No explanation is offered. The Lord is needed to facilitate the discovery of the body, but the actions and motivations of the Lord are confusing.

1950. villain.] D2,D3,D4; 1661,D1,B: villain:

1951. But,] D,B; 1661: But

1954. this, man,] D: this maid,

1957. at,] 1661,D1,D2,D3,B: at; D4: at:

1960. coy then.] D2,D3,D4: coy then? B: coy, then?

1961. honest;] D4: honest---

ladies.] 1661,D,B: Ladies:

1963. sate] D4: sat

1965. piecemeal] 1661: peicemeal

1966. again,] B: again

1968. Phoenix.] 1661: Phaenix, D1: phoenix, D2,D3,D4: phoenix! B: Phaenix:

1971. it.] 1661,D,B: it:

1973. king,] D4,B; 1661,D1,D2,D3: king;

1974. vertuous.] 1661: vertuous, D1,D2,D3: virtuous, D4: virtuous: B: vertuous:

1975. life;] D2,D3,D4,B; 1661,D1: life,

1976. men,] D4,B: men

1977. white,] D4; 1661,D1,D2,D3,B: white

1978. sir.] D3,D4,B; 1661,D1,D2: sir;

1980. Palermo.] B; 1661:Parlermo; D1,D2,D3: Palermo; D4: Palermo!

1981. valiant] 1661: valaint

men.] 1661,D,B: men:

1984. Christian;] D3,D4,B: Christian,

1986. cleanly.] D; 1661: cleanly, B: cleanly.---

1987. And] D4: Ere B notes that this emendation "gives no sense."

deed.] 1661,D,B: deed:

1989. flight,] 1661,D,B: flight

1990. captain,] D,B; 1661: Captain

gally.] D; 1661: Gally: B: Gally.---

1992. sea] D; 1661,B: sea,

1995. world.] D; 1661,B: world;

twilight;] 1661,D,B: twilight:

1996. pistol.] D; 1661,B: pistol:

1997. Laugh,] D,B; 1661: Laugh

prophet;] 1661,D: prophet, B: prophet:

1999. more,] D,B; 1661: more

sir;] D2,D3,D4: sir:

2001. hold,] D2: hold; D3,D4: hold!

you,] D,B; 1661: you

2002. back,] D,B; 1661: back

sir.] 1661,D,B: sir---

2003. Hold,] D; 1661,B: Hold

2004. not.] 1661,D,B: not---

thou?---] 1661,D,B: thou?

2006. me,] D1,D2: me; D3,D4: me:

'tis] D2,D3: 'tis,

2007a. Enter Lorenzo.] This is not a new scene, since the body lies on stage until carried off at l. 2045.

2008. Lor.] 1661 fails to note speaker.

not sure] D4: not, sure,

Millain.] 1661,B: Millain: D1,D2,D3: Milan: D4: Milan!

2009. habit,] D4: habit

Verona,] D4: Verona

2010. here.] D,B; 1661: here:

Oh Abstemia!] D1,D2: Oh, Abstemia! D3: Oh Abstemia, D4: O Abstemia,

2011. now?] D2,D3,D4: now!

2012. than] D; 1661,B: then

modestie] D: modesty,

2014. softly.] D3,D4,B; 1661,D1,D2: softly:

2015. How,] D2,D3,D4,B; 1661,D1: How

2017. look'd.] D3,D4; 1661,D1,D2,B: look'd:

Oh] D4: O,

2019. cloud] D4: cloud,

2021. more.] 1661,D,B: more:

2023. finde] D,B; 1661: finde,

2028. sir.] 1661,D,B: sir:

2029. him;] D2,D3,D4; 1661,D1,B: him,

2030. Certain] D4: Certain,

2031. Ha---] D2,D3: Ha!--- D4: Ha!

sir.] 1661,D,B: sir:

Oh] D4: O,

2033. Lord.] B: Lord!

2036. gone;] D2,D3,D4: gone!

yet,] D4: yet?

fresh,] D2,D3: fresh; D4: fresh? B: fresh!

2039. lodge.] D2,D3,D4; 1661,D1,B: lodge:

Oh] D1,D2,D3: Oh, D4: O,

2040. face,] D2,D3,D4: face

2041. life,] 1661,D,B: life:

2042. horse,] D3,D4,B: horse!

2043. wood,] D4: wood: B: wood!

way,] B: way!

2044. day.] D3,D4: day!

2045. pursuit.] D4,B: pursuit!

2045a. SCENE II] B continues as Scene I.

2046. Oh] D4: O,

name,] D2,D3,D4,B; 1661,D1: name

winds,] D2,D3,D4,B; 1661,D1: winds

2048. her.] D3,D4; 1661,D1,D2,B: her:

2050. sides.] 1661,D,B: sides:

2051. endeavours,] 1661,D,B: endeavours:

2053. upon.] 1661,B: upon, D: upon it.

lost.] 1661,D1,B: lost; D2,D3,D4: lost!

Oh] D1,D2,D3: Oh,

she,] D2,D3,D4; 1661,D1,B: she

2055. conquer'd.] 1661,D,B: conquer'd:

2056. sword] D: sword,

[shouts]] not in 1661,D,B.

follow.] D4,B: follow!

2057. way.] D4; 1661,D1,D2,D3: way, B: way:

2058. murderer,] D2,D3,D4; 1661,D1,B: murderer

2059. beset;] D4; 1661,D1,D2,D3,B: beset,

2060. Speak,] D,B; 1661: Speak

2063. sir;] D3,D4: sir:

2065. lyes,] D4: lies;

2066. Out] D,B: Out,

2067. feast] B; 1661: fedst D: feed

thee.] 1661,D,B: thee:

2068. wound,] D: wound

2070. Lor.] D,B; 1661: Lod.

2071. regular;] D3,D4,B: regular.

nothing.] 1661,D,B: nothing:

2075. Lead] In a note, D3, suggests "Lead" which D4 adopts within the text. 1661,D1,D2,B: Leave

tortures] D2,D3,D4,B: tortures,

2076. Oh] B: Oh,

2077. winter] D,B; 1661: winter,

2078. Oh] D1,D2,D3: Oh,

2079. affliction,] B: affliction

2079a. SCENE III] B continues as scene I.

2084. cause.] 1661,D,B: cause:

2087. paleness] D,B; 1661: paleness,

2088. fie.] D4,B: fie!

2089. Go,] D,B; 1661: Go

he,] D,B; 1661: he

than] D; 1661,B: then

woman,] D4: woman---

2090. (And] D4: And

saint)] D4: saint;

2092. heart,] D,B: heart

2093. Came] D4: Came,

flowing;] D,B: flowing,

2094. will,] D4,B: will

2095. Antonio.] D2,D3,D4,B; 1661,D1: Antonio:

Oh] D1,D2,D3: Oh, D4: O,

2096. fortune] D4: fortune,

2098. S.D.] not in 1661,D,B.

Lorenzo.] 1661,B: Lorenzo: D: Lorenzo,

2099. denial,] D: denial:

2101. makes] D4: make

2103. yonder,] D2,D3,D4,B: yonder:

2104. Ambo.] B: Anto.

How?] D: How!

2105. Nay,] D; 1661,B: Nay

2107. Verona.] 1661,D,B: Verona:

2108. S.D.] not in 1661,D,B.

wonder;] D2,D3,D4,B; 1661,D1: wonder,

slave,sure.] B; 1661,D1: slave sure. D2,D3: slave sure! D4: slave, sure!

2110. What,] D2,D3,D4; 1661,D1,B: What

2112. corns.] 1661,D,B: corns:

2113. Lady.] 1661,B: Lady: D: lady;

2114. house,] D4: house;

2115. thither.] D3,D4; 1661,D1,D2,B: thither:

2116. S.D.] not in 1661, D,B.

2118. Oh] D4: O,

me, I] D4: me: I

distraction,] D4,B: distraction;

2120. S.D.] not in 1661 or D; B, with dashes, marks ll. 2121-2122 only as an aside.

come.] 1661,B: come: D: come!

2121. too?] D2: too! D3,D4: too.

by;] 1661,D,B: by:

2123. S.D.] not in 1661 or D; B indicates with dashes.

he.] 1661,D,B: he:

2126. rather,] D4: rather:

2127. temples,] D3: temples

2128. Ha?] D3,D4,B: Ha!

2129. Wedlock!] D2,D3,D4,B; 1661,D1: Wedlock.

2131. far.] 1661,D,B: far:

come,] D4; 1661,D1,D2,D3,B: come

2132. deed.] D3,D4; 1661,D1,D2,B: deed:

2135. Abstemia!] D,B; 1661: Abstemia?

2136. look,] D,B; 1661: look

ye;] D2,D3,D4: ye! B: ye:

by,] D4; 1661,D1,D2,D3,B: by

2137. day,] D2,D3,D4: day; B: day:

2139. mine;] 1661,D1,B: mine, D2,D3,D4: mine:

sir,] D2,D3,D4,B: sir;

2140. together.] 1661,D1,D2,B: together: D3,D4: together;

I] D4: I,

2141. Prince] D4: prince,

son] D4: son,

2143. dead,] D4,B: dead

2146. knife] D2,D3,D4,B: knife,

2147. resistance,] D2,D3,D4,B; 1661,D1: resistance

2148. eye.] D3,D4; 1661,D1,D2,B: eye:

2150. me;] D4; 1661,D1,D2,D3,B: me,

him.] D3,D4; 1661,D1,D2,B: him:

2151. He] D4: He,

2152. writ, that] D4,B: writ that,

flattering] D: flatt'ring

2153. off] D: off,

2154. himself;] D3,D4: himself,

2156. languish] D: languish,

dye.] 1661,D1,D2,D3,B: die: D4: die---

2157. for] D4: for,

2159. sword,] D4: sword

2161. then,] D4: then;

2164. her self,] D4,B: her self

truth.] 1661,D,B: truth:

2165. months.] D; 1661,B: months:

2167. S.D.] not in 1661,D,B.

2168. justice; speak,] D2,D3,B; 1661,D1: justice; speak D4: justice. Speak:

soul,] B: soul

2169. hand] D,B; 1661: hand,

2170. life;] D2,D3,D4,B; 1661,D1: life,

2173. accuser.] D2,D3,D4; 1661,D1,B: accuser:

2174. thou] D: thou,

remembrance,] D2,D3,D4: remembrance:

2175. thee;] D2,D3,D4: thee,

2176. tears] D4: tears,

2178. her] D2,D3,D4 omit.

2180. me] D4: me,

2181. me.] D,B; 1661: me?

2182. jugling, sir,] D,B; 1661: jugling sir

this;] D1,D2,B; 1661: this, D3,D4: this:

2186. *Verona,*] D2,D3,D4,B; 1661,D1: *Verona*

2187. gentlemen,] D,B; 1661: gentlemen

2189. prison] B; 1661,D: prison,

2190. entertainment] D4,B; 1661,D1,D2,D3: entertainment,

2191. shew.] 1661,D1,D2,D3,B: shew: D4: show:

time,] D4; 1661,D1,D2,D3,B: time

2193. wife.] D2,D3: wife:

2193a. *Exeunt;*] 1661: *Exeunt:* D,B: *Exeunt.*

2196. ne'er] D2,D3,D4: never B: ne're

saw.] D2,D3,D4,B; 1661,D1: saw:

2197. dearly.] D2,D3,D4; 1661,D1,B: dearly:

trick,] D,B; 1661: trick

2200. nonplus,] B: nonplus

2201. stranger.] D2,D3,D4; 1661,D1,B: stranger:

2202. death.] D2,D3,D4,B; 1661,D1: death:

2204b. *without* . . . *Antonio*] not in 1661,D,B.

2207. S.D.] not in 1661,D,B.

unravell'd;] D2,D3: unravell'd. D4: unravell'd,

2208. me;] D2,D3,D4: me:

2209. slave doubtless] D4: slave, doubtless,

2210. spleen.] D2,D3,D4; 1661,D1,B: spleen:

2213. him;] D2,D3,D4: him.

2214. him] D4,B; 1661,D1,D2,D3: him,

2215. And,] D4,B; 1661,D1,D2,D3: And

2216. it seems] D2,D3: it seems, D4: (it seems)

hands.] D2,D3,D4,B; 1661,D1: hands:

2218. me.] D2,D3,D4; 1661,D1,B: me:

2218a. S.D.] D3 and D4 place after l. 2220.

2219. that.] D2,D3,D4; 1661,D1,B: that:

so,] D4: so:

fitted,] D4: fitted;

2223. Come,] D,B; 1661: Come

other] D3,D4: another

afoot;] D2,D3,D4: afoot:

2224. sir;] D2,D3,D4: sir.

ye.] 1661,B: ye: D: you;

2225. counsel;] D2,D3,D4: counsel.

2226. than] D; 1661,B: then

thee] D,B; 1661: thee,

2228. knave.] 1661,D1: knave, D2: knave; D3,D4,B: knave:

2230. belief.] D2,D3,D4; 1661,D1,B: belief:

2232. than] D; 1661,B: then

me,] D,B; 1661: me

sir.] 1661,D1,B: sir: D2,D3,D4: sir;

2233. Pray,] D2,D3,D4; 1661,D1,B: pray

before;] 1661,D1,B: before, D2,D3,D4: before.

private] D omits.

2234. custody,] D,B: custody

2235. you.] D2,D3,D4; 1661,D1,B: you:

comfort,] D4: comfort---

2237. dance.] D2,D3,D4; 1661,D1,B: dance:

prethee,] 1661,B: prithee D1: pr'ythee D2,D3: pr'ythee, D4: prythee,

2239. Oh] D1,D2,D3: Oh,

justice's] D4: justices'

clarke] 1661,B: clarke, D: clerk

2240. poor.] D2,D3,D4; 1661,D1,B: poor;

Pray,] D4; 1661,D1,D2,D3,B: pray

2241a. SCENE IV] B numbers as Scene II.

2246. Oh] D4: O,

2247. crowns,] D4: crowns

2248. good.] D2,D3,D4; 1661,D1,B: good;

2249. a young] D4: young

2253. integrity.] D2,D3,D4; 1661,D1: integrity; B: integrity:

fall,] D2: fall;

2256. eye] D2,D3,D4,B; 1661,D1: eye,

2257. vow;] D2,D3,D4,B: vow.

2259. merit.] D,B; 1661: merit,

2260. gale] D4,B; 1661,D1,D2,D3: gale,

2261. us),] D4,B; 1661,D1,D2,D3: us)

2262. nimbler] Library of Congress and Huntington copies: mimbler
This is apparently the only correction made during the press run.

rows,] D1,D2: rows; D3,D4,B: rows:

2264. thee.] 1661,D1,B: thee: D2,D3,D4: thee!

S.D.] not in 1661 or D; B indicates with a dash.

2265. cloud.] D2; 1661,D1,D3,B: cloud: D4: cloud!

2266. fruitful.] D2,D3,D4; 1661,D1,B: fruitful:

2269. stranger,] D1,D2,B: stranger; D3: stranger: D4: stranger!

2271. vertue.] 1661: vertue, D: virtue. B: vertue:

2272. innocence] D2,D3,D4,B: innocence,

2273. Look'd] D; 1661,B: Lookt

than] D; 1661,B: then

death,] D4,B: death

2276. innocence] D,B: innocence,

2278. Why, then,] D4,B; 1661: Why then? D1,D2,D3: Why then

you,] D4,B: you

2280. Oh] D4: O,

2281. sorrow.] D2,D3,D4; 1661,D1,B: sorrow:

her] 1661,D,B: her,

2282. (Since] D4: Since

married,] D2,D3,D4: married

us),] 1661,D1,D2,D3,B: us) D4: us,

2284. prey;] D1,B; 1661: prey, D2,D3,D4: prey:

2286. than] D; 1661,B: then

2287. S.D.] indicated in D4 and B only.

2288. than] D; 1661,B: then

2289. terrour] D2,D3,D4,B; 1661,D1: terrour,

2290. would snail-like] D2,D3,D4: would, snail-like,

2292. S.D.] indicated in D4 and B only.

better!] D3,D4: better.

2293. confess?] D,B: conceive

2294. love.] D,B: love?

2295. life?] 1661,D: life, B: life

2298. weather,] D2,D3,D4,B: weather:

2299. know] D2,D3,D4: know,

2301. (in] D4: in

2302. friend)] D4: friend,

2304. Lorenzo.] D4: Lorenzo!

2305. You will] B; 1661,D: Will you

2306. suspence;] D: suspense.

but,] D2,D3,D4,B; 1661,D1: but

say] D2,D3,D4: say,

2307. Portia] 1661: Protia

2309. still] D4: still [do]

2311. rate.] 1661,D,B: rate:

2312. murderer, you see,] D,B; 1661: murderer you see

2316. husband---] D,B; 1661: husband.

2318. Pray] D4: Pray,

me.] 1661,D,B: me:

2319. law.] D2,D3,D4; 1661,D1,B: law:

2321. transportation,] D2,D3,D4: transportation;

live] D: live,

2324. ye.] 1661,D,B: ye---

2325. fitted] D,B; 1661: fitted,

2326. weather.] D2,D3,D4; 1661,D1,B: weather:

2327. ear.] 1661,D,B: ear:

2329. it;] D2,D3,D4,B: it:

2333. loves.] 1661,B: loves: D: loves;

2336. meets the] 1661: the meets

eye.] D; 1661,B: eye:

2337. this,] D: this

2338. minutes.] D2,D3,D4; 1661,D1,B: minutes:

thriftiest] D,B; 1661: thirstiest

2339. harm,] D,B: harm

2340. wearing.] D; 1661,B: wearing:

you, sir,] D1,D2,D3,B; 1661: you sir D4: you, sir

2341. worne)] D4: worn),

2342. up)] D4: up)---

2347. Oh] D4: O,

2348. be] B: buy

2349. Now] D2,D3,D4: Now,

yel] Perhaps should be emended to: me!

2351. love.] D2,D3,D4; 1661,D1,B: love:

2352. profess,] D4: profess

2353. life,] D: life;

now] D,B: now,

2354. giv'st] D3,D4: givest B: giv[e]st

back,] D2,D3,D4,B; 1661,D1: back

2358. that?] D2,D3,D4: that!

2359. knowledge.] D; 1661,B: knowledge:

2360. tell,] D,B: tell

2362. ye] D: you

2363. do't,] D: do't

2364. I] D: Ay

2365. jealousie,] D: jealousy B: jealousie

judges.] D2,D3,D4; 1661,D1,B: judges:

2367. Oh] D4: O,

2368. daintily,] D2,D3,D4,B: daintily;

2369. death,] D2,D3,D4,B: death;

2371. That dead,] D2,D3; 1661: That dead D1,B: That, dead,
D4: That (dead)

2374. that] D4: that,

dying,] D4; 1661,D1,D2,D3,B: dying

2375. love;] D2,D3,D4: love:

2377. Oh] D4: O,

2380. me!] D3,D4: me.

learn'd] D; 1661,B: learn'd,

2382. snare.] D; 1661,B: snare:

2385. aconite.] D; 1661,B: Aconite:

hypocrite;] D2,D3,D4; 1661,D1,B: hypocrite:

2386. stick] D: stick,

2389. Away,] D2: Away; D3,D4: Away!

2390. mud.] D2,D3,D4; 1661,D1,B: mud:

2394. No] D: No,

not;] D2,D3,D4: not:

death,] D2,D3,D4: death;

2395. pleasure.] D2,D3,D4; 1661,D1,B: pleasure:

2397. Than] D,B; 1661: Then

baseness.] D; 1661,B: baseness:

2399. Oh] D4: O, B: Oh,

not,] D2,D3,D4,B: not

2400. honour.] D2,D3,D4,B; 1661,D1: honour;

2403. face.] D; 1661,B: face:

2404. more] D4: more,

then;] D; 1661,B: then,

but,] D,B; 1661: but

2406. than] D; 1661,B: then

kingdoms,] D3,D4,B: kingdoms!

confirm'd,] D,B: confirm'd

2407. suspition;] 1661,D,B: suspition,

2408. than] D; 1661,B: then

2409. garlands.] D2,D3,D4; 1661: garlands: D1: garlands; B: garlands!

winds] D: winds,

2412. thee.] D; 1661,B: thee:

2413. desires;] D: desires!

2414. marriage,] D: marriage;

and] D: and,

2416. hot room,] D1,B; 1661: hot room; D2,D3,D4: hot-room,

2417. Shall lawrel-like] D: Shall, lawrel-like,

2418. S.D.] not in 1661,D,B.

2418a. <u>and Philippo</u>] 1661,D,B fail to indicate that Philippo enters at this point, as he speaks at l. 2421.

2419. Ha,] D: Ha!

2421. Sir!] D,B; 1661: Sir.

2422. Sister?] D,B: Sister!

2423. shame,] D: shame!

2427. me,] D1: me; D2,D3,D4: me:

murder.] 1661,D1,B: murder: D2,D3,D4: murder;

2428. deed,] D2,D3,D4: deed

2430. us,] D3,D4: us:

all---] D,B; 1661: all.

2431. lives] D4: lives,

silent!] 1661,B: silent; D1: silent: D2,D3,D4: silent.

sir,] 1661,D2,D3,D4,B: sir: D1: sir;

2433. sir.] D2,D3,D4; 1661,D1,B: sir:

2434. it,] D1: it; D2,D3,D4: it:

2435. murderer.] D; 1661: murderer: B: murderer;

you] D4: you,

audience,] D: audience;

2437. Silence.] D: Silence!

2438. and,] D1,B; 1661,D2,D3,D4: and

truth's truth,] D2,D3,D4: (truth's truth)

2441. Nay,] D; 1661,B: Nay

2445. death.] D; 1661,B: death:

said] D: said,

2446. manners.] D2; 1661,D1,D3,D4,B: manners:

2449. dead.] 1661,D,B: dead:

2450. her] D2,D3: her,

2451. nobly,] D: nobly

2452. Belike] D4: Belike,

2453. him] D: him,

2454. tryal.] 1661,B: tryal: D: trial:

2456. *Lor.*] 1661,D,B: *Lod.* Lodovico is present, speaking at ll. 2475-2478, but it seems logical that Lorenzo would speak this line, since Lodovico has not been involved in the action.

twice;] D; 1661,B: twice,

2458. again;] B: again

2460. eyes.] 1661,D,B: eyes:

2461. Oh] D4: O,

Prince,] D4: prince

2462. lust,] D4: Lust

else)] D4: else),

2464. then] D: then,

2467. alive.] 1661: alive

2468. *Antonio?*] D: Antonio!

2469. Prince!] D; 1661,B: Prince.

2470. home, my sister,] D,B; 1661: home my sister

2472. Oh] D1,D2,D3,B: Oh,

2473. large,] D2,D3,D4: large

2475. then.] 1661,D,B: then:

2476. book] D: book,

sexto] D: *sexto,*

2478. shops.] 1661: shops

2479. wonder;] D,B; 1661: wonder,

2481. *Aside*] not in 1661,D,B.

2482. *Ferrara*---] D,B; 1661: *Ferrara*.

2483. S.D.] not in 1661,D,B.

noble.] D,B: noble---

2484. fight.] 1661,D,B: fight:

2485. *Palermo*;] D: Palermo:

2486. equal.] 1661,B: equal: D: equal;

2488. t'other] 1661,D,B: the t'other

2490. kick;] D: kick:

2491. t'other] 1661,D,B: the t'other

2492. Prince;] D4: prince,

2493. swear] D3,D4: swear,

2495. fairly.] D2,D3,D4: fairly?

2497. then;] 1661,D,B: then:

dyes,] D4: dies

2499. you,] D1,D2,D3: you D4: you:

noble;] D1,D2,D3; 1661,B: noble, D4: noble.

2502. honour.] 1661,D,B: honour:

me] D: me,

2503. person] D: person,

S.D.] not in 1661,D,B.

2505. ill (as 't happen'd)] D4: ill---as 't happen'd,

2506. end.] 1661,D,B: end:

kill'd,] D2,D3,D4: kill'd

2507. you.] 1661,D,B: you:

paper] D: paper,

2509. it.] D; 1661,B: it:

2510. just] D: just,

2513. love] D: love,

2517. At court,] D4: At court [a] B: At Court, [a]

2518. distinguish,] D4; 1661,D1,D2,D3,B: distinguish

2519. Excellent Lady,] D4; 1661,D1,B: (Excellent Lady) D2,D3: (Excellent lady!)

2520. women] D,B; 1661: women,

2521. clouds] D: clouds,

shine;] D3,D4: shine:

2522. S.D.] indicated only in D.

LIST OF WORKS CITED

Adams, Joseph Quincy, ed. The Dramatic Records of Sir Henry Herbert. [1917]; rpt. New York: Benjamin Blom, n.d.

Arber, Edward, ed. A Transcript of the Registers of the Company of Stationers of London, 1554-1640. 5 vols. 1877; rpt. New York: Peter Smith, 1950.

A Transcript of the Registers of the Worshipful Company of Stationers; from 1640-1708. 3 vols. 1914; rpt. New York: Peter Smith, 1950.

Beaumont, Francis, and John Fletcher. The Dramatic Works in the Beaumont and Fletcher Canon. Ed. Fredson Bowers. Cambridge: the University Press, 1966. Vol. 1.

Behn, Aphra. The Amorous Prince. Ed. Montague Summers. London: William Heinemann, and Stratford-on-Avon: A. H. Bullen, 1915. Vol. 4.

Bentley, Gerald Eades. The Jacobean and Caroline Stage. 7 vols. Oxford: the Clarendon Press, 1941-1968.

Boccaccio, Giovanni. The Decameron. The Tudor Translations, First Series. 1909; rpt. New York: AMS Press, Inc., 1967. III, 204-212.

Bowden, William R. The English Dramatic Lyric, 1603-42. New Haven: Yale University Press, 1951.

Brooks, Harold F. and Harold Jenkins, gen. eds. The Arden Edition of the Works of William Shakespeare. London: Methuen and Co., and Cambridge: Harvard University Press, v. d.

Busby, Olive Mary. Studies in the Development of the Fool in Elizabethan Drama. London: Oxford University Press, 1923.

Cervantes, Miguel de. The History of Don Quixote of the Mancha. Trans. Thomas Shelton. The Tudor Translations, First Series. London: David Nutt, 1896. II, 61-113.

Davenport, Robert. "A Dialogue Between Policy and Piety." Folger Shakespeare Library MS. 1919.3.

Davenport, Robert. The City-Night-Cap. London, 1661 (Wing D-369).

Davenport, Robert. The City-Night-Cap. In A Select Collection of Old Plays, Ed. Robert Dodsley. London: R. Dodsley, 1744. IX, 253-328.

Davenport, Robert. The City-Night-Cap. In Dodsley's Select Collection of Old Plays. Ed. Isaac Reed. London: J. Dodsley, 1780. XI, 265-365.

Davenport, Robert. The City-Night-Cap. In Dodsley's Select Collection of Old Plays. Ed. John Payne Collier. London: Septimus Prowett, 1827. XI, 261-345.

Davenport, Robert. The City-Night-Cap. In Dodsley's Select Collection of Old Plays. Ed. W. Carew Hazlitt. London: Reeves and Turner, 1875. XIII, 99-197.

Davenport, Robert. The City-Night-Cap. In The Ancient British Drama. Ed Sir Walter Scott. London: William Miller, 1810. III, 324-353.

Davenport, Robert. The Works of Robert Davenport. Old English Plays, III. Ed. A. H. Bullen. London and Redhill: Hansard Publishing Union, 1890.

Davenport, Robert and William Lower. The Enchanted Lovers and The City-Night-Cap. Folger Shakespeare Library, MS. J. b. 2.

Davis, Joyce Outten. "Robert Davenport's King John and Matilda: A Critical Edition." Diss. Tulane 1969.

Dean, James S., Fr. "Borrowings from Robert Greene's Philomela in Robert Davenport's The City-Night-Cap." Notes and Queries, 13 (1966), 302-303.

Dunlop, John. The History of Fiction. 2nd ed. 3 vols. Edinburgh: James Ballantyne and Co., 1816.

Durfey, Thomas. Squire Oldsapp. London, 1679. (Wing D-2786.)

Fane, Sir Francis. Love in the Darke; or the Man of Business. London, 1675. (Wing F-408.)

Farmer, John S., and W. E. Henley, eds. Slang and Its Analogues. 7 vols. in 1. 1890-1904; rpt. New York: Arno Press, 1970.

Florio, John. Queen Anna's New World of Words, Or Dictionarie of the Italian and English Tongues. 1611; rpt. in facsim. Menston, England: The Scolar Press, 1968.

Gosse, Edmund and Thomas James Wise, eds. The Complete Works of Algernon Charles Swinburne. 20 vols. 1925; rpt. New York: Russell & Russell, 1968.

Greg, W[alter] W[illiam]. The Editorial Problem in Shakespeare. Oxford: The Clarendon Press. 1942.

Greg, W[alter] W[illiam]. "The Rationale of Copy-Text." Studies in Bibliography, 3 (1950), 19-36.

Greg, W[alter]W[illiam], ed. The Second Maiden's Tragedy. The Malone Society Reprints. 1909; rpt. Oxford: University Press, 1964.

Grosart, Alexander B., ed. The Life and Complete Works in Prose and Verse of Robert Greene. 15 vols. Rpt. New York: Russell & Russell, 1964.

Harbage, Alfred. Annals of English Drama. Rev. S. Schoenbaum. London: Methuen and Co., 1964.

Harbage, Alfred. "Elizabethan-Restoration Palimpsest." Modern Language Review, 35 (1940), 310-318.

Holden, William P. Anti-Puritan Satire 1572-1642. 1954; rpt. n.p.: Archon Books, 1968.

Hoy, Cyrus. "On Editing Elizabethan Plays." *Renaissance and Reformation*, 8(1972), 90-99.

Ingleby, C. M., et al., comps. *The Shakespeare Allusion Book: A Collection of Allusions to Shakespeare from 1591 to 1700*. 2 vols. London: Humphrey Milford, Oxford University Press, 1932.

Jones, Robert C. "Italian Settings and the 'World' of Elizabethan Tragedy." *Studies in English Literature, 1500-1900*, 10 (1970), 251-68.

Jordan, John Clark. "Davenport's *The City-Night-Cap* and Greene's *Philomela*." *Modern Language Notes*, 36 (1921), 281-84.

Knappen, Marshall M. *Tudor Puritanism*. 1939; rpt. Gloucester, Mass.: Peter Smith, 1963.

Langbaine, Gerard. *An Account of the English Dramatick Poets*. 1691; rpt. in facsim. Hildesheim: Georg Olms Verlagsbuchhandlung, 1968.

Levin, Richard. *The Multiple Plot in English Renaissance Drama*. Chicago: University of Chicago Press, 1971.

McManaway, James G. "Latin Title-Page Mottoes as a Clue to Dramatic Authorship." *Library*, 4th ser., 26 (1945), 28-36.

McManaway, James G. and Mary R., eds. *Dick of Devonshire*. The Malone Society Reprints. Oxford: University Press, 1955.

The National Union Catalog, Pre-1956 Imprints. London and Chicago: Mansell, 1968-----.

Olive, W. J. "Davenport's Debt to Shakespeare in *The City-Night-cap*." *Journal of English and Germanic Philology*, 49 (1950), 333-344.

Olive, W. J. "Shakespeare Parody in Davenport's *A New Tricke to Cheat the Divell*." *Modern Language Notes*, 66 (1951), 478-480.

Ouvry, Frederick, ed. *The Cobler of Caunterburie, Or An Invective Against Tarlton's Newes Out of Purgatorie*. London: Frederick Ouvry, 1862.

Peery, William, ed. The Plays of Nathan Field. Austin: University of Texas Press, 1950.

Plomer, Henry R. A Dictionary of the Booksellers and Printers Who Were at Work in England, Scotland and Ireland from 1641 to 1667. 1907; rpt. The Bibliographical Society, 1968.

The Politick Whore: or the Conceited Cuckold. In The Muse of Newmarket. London, 1680, pp. [39]--61.

Ravenscroft, Edward. The London Cuckolds. London, 1682. (Wing R-332.)

Rosenbach, A. S. W. "The Curious Impertinent in English Dramatic Literature Before Shelton's Translation of Don Quixote." Modern Language Notes, 17 (1902), 358-367.

Rosenfeld, Sybil. Strolling Players & Drama in the Provinces 1660-1765. 1939; rpt. New York: Octagon Books, 1970.

Schoenbaum, Samuel, ed. The Bloody Banquet. The Malone Society Reprints. Oxford: University Press, 1961.

Scott, Mary Augusta. Elizabethan Translations from the Italian. Boston and New York: Houghton-Mifflin, 1916.

Sugden, Edward H. A Topographical Dictionary to the Works of Shakespeare and His Fellow Dramatists. Manchester: University Press, 1925.

Thorn-Drury, G., comp. and ed. A Little Ark. London: P.J. and A. E. Dobell, 1921.

Tilley, Morris Palmer. A Dictionary of the Proverbs in England in the Sixteenth and Seventeenth Centuries. Ann Arbor: University of Michigan Press, 1950.

Van Lennep, William, ed. The London Stage, 1660-1800. Part 1. Carbondale: Southern Illinois University Press, 1965.

Wright, Herbert G. The First English Translation of the 'Decameron,' 1620. Upsala: Lundequistska bokhandeln, 1953.